The Jewish Family

THE JEWISH FAMILY
Metaphor and Memory

Edited by David Kraemer

New York   Oxford
OXFORD UNIVERSITY PRESS
1989

Oxford University Press

Oxford   New York   Toronto
Delhi   Bombay   Calcutta   Madras   Karachi
Petaling Jaya   Singapore   Hong Kong   Tokyo
Nairobi   Dar es Salaam   Cape Town
Melbourne   Auckland
and associated companies in
Berlin   Ibadan

Published by Oxford University Press, Inc.,
200 Madison Avenue, New York, New York 10016

Oxford is a registered trademark of Oxford University Press

Library of Congress Cataloging-in-Publication Data
The Jewish family : metaphor and memory /
edited by David Kraemer. p. cm.
Based on papers delivered at the First Henry N. Rapaport Memorial Conference,
held at the Jewish Theological Seminary, May 1985.
Bibliography: p.   Includes index.
ISBN 0-19-505467-9
1. Jews—Families—Congresses.   I. Kraemer, David Charles.
II. Henry N. Rapaport Memorial Conference
(1st : 1985 : Jewish Theological Seminary)
HQ525.J4J39 1989   306.8'5' 089924—dc19   88-4008 CIP

9 8 7 6 5 4 3 2 1
Printed in the United States of America
on acid-free paper

Acknowledgments

Despite ever-increasing interest in the Jewish family in recent years, relatively few volumes have been devoted, in whole or in part, to this subject. For this reason it is with satisfaction that I see this book brought to publication. Given the range of its subjects, it is safe to say that this volume's contribution to the study of the Jewish family and its history is a significant one. However, such an endeavor could not have been carried out without the support and assistance of many people.

To begin with, the conference for which these papers were first produced, the First Henry N. Rapaport Memorial Conference, would not have been possible without the generous endowment of Mrs. Selma Rapaport, who established the Henry N. Rapaport conferences and lectures in memory of her late husband. These events, held annually at the Jewish Theological Seminary, have provided the occasion for many exciting contributions to the world of Jewish scholarship and thought. This is the first book to emerge from that series, and it is evidence that the memorial which Mrs. Rapaport wished to establish will be a lasting one.

The topic for the first conference was initially proposed by the then chancellor of the Jewish Theological Seminary, Dr. Gerson Cohen. The primary responsibility for attending to details and assuring that this conference would come to fruition was shouldered by Dr. Neil Gillman. The quality of the conference and the excellence of the scholars who agreed to participate testify to the capable direction Dr. Gillman provided, as well as the high esteem with which he is regarded by his colleagues. Though several changes in format and a few substantive differences distinguish this book from the conference that produced it, it is nevertheless fair to say that Dr. Gillman was the first "editor" of this volume.

The direction provided by the editorial and production staff at Oxford University Press has been, without exception, first-rate. In particular, the copy editing done by Cecil P. Golann was meticulous and precise, and the final quality of the text is due, in large part, to her discerning eye. On the other hand, any errors or inconsistencies that remain are due to my own oversight.

Finally, my own task as editor was greatly facilitated by the cooperation of the contributors to this volume. As many readers are aware, these scholars are among the most prominent in their respective fields; they must consequently often attend to many projects simultaneously. That they did, when necessary, make this project a priority demonstrates their commitment to the subject at hand. I am personally gratified by the support they chose to offer.

Despite the occasional tedium of editing and re-editing a volume such as this, the excitement of doing so was far more profound. Each of these essays provides the opportunity for a new discovery. Each asks a question or offers a perspective that has not previously been presented. Collectively these studies make us aware of the vast fields that have yet to be examined, and of the immense treasures that have yet to be mined. They ask us to consider with a fresh eye the history and variety of the Jewish family. As volume editor, I have had to familiarize myself with these challenges. For this reason, and for all that I have learned as a consequence, I am grateful that the task of shaping this important book fell to me.

New York   D.K.
April 1988

Contents

Part III Family and Community

Part IV Family Relations as Metaphor

Contributors

Robert Alter is Professor of Hebrew and Comparative Literature at the University of California, Berkeley. He has written critical studies of Fielding, Stendhal, and various aspects of the evolution of the novel. He has also published work on biblical literature as well as on modern Hebrew literature and on modern Jewish authors writing in other languages.

Immanuel Etkes is Senior Lecturer in Modern Jewish History and History of Jewish Education at the Hebrew University. His areas of research include ideological trends and social movements in East European Jewry (Hasidism, Musar movement, Haskalah), and modern Jewish education.

Mordechai A. Friedman is Professor of Talmud at Tel Aviv University. His main fields of scholarly research are marriage and the family in the Talmud, medieval Jewry under Islam, and the legal documents of the Cairo genizah.

Isaiah M. Gafni is Associate Professor of Jewish History at Hebrew University in Jerusalem. His research is primarily devoted to the history of rabbinic Judaism and its institutions, and to the Jews of classical antiquity in general. His book on the history of the Jews in Babylonia is scheduled to appear shortly.

Harvey E. Goldberg is Associate Professor and Chairman of the Department of Sociology and Social Anthropology at the Hebrew University. His research interests include the Jews of North Africa and ethnicity in Israeli society.

Avraham Grossman is Professor of Medieval Jewish History at the Hebrew University. He has written extensively on the history of the Jews during the Middle Ages both in Moslem and Christian countries and is also the author of *The Early Sages of Ashkenaz*. His current research interests include the exilarchate in the Eastern Caliphate and the Jewish family and community organization.

Joseph Gutmann is Professor of Art History at Wayne State University and Adjunct Curator at the Detroit Institute of Arts. His areas of research include biblical archaeology, Jewish art history, medieval Jewish history, and medieval Christian art. He has published extensively on synagogue art and architecture, Jewish ceremonial art, and medieval Hebrew manuscripts.

Gershon David Hundert is Associate Professor of History and Director of the Jewish Studies Program at McGill University. He has published articles on the Jews in early modern Poland and coauthored *The Jews in Poland and Russia*.

Paula E. Hyman is Lucy Moses Professor of Modern Jewish History at Yale University and a former Professor in Jewish History at The Jewish Theological Seminary of America. Author of *From Dreyfus to Vichy: The Remaking of French Jewry, 1906–1939*, she is coeditor, with Steven M. Cohen, of *The Jewish Family: Myths and Reality*. Professor Hyman is currently working on a book entitled *Emancipation and Social Change: Alsatian Jewry in the Nineteenth Century*.

Moshe Idel is Senior Lecturer in the Department of Jewish Thought at The Hebrew University. He is an established authority on kabbalistic literature and the author of scores of studies on all aspects of that tradition.

David Kraemer is Assistant Professor of Talmud and Rabbinics at The Jewish Theological Seminary of America. He is also a Program Associate at the National Jewish Center for Learning and Leadership (CLAL).

Anne Lapidus Lerner is Assistant Professor in Hebrew Literature and Dean of the List College at The Jewish Theological Seminary of America. Her publications include "Who Hast Not Made Me a Man: A Study of the Movement for Equal Rights for Women in American Jewry," *Passing the Love of Women: A Study of Gide's "Saul" and Its Biblical Roots*, and articles in the field of modern Jewish literature.

The Jewish Family

Introduction

DAVID KRAEMER

To many the social stability of earlier generations must seem irretrievable. In the absence of established alternatives, the choices made available by the collapse of traditional role models often yield not liberation but ambivalence. Particularly with respect to the family, the breakdown of definitions has led to confusion, conflict, and—with frightening frequency—the breakdown of the family itself.

Although fewer and fewer of those who establish families expect that the woman will remain in the home and raise children while the man works to support his family, many, nevertheless, persist in harboring expectations regarding family relationships that derive from an earlier, more romantic age. This tension between rapid change and unrealistic expectations has often been the cause of the family's disintegration. In reaction to this—and in response to the palpable instability that emerges from these conditions—the return to familial and social roots, which has engaged the attention of many observers in recent years, has taken on a kind of urgency.[1]

In part this urgency stems from our belief that by studying our recent ancestors and examining the way they conducted their personal affairs, we might somehow be able to share the stability that we imagine characterized their lives. As the rate of change in earlier generations was slower than our own, we assume—in some matters correctly—that the experience of our grandparents or great-grandparents reflects the conventions of generations. But by assuming the longevity of their experience, we also tend to idealize it. We too often ignore the upheavals that befell them, and we neglect to notice that changes made demands of them much as they do of us.

The commonly held beliefs that are the source of this misperception are manifold. For example, based on the demographic data of the middle part of this century, many have assumed that recent trends favoring later marriage and childbearing are aberrant. Research has shown, however, that the age of such transitions today only begins to surpass what was common much earlier this century, and in many contexts present conventions were far more typical.[2] Similarly, the picture of women generally staying in the home and raising children is woefully incomplete. The truth is that in some settings and social classes children were farmed out to nurses and others to enable the woman to help support the household. Only the affluence of a middle-class life-style afforded many families the luxury of having the woman remain in the home.[3]

More than mere academic interest makes such corrected assumptions compelling. If we understand the dynamism of earlier social conditions, we will appreciate the fact that contemporary experience represents less of a break with the past than we might have believed. Furthermore, though the discovery of past familial instability offers us no ready-made solutions for our own confused state, we may still derive some comfort in knowing that we are hardly unique in having to face upheaval and change. The challenge that confronts us might in some ways be more extreme, but it is only a difference in degree, not in kind.

What has been said of the family in general relates even more closely to the Jewish family. The families of many contemporary Jews have emerged from the Middle Ages to modernity not in the space of centuries but in only one or two generations. A Jew today may look to a grandparent or great-grandparent to find someone who was literally untouched by Enlightenment thinking that had transformed West European society long ago. Moreover, in coming to the New World, these Jews modernized and adapted almost with a vengeance. American Jews today have a low birth rate, an escalating divorce rate, and an almost unparalleled rate of assimilation. The danger (demographically at least) that this represents has caused great alarm among Jewish social scientists and community leaders, who have not hesitated to sound this alarm to the general Jewish population. As a result, the confusion experienced by many as they confront modern society is among Jews often compounded by feelings of guilt.

The degree of idealization that frequently characterizes representations of the premodern Jewish family has not made matters easier. Though most contemporary Jews would not choose to revive the role definitions that governed earlier family groups, many are still attracted by the warmth and stability with which these are remembered. If the testimony of the popular media is to be accepted, the traditional Jewish family consisted of a large nuclear core with strong ties to the extended family. Weddings took place under a huppah (canopy), accompanied by the reading of a traditional ketubah (marriage contract) whose text had remained unchanged since antiquity. Following marriage—usually at a very young age—came the bearing of many children, who were named after deceased relatives. The strong, caring wife generally stayed in the home, often supplementing her husband's modest income through handiwork or by running a shop. The husband simultaneously attended to both the support of his family and his religious commitments to synagogue and house of study.

Some of these depictions are undoubtedly accurate for a particular Jewish society at a given time, but, as the essays in this volume demonstrate, none fits all Jewish societies at all times. Rather, what emerges from these studies is a picture of immense variety and the realization that down through the ages the Jewish family has adapted almost "organically" to the many and varied environments within which it has had to survive.

If common misconceptions do not correspond to historical reality—a reality that the present generation now seeks—how should this problem be addressed? The answer must be in the publication of scholarly works on the history of the Jewish family that are made accessible to a general readership. Regrettably, there has been very little scholarship on the subject, especially for nonspecialists. It is this absence that the present volume attempts to redress.

There are few earlier studies on the history of the Jewish family. The most significant contribution to this field, representing as well a major contribution to the history of the family in general, is *The Family*, the third volume of S. D. Goitein's *A Mediterranean Society*, which is entirely devoted to the family.[4] Based on evidence found in the Cairo genizah, it describes the Jewish family in Islamic society from the tenth to the thirteenth centuries. A true tour de force, the volume has much to offer to a scholar engaged in the study of the family; but, being a work addressed to scholars, it does not meet the needs of the general reader.

The Jewish Family: Myths and Reality,[5] edited by Steven M. Cohen and Paula E. Hyman (the latter is a contributor to this volume), also makes a significant contribution to the history of the Jewish family. Based on an earlier conference on the Jewish family, it contains essays that vary in terms of accessibility to the nonscholarly reader. Yet it has much to offer even to the nonspecialist. Its one serious limitation—which is also its greatest strength—is its (almost exclusive) concentration on post-Enlightenment Western Jewry.

Other works, though not devoted to the family as such, do address issues of interest to the study of the family. An outstanding example is Mordechai Friedman's *Jewish Marriage in Palestine: A Cairo Geniza Study*.[6] Friedman, who is also a contributor to the present volume, analyzes in detail the marriage contracts of the Cairo genizah and reconstructs the Jewish marriage ceremony of the communities represented. Naturally, many other details of interest in the study of the family are revealed by his research. However, the volume is strictly a scholarly work and much too difficult for a nonspecialist. Also unavailable to the general reader are numerous scholarly articles on the history of the Jewish family published over the years in various hard-to-find scholarly journals.

The present collection of essays is based on papers delivered at the First Henry N. Rapaport Memorial Conference, held at the Jewish Theological Seminary in May 1985. This conference sought to make scholarly research on the history of the Jewish family accessible to specialists *and* nonspecialists alike. Given such a goal, it was inevitable that some papers failed to speak to both audiences with equal success; still, their present form reflects an attempt to establish a voice that facilitates access for all who might have an interest in this subject. To the degree that this goal has been accomplished, it is hoped that the foundation has been laid for a more accurate perception of the Jewish family in its many traditional forms.

The essays in this volume touch on nearly all categories in the history of the Jewish family: legal, economic, social, and psychological/behavioral.[7] In this examination of the Jewish family from antiquity to the present and from Persia and North Africa to Europe and the United

States, many common myths are scrutinized. The Jewish family emerges as an institution of great variety, possessing many guises in its different "homes."

The main divisions of this volume seek, in a general way, to parallel the development of a family and its concerns, beginning with marriage, continuing on to children and their place within the family, and concluding with the family as it relates to the community at large. The final section, dealing with the metaphorical and literary use of family relationships, is of course unrelated to this scheme. Within the individual sections the essays are arranged according to their chronological concerns.

Part I examines marriage as practiced by Jews in three different settings. Isaiah Gafni's study of marriage in rabbinic times describes the institution of Jewish marriage, with reference to Roman and early Christian marriage, during the classical rabbinic period (when the Mishnah and Talmuds were composed, from the first through the sixth centuries). Gafni considers the purported sanctity of rabbinic marriage, the presumed purpose of marriage, and the difference between the Palestinian and Babylonian (Persian) Jewish communities in terms of their conceptions of marriage.

Viewing the same part of the world but moving ahead several centuries, Mordechai Friedman presents a study of Jewish marriage under Islam. Friedman considers the legal relationship between husband and wife under Islam, beginning with the question of "property versus partnership." Parallels to Islamic practice in other cultures are examined extensively, and the influence of Islamic custom on the Jews is richly illustrated. Of great interest is Friedman's conclusion that polygamy among Jews under Islam was not as rare as had been previously believed.

In the third essay Joseph Gutmann traces the development of Jewish wedding practices in medieval Europe as revealed by evidence preserved in ceremonial objets d'art. Here he shows that many traditional wedding customs are borrowed from parallel Christian practices.

Part II considers the attitudes of Jews in various societies toward their children. My own contribution on childhood and adolescence as reflected in talmudic literature yields several surprising conclusions. Not only was a distinctive developmental continuum admitted in rabbinic society—unlike many premodern European societies—but there was a clearly discernible period of adolescence. Furthermore, the authors of the rabbinic corpus did not consider Jewish adulthood to begin at age thirteen (bar mitzvah), as is widely believed, but closer to age twenty.

Utilizing a very different sort of literature as his source, Gershon Hundert next examines Jewish childhood in early modern Europe as reflected in Jewish ethical literature. He studies contrasting attitudes toward male and female children, the role of the mother as ethical instructor, and the parents' aspirations for the growing child, providing a wealth of detail that considerably enriches our concept of the premodern Jewish child.

In the final essay in this section, Anne Lapidus Lerner turns to East European Hebrew literature to examine the child as symbol in the stories of Isaac Dov Berkowitz and Devorah Baron. Recollecting some of the most poignant moments in their works, Lerner brings to life the lost childhoods of these modern Hebrew writers.

Part III treats the relation of family and community and discusses the influence that each has had on the other. Avraham Grossman examines in detail the development of family "dynasties" in various Jewish societies. Beginning with talmudic times and continuing through the medieval period, he shows how these dynasties affected the quality of Jewish leadership in their respective communities.

Next, Harvey Goldberg brings an anthropologist's eye to a consideration of the relationship between family and community in Sephardic North Africa. In addition to his study of the relation of the family to the Jewish community and to the surrounding Arab population, he includes personal reminiscences of Israelis raised in this region. His discussion of Jewish laws governing family purity and their central place in the self-identification of Jewish women in these societies is of special interest.

The relation of family and community is also the subject of Immanuel Etkes's study of the conflict between family obligations and commitment to Torah study in nineteenth-century Lithuania. Etkes shows that early marriage and the need to complete advanced talmudic education combined to create immense difficulties in starting up a new family and also that the need to depend on the bride's family for support often led to resentment and unfulfilled expectations. A clear understanding emerges that the traditional Jewish family was not nearly as ideal as has been believed.

In the concluding essay in this section Paula Hyman discusses the changing character of the Jewish family in Europe following the legal emancipation and acceptance of its members as citizens. Particularly noteworthy is Hyman's suggestion that "by the second half of the nineteenth century . . . the family [had] become the issue upon which concern for assimilation had focused." In connection with this claim, she examines—from an incisive feminist perspective—the Jewish woman's role as the "last great hope" for providing a religious and ethical education for her children.

In Part IV family relations are considered in terms of their metaphorical usage within two kinds of Jewish literature. Moshe Idel, treating the kabbalah, describes how that tradition views the human sexual act as affecting the relationship among different aspects of the Divine (the sephirot) and how, at the same time, the relationship between mystics and the Divine is viewed in more or less literal sexual terms.

Finally, Robert Alter speaks of the modern Jewish family as it is reflected (Alter prefers "refracted") in the works of Kafka, Agnon, and Bellow. The author has a dual purpose: to critique those who have employed literature as too literal a record of the times they are thought to represent and to demonstrate how the writer's imaginative elaboration of the family can yield "secret hints of meaning about what we are and where we are headed."

The cumulative impact of the essays included in this volume should be felt both by specialists in family history and by anyone interested in the Jewish family. For the former, the most important contribution of this collection is the breadth of family types that are now made accessible to scholarly scrutiny. Because of the many ways families have been organized through the ages, family historians have long recognized the need for research in this field to be based on the broadest possible spectrum of samples, one that is greatly enhanced by the studies included here.[8] For those, on the other hand, whose interest is specifically Jewish, the contribution of this volume may be stated far more simply: to satisfy the desire to understand—even on a personal level—what it has meant historically to be part of a Jewish community.

Of course, a volume of this sort can only make a modest contribution to the task of writing a history of the Jewish family. What is still necessary are comprehensive studies for many more Jewish societies based on the model of Goitein's *Mediterranean Society*. If this volume succeeds in generating interest in the subject of the Jewish family and helps to demonstrate its importance, it will have made a lasting contribution.

NOTES

1. The thesis expressed in this paragraph and the next recapitulates the opinion of Lawrence Stone, "Family History in the 1980s," *The Journal of Interdisciplinary History* 12:1 (Summer 1981), 53–54.

2. See Stone, "Family History," p. 58.

3. Stone, "Family History," pp. 65–66.

4. 4 vols. (Berkeley and Los Angeles, 1967–83).

5. (New York and London, 1986).

6. (Tel Aviv and New York, 1980).

7. See Stone, "Family History," p. 55, for a list and description of these categories.

8. See Stone, "Family History," p. 81.

PART I

MARRIAGE AS AN INSTITUTION

1

The Institution of Marriage in Rabbinic Times

ISAIAH M. GAFNI

In his monumental study entitled *A Social and Religious History of the Jews*, Professor Salo Baron makes the following basic observation on the rabbinic concept of the institution of marriage: "The Talmudic legislators neither elevated marriage to the position of a sacrament, a supernatural sanction of what otherwise would be an unforgivable sin, nor did they regard it as a mere contract in civil law."[1] Clarification of this statement might serve as a fitting introduction to our study of Jewish marriage in the rabbinic period (ca. 70–600 C.E.), and we would do well to begin by taking up the first clause: Marriage was neither a sacrament nor supernaturally ordained. To be sure, the rabbis did not remove God from an involvement of sorts in the marriage process, and the idea that marriages, or matches, are made in heaven found its way into numerous legends and midrashim,[2] not the least amusing being the attempt of a Roman matron to emulate God by matching off one thousand of her slaves and maidservants, only to be encountered on the morrow by a horde of mutually bruised and battered couples.[3] God's matchmaking skills were thus made evident and appreciated, and the Babylonian sage Samuel could thereby conclude that on each and every day a heavenly voice issues forth proclaiming: "the daughter of X is for Y."[4] But even this idea had to be tempered when confronted with the real and legal world of marriage, and when the very same Samuel is quoted as permitting bethrothal of a woman on the intermediate days of a festival, the Talmud immediately raises the question, Why the rush? Has not the match already been divinely ordained? Samuel's explanation is revealing: although the voice has already made its announcement, we, nevertheless, fear someone else may show up first!

Marriage, then, was in fact contracted by individuals, and though God's presence—the Shekhinah—may be considered a sine qua non for a happy marriage,[5] we do not find the rabbis suggesting—as did the Church—that the institution was, in and of itself, a sacred institution or a sanctifying one. For the early Christian church marriage as a sacrament was a central idea. Not only is it God who has joined together (or rejoined) two into one,[6] with all the ensuing implications negating divorce, second marriages, and the like; but Paul's reference to marriage as a *sacramentum* (or *mysterion*)[7] was understood as a reflection of the union of Christ and his church, so that marriage in human society, to the extent that it would be allowed, derives its legitimacy and sanctity directly from the spiritual nuptuals between Christ and church.[8]

The rabbis saw no equivalent kedushah (sanctity) in Jewish marriage.[9] The bethrothal benediction, unlike those blessings that stress the sanctity of Sabbath ("who hallows the Sabbath") or of Israel and the holidays ("who hallows Israel and the festivals"), does *not* refer to the sanctification of *marriage* but rather to the sanctification of *Israel* by *means* of huppah and kiddushin,[10] and even here a major qualification must be introduced. The conclusion to the benediction as it appears in b. Ketubot 7b ("Blessed are you, Lord, who hallows Israel by *means* of huppah and kiddushin") was not, at first, a tradition universally maintained by all Babylonian authorities. More interesting, however, are the textual variants that completely omit the last clause and read merely "Blessed are you, Lord, who hallows Israel."[11] A responsa of Rav Hai Gaon (tenth and eleventh centuries) not only supports this reading ("and thus do the two academies conclude, from the days of the first sages to the present") but goes on to say that those who would add "by means of huppah and kiddushin" in fact distort the issue, "for the sanctity of Israel is not dependent on this."[12] Even the term kiddushin was not understood by the Talmud to imply a *sacred* or *sanctified* event, but rather the rendering of the bethrothed woman forbidden to the rest of the world as are sacred objects.[13]

By the removal of this particular idea of sacramentum, marriage was rendered, to a degree, a willful arrangement or contract, the conditions of which—while ascribing to certain stipulations—could nevertheless be concluded on an individual basis by the parties concerned. In this respect, all the forces governing a free and fluctuating market might affect the arrangement. Thus, whereas the point of departure assumed certain basic requirements on the part of both parties, such as the husband's obligation to provide "food, raiment and conjugal duties"[14] and the wife's responsibility to perform various household chores (grinding flour, baking bread, washing clothes, cooking food and so forth),[15] all this was contracted with the understanding that precisely *because* marriage provided both parties with certain benefits, each party's relative interest in the agreement might determine the precise nature of the contract.

In this context, certain determining social factors were considered fairly stable, whereas others were liable to change owing to ongoing developments. For example, the dominant market appraisal in the rabbinic period was that the woman—notwithstanding her social or economic status—was more eager to enter a marriage relationship than a man.[16] The sages of the Mishnaic period cite this eagerness as justification for exacting payment of the ketubah from the poorer fields of the husband and add a psychological interpretation to what they perceived as the woman's concession: "It is more of an embarrassment for her (to be alone) than for him."[17] Although we can assume that such an evaluation is the natural consequence of a patriarchal society,[18] the woman's situation in second-century Palestine must have been exacerbated even further by the death of tens of thousands of Jewish soliders in the two great wars against Rome (66–73 and 132–135 C.E.). The number of available bachelors, as a consequence, was considerably diminished, and the pressure of supply and demand would have lent credence to statements such as the preceding or the equivalent one attributed to Resh Lakish: "Better to sit as two than to sit alone."[19] It was this eagerness to marry—almost at all costs—that justified in rabbinic eyes a blanket concession on the part of the woman.

But if this concession was a permanent one, other examples have been cited of changes in the perceived conditions accepted by both parties, reflective of changes on the economic or social scene. Thus, for instance, Professor Y. D. Gilat has shown[20] that, whereas earliest rabbinic authorities considered the husband's obligation to provide food a requirement of Torah, later discussion of the issue gradually reverts to a consensus that this was only a rabbinic obligation. As such, this requirement was now exposed to bargaining on the part of both sides, and the agreement achieved would reflect the respective interests and bargaining power of each partner. Whether the economic conditions in post-Temple Judaea were indeed the underlying factor in this change is open to debate, but the result nevertheless was to leave open yet another aspect of the matrimonial undertaking to the free choice of the involved parties. Thus, we already find in the late second century the following: "A man may marry a woman and stipulate the condition that he *not* supply food, that he *not* support. Moreover, he may stipulate *with her*, that *she* will feed *him*, support him and teach him Torah. And it happened that Yehoshua, son of R. Akiba, married a woman and stipulated with her that she would feed and support him and teach him Torah. . . ."[21]

If this is the case, why *not* view marriage as a contract in civil law? The legal system of Rome that encompassed the Jews of Palestine and the empire had begun to consider marriage precisely such an affair. Not only had Roman practice, by the time of Augustus, done away with most of the vestiges of religious marriage known as *confarraetio* (save for those interested in higher priesthood),[22] but even the marriage form of *cum manu*, by which a woman passed into the manus, or hand, of her husband as his possession, had fallen into disuse. The prevailing practice by this time was marriage without manus, a free consensual union, which was usually accompanied by marriage settlements with detailed provisions concerning dowry and antenuptual gifts and which might also be terminated by either mutual consent or the unilateral decision of either party.[23]

Here, however, the rabbinic concept, and resulting laws, of marriage parted with the Roman idea. For Jewish marriage, though requiring mutual consent in a manner outwardly similar to Roman custom, was also intrinsically linked to the mitzvah (divine commandment) of procreation, and the concomitant obligations governing marriage reflect the rabbinic interpretation of that commandment.[24] It was only through marriage that a Jew could properly meet the standing obligation to reproduce, and the connection between the two was succinctly stated by Josephus: "What are our marriage laws? The law recognizes no sexual connections, except the natural union of man and wife, and that—only for the procreation of children."[25] We may note, however, that Josephus does not merely link marriage with procreation but actually claims that *the sole purpose* of marriage was to have children. Here rabbinic attitudes are not uniform, and to understand the various nuances we would do well to again draw a comparison with the early Church. At first glance it would appear that major Christian authors were at one with Josephus. Tertullian, in his *Letter to His Wife*, says that marriage was "blessed by God for the reproduction of the human race. It was planned by Him for the purpose of populating the earth,[26] and to make provision for the propagation of humankind. Hence it was permitted."[27] This stand would ultimately evolve into the constant position of the Church.[28] However, this was in fact only a grudging acceptance of a reality that could not be changed. Every church father who addressed himself to the issue could not ignore Paul's famous proclamation in 1 Cor. 7:1–9: "It is good for a man not to touch a woman. Nevertheless, to avoid fornication, let every man have his own wife, and let every woman have her own husband . . . I say this by way of *concession*, not of *command* . . . for it is better to marry than to burn." Tertullian clearly saw this for what it was: "We understand that it is better to marry than to burn in the same sense in which it is better to have one eye than none . . . It is not so much a *good*—as it is a kind of lesser evil."[29]

Jerome follows him closely, seeing marriage as a poor second best; virginity is the original state willed by God, and sexual intercourse came along only after man's fall.[30] "While marriage replenishes the earth—virginity replenishes paradise."[31] Jerome also takes up both the semantic implications of Paul's declaration and the difference between "good" and "better": "When you come to marriage, you do not say it is *good* to marry, because you cannot then add 'than to burn,' but you say it is better to marry . . ."[32]

But if in Christian minds marriage was barely "good," in rabbinic eyes the fact that it maintained the world rendered it literally "*very* good": "Naḥman in the name of R. Samuel said: And God saw everything that he had made and behold—it was very good (Gen. 1:31). 'Good'—that is yetzer tov (the good impulse), 'Very Good'—that is yetzer hara (the evil impulse).[33] But is the evil impulse very good—I wonder! Yes, for were it not for the evil impulse, a man would not build a house, *marry a wife*, and have children."[34]

The place accorded childbearing as a main purpose in marriage could easily affect the practical guidelines of marriage set down by the rabbis, and it is in contexts such as this that the institution was affected by religious ideas rather than social pressures.

For example, if a ten-year marriage produced no offspring, the sages of the Mishnah require the husband to marry another woman.[35] Whether this necessarily entailed divorce of the first wife is unclear in the Mishnah, but this was at least one probable consequence, as was in fact spelled out in the Tosefta.[36] Should a woman conceive but repeatedly miscarry, the end result for the husband would be the same; inasmuch as the mitzvah is procreation, he is again required to marry another woman.[37]

The barren and divorced woman, however, is entitled to remarry at least two more times,[38] until we are convinced that the problem lies with her rather than her various husbands. If the problem turns out to be hers, she would be permitted to marry only a man who has already fulfilled the requirements of procreation. This law, as stated in the Tosefta, is a particularly interesting one, for it is just possible that in discussing the question of permitting a childless marriage, the rabbis knowingly attempted to place some distance between themselves and the Church.

If a woman has married three times and not produced children, she may marry only one who has a wife and children, but if she married one who has no wife and children, she is sent out without a *ketubah*, for her marriage is a *mistaken marriage* (*nissu'ei ta'ut*).[39] At least two textual witnesses, however, attest here to an interesting variant: "For her marriage is a marriage of *minnut*."[40] That is, a woman entering a marriage that cannot produce children is marrying after the manner of the *minnim* (lit. sectarians, often understood to refer to Christians). Lieberman, albeit with great hesitation, wonders whether we have not come up against the rabbinic answer to 1 Cor. 7, which, as we have seen, grudgingly permitted marriage only to avoid fornication and placed no import on procreation. This type of marriage is "sectarian marriage," for it does not recognize the positive commandment of reproduction as an underlying purpose of matrimony.

Even if the reading "sectarian marriage (*nissu'ei minnut*)" is a scribal error, we have begun to grasp the complexity of the marriage institution, embracing as it did social and religious elements that might not always complement each other. Whereas socially marriage was seen (among other things) as a solution to a woman's need for masculine companionship, protection, and support and hence her willingness to accept concessions, the religious requirement of marriage—procreation—which the Mishnah understood to be the man's obligation, might ultimately prevent the partners from achieving their other goals.

The rabbis were thus forced to subject the marriage institution to a wider appraisal, and various statements on marriage go beyond an analysis of the immediate religious and social benefits. If the Church ultimately conceded that marriage was not only a means of overcoming fornication but also the basis for maintaining the human race, the rabbis in turn advanced beyond the commandment to "be fruitful and multiply" and expre sed appreciation of marriage in a broader sense. In stressing the greater advantages of marriage, however, the sages of Palestine appear to be divided into two camps. One group might be defined as maximalist; that is, they see nothing merely *relative* in the positive aspects of marriage, nor do they stress the *practical* advantages of attaining a wife. For them marriage is good—period. With reference to Scripture "it is not good that man be alone (Gen. 2:18)," the Palestinian midrash taught: "It has been taught: He who has no wife lives without *goodness*, without *help*, without *joy*, without *blessing*, without *atonement*."[41] The Babylonian Talmud parallel makes an interesting distinction: "R. Tanḥum in the name of [Munich Ms. reads: son of] R. Ḥanilai says: 'He who has no wife lives without *joy*, without *blessing*, without *goodness* [*help* and *atonement* are missing here]. *In the West* [Palestine] they say: without *Torah*, without a *(protecting) wall*."[42] Although R. Tanḥum was also Palestinian, the difference between his statement and that attributed to "the West" is clear. Whereas attributes of joy, goodness, and blessing reflect on a mutually favorable atmosphere created through matrimony and, in no slight degree, reflect on the very nature of woman, the second statement is utilitarian, with the husband squarely in the center, requiring a wife as a means of fulfilling his particular obligations.[43]

The logical conclusion of this second approach—possibly condoning bachelorhood (should a man's goal be achievable without marriage) or foregoing marriage (should it prove a hindrance)—was, of course, counterbalanced by the mitzvah of procreation, and so marriage was universally prescribed by the Palestinian sages. Nevertheless, the utilitarian rationale for marriage provided at least some justification for attitudes such as that of Ben Azzai, who remained single because his soul "yearned for Torah,"[44] and left propagation of the human race to others. These sentiments were not unknown in the Roman world as well, and Ben Azzai's contemporary, Epictetus, explains in his *Discourses* (3, 22, 8) that the cynic philosopher cannot marry because he is entirely attentive to the service of God. Epictetus, in fact, expresses yet another sentiment that is parallel to rabbinic views, for he explains in the same context that the philosopher "who is tied down to vulgar duties," such as providing clothes for children, simply has no time for the greater issues.[45] This immediately brings to mind the well-known discussion in b. Kiddushin 29b, wherein Samuel decrees: "A man should marry first and then study Torah. R. Yoḥanan says: *A millstone around his neck* and he will study Torah?" Relating to the dispute, the anonymous Bavli concludes: "This [Samuel's statement] is for *us*, that [Yoḥanan's statement] for them [the Palestinians]."

In the light of Palestinian statements on marriage, as well as those of Epictetus, must we accept the popular interpretation that sees the Kiddushin debate reflecting an *economic* disparity: prosperous Babylonians who can afford to marry first, on the one hand, and inflation, tax-ridden Palestinians on the other?[46] It is equally feasible that we are confronted here by varying attitudes toward the role of marriage within the framework of one's total life commitment, which also includes the study of Torah. In this context one must note what emerges from other Babylonian rabbinic sources, for in Babylonia we encounter no divisions regarding the relative advantages of marriage nor the linkage of marriage primarily to procreation. The institution is completely desirable and mandatory on its own intrinsic merits, and the same Samuel who requires marriage before Torah study also decrees: "Even though a man has children, he must not remain without a wife."[47] Whereas Palestinian tradition knew of other cases—even before the rabbinic period—of those who put off marriage because of other important pursuits (cf., e.g., The Testament of Issachar 3:5—who explains that he married at age thirty-five because of his *labor* up to then; Issachar's labor in rabbinic sources was the study of Torah),[48] the Babylonian rabbis would hear nothing of this. Rav Huna would not even look at Rav Hamnuna before he was married,[49] and it was the Babylonians who elaborately described how and when God loses His patience with those who have not yet wed.[50] Rav Ḥisda, who married at sixteen, had only one regret: that he did not marry at fourteen!

Babylonian Jews, in fact, were rather militant about the requirement of marriage and may have used the issue as ammunition in their confrontation with Christians in fourth-century Mesopotamia. The eighteenth demonstration of Aphrahat, written around the year 344 C.E., was devoted to a defense against Jewish attacks on Christian celibacy, and this, as I have discussed elsewhere,[51] was not merely an academic discourse but a direct rebuttal to actual confrontations. Aphrahat notes that "they [the Jews] change and weaken the minds of simple and ordinary folk who are attracted and captivated by this argument [against celibacy],"[52] and he even alludes to actual instances of their success: "I have written to you, my beloved ones, on the issue of virginity and sanctity because I heard of a Jew who embarrassed one of our brethren of our community and said to him: 'You are impure because you take no wives, whereas we who procreate and increase the world are holy and excellent.' Therefore I have written this argument for you."[53]

The Jews of Babylonia were joined in these attacks on Christian celibacy by the local Persian church[54] and this leads us to the obvious question: To what extent were rabbinic attitudes toward marriage in the two large centers, Palestine and Babylonia, influenced by varying ideas and attitudes in the different societies and cultures?

The Persian world certainly encouraged marriage; and, as we shall see shortly, it is even possible that certain Persian practices are alluded to in the Babylonian Talmud. The importance of bearing children is attested in Pahlavi texts, such as in the following chapter of the *Dātestān i Denig* (36.29):

> Through the great mystery full of marvel, he gave to the living [people] long immortality: the descent of offspring, that which is the best and most excellent immortality of that which has adversity. For an eternal being, who has adversity, suffers always pain. That one has wondrous power who *has been endowed with offspring*, he is constantly young in adversity thanks to his good offspring, family, and descendants. The constancy of his life is eternal [a gloss reads: that is, their living continues through their children and descendants].[55]

If the monogamous Roman society established monogamy as a norm throughout most of the Empire, this was *not* the case in Sassanian Persia. Polygamy, the antiquity of which is attested in the Avesta, continued down to the Sassanian period, at least among the aristocracy that could afford a plurality of wives.[56]

The Jews of Palestine and the Roman Empire, on the other hand, had by the period of the Talmud encountered other pressures and ideas. A Roman reading Tacitus then knew that Jews, although they abstain from intercourse with foreign women, are nevertheless "a race prone to lust."[57] The monogamy of the Roman Empire twice forced Josephus to insert into his text explanatory notes describing the polygamous behaviour of Herod as nevertheless being permitted by Jewish ancestral custom.[58] With the growth of the Church, Jews would now find themselves attacked by the likes of Justin Martyr for their acceptance of polygamy.[59] While the Church succumbed on the issue of universal celibacy, the Fathers made a stand regarding polygamy in all its forms, including concurrent marriage to more than one wife, as well as consecutive marriages to different women (or men). Paul's various statements on the issue were cited (Titus 1:6; 1 Tim. 3:2, 12), and elaborate arguments were produced to explain the polygamous life-styles of the biblical patriarchs. Adam and Eve, on the other hand, became the natural archetypes, as Tertullian claims: "For Adam was the only husband that Eve had, and Eve was his only wife; *one rib, one woman!*" (*Ad uxorem*, 2).

Although not sufficient to engender an outright revision of Jewish law, one cannot help but wonder—as indeed a number of historians have suggested[60]—whether these ideas might not have shaped certain nuances towards marriage in Palestinian rabbinic thought. To be sure, the issue of monogamy and polygamy in the rabbinic period has been an extremely popular topic in scholarly and semischolarly research, although frequently not devoid of more than a measure of apologetic rhetoric.[61] In brief, it is clear that Palestinian rabbinic sources, to the extent that they allude to actual historical events, imply a predominantly monogamous society. The Mishnah, it must be said, certainly discussed in legal context problems arising out of a polygamous state, whether in the framework of levirate marriage,[62] inheritance,[63] or other aspects of family law.[64] But these are not different from so many other talmudic discussions of legal doctrine, particularly in the realm of issues such as levirate marriage, that appear to be either hypothetical or legendary.[65] Thus one can enjoy the remarkable story of the poor soul whose twelve brothers die, all childless—leaving him to contract levirate marriage with twelve widows—without necessarily assuming that we are confronted with reality (three years later we find our hero the proud father of 36 children!).[66] At least one frequently cited Mishnah, in fact, appears to reflect, en passant, a monogamous tendency: "If a sage caused a woman to be forbidden to her husband by [upholding] her vow [not to derive any benefit from him]— the sage may not marry her (the appearance of impropriety exists—his interest may have influenced his ruling). . . ." But if the sage had a wife at the time of his ruling and she died, then he may marry the first woman (Yemavot 2:10). In other words, the Mishnah presupposes that *a married man* might have no designs in marrying another woman.

More important, however, for our purposes are all the Palestinian aggadic statements that tend to frown on bigamy or polygamy:[67] "If Adam was intended to be polygamous, God would have given him ten wives, not one (compare Tertullian);"[68] Elkana's piety is tainted by the fact that he took two wives;[69] the functions of Lemekh's two wives are described in a most unbecoming way[70] (Lemekh, in Tertullian's eyes, was a degenerate).

These statements seem to reflect a growing Palestinian consensus. Taken together with the unequivocal declaration of R. Ami—"he who takes a second wife should release the first and pay her ketubah"[71]—it appears that the monogamous atmosphere of Roman society (and legislation),[72] as well as the preaching of church fathers throughout the empire, coincided with a similar standard among the Jews of the empire. To this we might add, as correctly noted by Juster,[73] that the scores of Jewish inscriptions throughout the Diaspora, usually in the form of epitaphs, fail to refer even once to a case of polygamous marriage (although here one wonders what we might hope to find. Would the bereaved husband inscribe "you were my favorite" and then go home to the others? Might a band of recent widows, who probably never got along too well, bid their husband good-bye with "we *all* loved you"?). The overall picture, however, is clear.

As for the situation in Babylonia, although this will be denied by some scholars,[74] the picture that emerges from our sources is anything but similar. Not only does Rava's clear-cut statement: "A man may marry several wives in addition to his wife"[75]—seem to indicate his stand regarding marriages in *general*[76] and not just the specific case at hand in b. Yemavot, but other Babylonian pronouncements connected with Rava appear to support this idea.[77] Moreover, the anonymous Bavli understands the Mishnah—"If four brothers married to four women died, their elder brother may perform levirate marriage with all"—as dispensing sound practical advice: A man should marry only up to four wives, so that each may receive one marital visit a month (scholars attend to this duty on Friday nights).[78] The same number (or *up* to four) already appears in the Qur'an (Sura 4:3)[79] and became binding in Islam, but other numbers also appear among Babylonian Jews. Rav advises Rav Asi not to marry two wives, but if already two, then three is better! (b. Pesaḥim 113a). Granted, statements like these are not yet proof of a reality, and economic conditions must have placed polygamous marriage beyond the reach of most men (the Aramaic stipulation added to Rav's statement in the Talmud—that polygamy is conditional on the husband's capability to maintain more than one wife—is apparently echoed in the Qur'an's qualification: "[I]f you fear you cannot act equitably toward so many, marry only one"). But even these statements are illuminating in that they appear beyond the framework of purely hypothetical legal discussion, which is the case in most of the Palestinian Mishnayoth that allude to polygamous situations. In this context one cannot overlook the well-known anecdotes regarding the Babylonian sages, Rav and Rav Naḥman: "When Rav would come to Darshish [in Yevamot, "Darda-shir" = be-Ardashir][80] he would declare: 'Who will be [my spouse] for the day (or: days)?'[81] When Rav Naḥman came to Shekhunẓib,[82] he declared: 'Who will be [my spouse] for the day?' "[83] Understandably, these stories gave rise to a long and frequently entertaining list of ex-planations, all with the same urgent apologetic tendency and all with the natural assumption that things cannot be what they seem.[84] And so, we are told, the two itinerant rabbis were really issuing proclamations stressing the importance of arranged marriages, or they married for the day only when their wives had their period. One suggestion assumes that unaccompanied scholars visiting Persian dignitaries were automat-ically given women for the night, hence the need to produce a wife fast and prevent the unthinkable. And then there is the more "sophisticated" solution: Rav and Rav Naḥman are known to have encountered trouble with their wives; hence what we have here are *threats* aimed at them (i.e., there are more fish in the sea!). To this yet another historian adds conversely: "One may well understand why Rav's wife behaved like a shrew," seeing how he behaved on his business trips.[85]

The only source, in fact, that was not aghast at what the story was saying was the Talmud itself,[86] which raised the issue as a case in contrast to the established halakhah that a man should not have wives in two different cities lest his offspring unwittingly marry one another. The whole discussion revolves around the assumption that the two rabbis were indeed looking for temporary wives. Urbach goes so far as to quote a statement attributed to Rav that he surmises may even explain that sage's out-of-town behavior: "A man will have to give account for all that his eye saw but did not enjoy."[87] More important, however, is the fact that what the Bavli alludes to was in fact a fairly widespread practice in the East. Particularly striking is the similarity of the described practice to the temporary marriage practiced among the Shiites, known as Muta (marriage of pleasure)—a practice possibly referred to in the Qur'an itself (Sura 4, 28). Just as in the Talmud text, muta marriage was in-tended for men traveling to other towns for extended periods.[88] Justin Martyr's words on Jewish polygamy take on a new significance in light of this phenomenon, for he does not merely accuse the Jews of marrying more than one wife, but rather says that they do this "in every land where they sojourn or are sent—taking women under the name of marriage."

As for the Babylonian setting, it appears that marriage "for a definite period" was also known in Sassanian Persia. The major collection of legal decisions, the *Mātakdān ī hazār dātastan*, describes instances when a woman, even a married woman, might be given through a formal procedure to another man as a temporary wife for a definite period. A father could also bestow his daughter in temporary marriage.[89] Whereas no one would suspect a case of adultery (e.g., marrying an already married woman) before us in the Talmud, phrases such as "who will be [my spouse] for the day?" might nevertheless reflect types of marriage "for a definite period" that existed in the surrounding culture. In any case, anecdotes such as these are totally alien to the Palestinian Talmud and would have been impossible in Palestine.[90]

In conclusion, it appears that the underlying factors that determined attitudes toward marriage, both in Palestine and Babylonia, present a complex picture. Although basic Jewish concepts of marriage were certainly primary, other factors that were the consequence of surrounding social and economic conditions might also determine the particular nature of the marriage arrangement. In this context, social factors include both an ongoing practical evaluation of the forces pressing both parties into accepting matrimony, as well as external religious ideas that exerted tremendous influence on vast numbers of human beings in late antiquity.

All this, then, contributed to what we have called the *institution* of marriage in rabbinic times. The rabbis, however, were the first to realize that we are dealing not only with an institution, but with *people*. One of the most touching stories in the Babylonian Talmud describes how delicate a balance must be maintained, if the institution is to survive:

> R. Reḥumei frequented (the school of) Rava at Maḥoza and would customarily return home on every eve of the Day of Atonement. One day he got carried away with his studies. His wife was expecting him, saying: "He is now coming, he is now coming." But he did not appear, and she was distressed, and a tear ran down from her eye. At that precise moment R. Reḥumei was sitting on a roof, the roof collapsed under him, and he died. (b. Ketubot 62b)

One wife's tear, at least in heaven, took precedence over all the studies of the Maḥozan academy.

NOTES

1. Salo Baron, *A Social and Religious History of the Jews*, 18 vols. (New York, 1952) II, 218.

2. See the sources by L. Ginzberg, 7 vols. *Legends of the Jews* (Philadelphia, 1909–38) V, 76, 262.

3. Gen. Rabbah 68:4 (ed. Theodore–Albeck, pp. 771–72) and parallel sources cited there (note the apparatus criticus for various versions on the wounds sustained by the "newlyweds").

4. b. Moed Katan 18b; compare b. Sotah 2a; b. Sanhedrin 22a.

5. E.g., Gen. Rabbah 8:9 (p. 83); id., 62:2 (p. 206); b. Sotah 17a.

6. Matt. 19:4–6; Mark 10:6–9. For early Christian and possibly Jewish interpretations of Gen. 2:24 in this connection, see D. Daube, *The New Testament and Rabbinic Judaism* (London, 1956), pp. 71–86.

7. Eph. 5:32.

8. See Tertullian, *De exhortatione castitatis*, 5, in W. P. Le Saint, trans., *Tertullian: Treatises on Marriage and Remarriage* (New York, 1951), p. 51; for marriage as a sacrament, see also St. Augustine, *De Nuptiis et Concupiscentia*, I, ii in Migne, *Patrologia Latina* 44, p. 420.

9. The following point has been succinctly presented by M. D. Herr, "The Socioeconomic Aspects of Marriage According to the Halakha" [in Hebrew], in *Mishpaḥot Bet Yisrael*, 1976, pp. 37–46.

10. One version of the She'iltot reads: "kiddushin and huppah." See Masekhet Ketubot, ed. M. Hershler (Jerusalem 1972), p. 39. This variant could apparently answer the frequently repeated question regarding the accepted version, which cites the two main stages of marriage in reverse order (huppah before kiddushin). A brilliant study by S. Friedman, however, has shown that our common version follows a well-documented stylistic norm of listing short words first; see "The Law of Increasing Numbers in Mishnaic Hebrew ("kol ha-katzar kodem")," *Leshonenu* 35 (1971), 201. Friedman also notes that most She'ilta variants follow the customary order.

11. Vat. ms. 130, geonim and rishonim; see Hershler, Masekhet Ketubot, p. 39, n. 78.

12. *Ginzei Kedem*, IV, 47; Otsar Ha-Geonim, Ketubot, p. 23.

13. "And what is the meaning of the rabbinic phrase ['the man hallows']? That he causes her to be forbidden to anyone else as though she were *hekdesh* [something devoted, or 'hallowed,' to the Temple service]." b. Kiddushin 2b; cf. Tosafot, ad loc.: "The simple meaning of the phrase 'hallowed to me' [is] 'she is unique to me'; 'she is set aside for me.' " Cf. Z. Falk, *Introduction to Jewish Law of the Second Commonwealth*, pt. 2 (Leiden, 1978), p. 285 and n. 2, who attempts to link the term *kiddushin* to aspects of purification. Falk's

suggestion in his earlier work *Jewish Matrimonial Law in the Middle Ages* (Oxford, 1966), pp. 41–42, that the term *kiddushin* (which he interprets as rendering the act "a religious ceremony of transcendental significance") was derived from the benediction itself is untenable in light of what has been noted earlier; cf. Herr, "Socioeconomic Aspects," p. 40, n. 12; Y. N. Epstein, *Mevo'ot Lesifrut Ha-Tannaim* (Jerusalem, 1957), pp. 53, 414.

14. Exod. 21:10. These requirements relate to a maidservant in the Torah but were understood to apply to all wives; see the following: Mekhilta d'Rabbi Yishmael, Mishpatim, Nezikin 3, ed. H. S. Horovitz-I. A. Rabin, (Jerusalem, 1970), pp. 258–59; Mekhilta d'Rabbi Shimon ben Yohai, ed. J. N. Epstein-E. Z. Melamed, (Jerusalem, n.d.) p. 167; b. Ketubot 47b. To these the rabbis added a variety of responsibilities, such as provision for her healing or ransom should she be taken captive; see m. Ketubot 4:8–9.

15. m. Ketubot 5:5.

16. t. Ketubot 12:3 (ed. S. Lieberman, p. 96); b. Ketubot 86a; b. Yevamot 113a; b. Kiddushin 7a; b. Gittin 49b.

17. t. Ketubot 6:8 (p. 77); 12:3 (p. 96); S. Lieberman, *Tosefta Kifshutah* (New York, 1967), p. 371.

18. See E. Westermarck, *The History of Human Marriage* (London, 1925) I, 46ff.

19. b. Kiddushin 7a and parallels.

20. Y. D. Gilat, "From Biblical Severity to Rabbinic Injunction," *Benjamin De Vries Memorial Volume*, ed. E. Z. Melamed (Jerusalem, 1968), pp. 84–93.

21. t. Ketubot 4:7 (p. 67); p. Ketubot 5:2, 29d; S. Lieberman, *Tosefet Rishonim*, II, 33, cites another example of twelve women who married Bar-Kappara and took it upon themselves to support him because of his wisdom; see also S. Lieberman *Tosefta Kifshutah*, Ketubot, p. 244.

22. See P. E. Corbett, *The Roman Law of Marriage* (Oxford, 1930), p. 77.

23. J. A. Crook, *Law and Life of Rome* (London, 1967), p. 105.

24. For an original thesis on the development of Jewish and Christian attitudes toward this commandment, see D. Daube, *The Duty of Procreation* (Edinburgh, 1977), esp. pp. 34–40.

25. *Against Apion* 2:199; cf. Philo, On Joseph 43: "The end we seek in wedlock is not pleasure but the begetting of lawful children"; cf. also Moses 1:28; The Special Laws 1:32, 113; The Worse Attacks the Better 102.

26. "replendo orbi." Cf. Gen. 1:28.

27. *Ad uxorem*, 2.

28. See St. Augustine, *De Nuptiis et Concupiscentia*, book I.

29. *Exhortatione* 3; Tertullian goes to great lengths to explain the nature of "good" in the context of marriage, noting that "the predicative 'good' is a forced predicative, because the true nature of the thing itself is obscured by the presence of a greater evil." Tertullian repeats the whole issue again in *De monogamia* 3.

30. Letter 22, 19–20; cf. J. N. D. Kelley, *Jerome: His Life, Writings and Controversies* (London, 1957), p. 102.

31. *Against Jovinianus*, 1:16.

32. *Against Jovinianus*, 1:9; the discussion of "good" versus "better" in this context spread throughout early Church literature; see, e.g., Aphrahat's eleventh demonstration, translated in J. Neusner, *Aphrahat and Judaism* (Leiden, 1971), p. 81.

33. This is the reading in Eccl. Rabbah 3:11.

34. Gen. Rabbah 9:7 (ed. J. Theodor and C. Albeck, pp. 71–72); Midrash Tehillim 9:1; cf. E. E. Urbach, *The Sages* [in Hebrew] (Jerusalem, 1975), pp. 474–75.

35. m. Yevamot 6:6.

36. "He is not permitted to neglect [performing the procreative act with her], rather he should divorce her and pay her her *ketubah*." t. Yevamot 8:5 (Lieberman, p. 25).

37. b. Yevamot 65b.

38. According to t. Yevamot 8:6 (p. 26); b. Yevamot 64b presents a tannaitic debate regarding the permissibility of a third marriage in this case.

39. See S. Lieberman, *Tosefta Kifshutah*, p. 72, for a discussion of this clause.

40. b. Yevamot 65a and Tosafot Ha-Rosh.

41. Gen. Rabbah 17:2 (ed. Theodor and Albeck, pp. 151–52).

42. b. Yevamot 62b.

43. Rashi explains that without a wife "he has to be involved in the needs of his household and [as a result] his learning is forgotten."

44. b. Yevamot 63b.

45. The similarity to Ben Azzai (but not to R. Yoḥanan) was noted by Daube, *Duty*, p. 38.

46. See Baron, *Social and Religious History*, II, 221.

47. b. Yevamot 61b; there is no parallel tradition in the Yerushalmi discussion of the same Mishnah (Yevamot 6:6), but the requirement is listed in t. Yevamot 8:4 (pp. 24–25).

48. See M. M. Kasher, *Torah Shlemah* 7 vols. (Jerusalem, 1938), VII, 1825–26.

49. b. Kiddushin 29b; Rav Hamnuna and Rav Safra (b. Pesachim 113a) are two well-known bachelors in Babylonia, but the motif of the scholar whose love of Torah keeps him single appears to be Palestinian.

50. b. Kiddushin 29b–30a.

51. See I. Gafni, "Converts and Conversion in Sassanian Babylonia" [in Hebrew], in M. Stern, ed., *Nation and History: Studies in the History of the Jewish People* (Jerusalem, 1983), pp. 205–6 and n. 42.

52. W. Wright, *The Homilies of Aphraates, the Persian Sage*. Vol. 1: *The Syriac Texts* (London, 1869), p. 345; Neusner, *Aphrahat and Judaism*, p. 76.

53. Wright, *Aphraates*, I, 355.

54. A. Vööbus, *A History of Asceticism in the Syrian Orient* (Louvain, 1958), I, 254 ff.; idem, *A History of the School of Nisibis* (Louvain, 1965), p. 2 and n. 8.

55. Cf. S. Shaked, "Esoteric Trends in Zoroastrianism," in *Proceedings of the Israel Academy of Science and Humanities* (Jerusalem, 1969), III, 209.

56. M. Shaki, "The Sassanian Matrimonial Relations," *Archiv Orientalni* 39 (1971), 338.

57. Tacitus, *Histories*, v, 5, 2, in M. Stern, *Greek and Latin Authors on Jews and Judaism* 3 vols. (Jerusalem, 1974–84), 26 (see also Stern's note on p. 40); J. N. Sevenster, *The Roots of Pagan Anti-Semitism in the Ancient World* (Leiden, 1957), p. 142.

58. *Antiquities* 17:14; *War* 1:477.

59. Justin, *Dialogue with Trypho*, 134,1; 141,4 (PG vi, 785, 800), translated, with an introduction and notes by A. L. Williams (London, 1930), pp. 276, 288.

60. Baron, *Social and Religious History*, II, 223 f.

61. For discussions of the issue and bibliography, see: S. Lowy, "The Extent of Jewish Polygamy in Talmudic Times," *Journal of Jewish Studies* 9 (1958), 115–38; Z. Falk, *Jewish Matrimonial Law* (Oxford, 1966), pp. 1–34; and, more recently, M. A. Friedman, *Jewish Polygyny in the Middle Ages: New Documents from the Cairo Geniza* [in Hebrew] (Jerusalem and Tel Aviv, 1986), esp. pp. 7–11. On the question of polygamy in the writings of the Dead Sea sect, see: G. Vermes, "Sectarian Matrimonial Halakha in the Damascus Rule," *Studies in Jewish Legal History*, ed. B. S. Jackson (London, 1974), pp. 197–202; Y. Yadin, *The Temple Scroll* (Jerusalem, 1983), I, 355–57.

62. Yevamot 1:1–4; 6:5; 13:8; 16:1.

63. Ketubot 10:2.

64. Gittin 8:6–7.

65. See Lowy, "Extent of Jewish Polygamy," p. 116, but compare Falk, *Jewish Matrimonial Law*, p. 3.

66. p. Yevamot 4:12, 6b.

67. At least two cases of bigamous Palestinian marriage are mentioned, both, however, in the Babylonian Talmud: Sukkah 27a (a Jewish official under Agrippa with two wives, one in Tiberias and one in Sepphoris); Yevamot 15a (Abba, brother of Rabban Gamaliel).

68. Avot of Rabbi Nathan, vers. B., chap. 2 (ed. Schechter, p. 9).

69. Pesikta Rabbati 43, p. 181b (ed. Braude, p. 765).

70. Gen. Rabbah 23.2 (ed. Theodor and Albeck, p. 222).

71. b. Yevamot 65a; M. A. Friedman, "Polygamy in the Documents of the Geniza," *Tarbiẓ* 40 (1971) 331, n. 50, suggested that this statement (and Rava's— see below, infra.) was made independently and not as part of the talmudic discussion on procreation. In another article (*Tarbiẓ* 43 (1974), 173), he supports this claim; cf. n. 21, which quotes the version recorded in a responsa of R. Sherira Gaon: "R. Ammi said: he should release [her] and pay her *ketubah*.

R. Ammi follows his reason [suggested elsewhere], for he said: he who marries
... " Thus, R. Ammi's rule was incorporated by the redactor into the *sugya*.

72. *Codex Iustinianus* 1,9,7 represents a law from Dec. 30, 393 c.e. prohibiting various acpects of Jewish marriage, including polygamy; see A. Linder, *Roman Imperial Legislation on the Jews* (Jerusalem, 1983), pp. 183–39.

73. J. Juster, *Les Juifs dans l'empire romain* (Paris, 1914), II, 52, n. 4.

74. Lowy, "Extent of Jewish Polygamy," pp. 115, 123f.

75. b. Yevamot 65a.

76. This has also been noted by Friedman. The Aramaic qualification "and that is under the condition that he can support her" (see Friedman, *Tarbiẓ* 40 (1971), 321, n. 3) is most likely an additional gloss (Friedman, "Polygamy," p. 358).

77. b. Ketubot 80b; b. Kiddushin 7a.

78. b. Yevamot 44a.

79. R. Roberts, *The Social Law of the Qur'an* (London, 1925), pp. 7–10.

80. For variants, see Herr, "Socioeconomic Aspects of Marriage," p. 40, n. 14; see, most recently, A. Oppenheimer, *Babylonia Judaica in the Talmudic Period* (Wiesbaden, 1983), pp. 223–35.

81. See Urbach, *The Sages*, p. 897, n. 47.

82. See Oppenheimer, *Babylonia Judaica*, pp. 397–401.

83. b. Yomah 18b; b. Yevamot 37b.

84. Cf. R. Margaliot, *Sinai* 21 (1974), 176–79; S. Krauss, "Who Would Be Mine for the Day" (in Hebrew), *Sinai* 22 (1948), 299–302; Lowy, "Extent of Jewish Polygamy," pp. 124–29.

85. J. Neusner, *History of the Jews in Babylonia* 5 vols. (Leiden, 1965), II, 130.

86. See Herr, "Socioeconomic Aspects of Marriage," p. 41 and n. 16.

87. p. Kiddushin 4:12, 66d; Urbach, *The Sages*, p. 898, n. 49.

88. See "Mutᶜa," *Encyclopaedia of Islam*, III, 774–76.

89. See *Cambridge History of Iran*, ed. Ilya Gershevitch (Cambridge, Eng., 1983), III, no. 2, p. 650. For polygamy in Sassanian Persia, see also A. A. Maharezi, *La Famille iranienne* (Paris, 1938), pp. 133–43.

90. Baron, *Social and Religious History*, II, 226.

2

Marriage as an Institution: Jewry Under Islam

MORDECHAI A. FRIEDMAN

Jews have lived in predominantly Islamic societies for over 1,350 years, from Spain in the West to Indonesia in the East. Jewish and Arab contacts began centuries before Muhammad's call, of course. From the beginning the two cultures have adapted to, influenced, and nurtured one another; and this process encompassed, inter alia, matters concerning marriage and the family. Such influence is reflected in an often quoted second-century passage from the Mishnah that describes the Jewish women of Arabia as going about veiled, and the Talmud notes that these women collected their ketubah payments from spices or camels.[1] The coexistence of these cultures over two millennia, with extended and repeated periods of mutual fructification, has been described by the late S. D. Goitein as a Jewish-Arab symbiosis.[2] Given the multifarious vicissitudes within these chronological and geographical spans, it would be irresponsible for me to attempt to discuss marriage as an institution among Jewry under Islam as a whole. In my following remarks, therefore, I shall confine myself to the Jews of the Near East, with special emphasis on Palestine and Egypt, particularly during the High Middle Ages (from the tenth to thirteenth centuries). I do so for two reasons. First, this period coincides with the zenith of the Jewish-Arab symbiosis. It is a formative period within Judaism, molded by the writings of the geonim (central authorities in the Babylonian academies), Maimonides, and the luminaries of Spain. Second, it has been blessed by a wealth of documentation in the papers discarded and preserved in the Cairo genizah, that treasure trove of manuscripts whose greatest "discoverer" was the Jewish Theological Seminary's own Solomon Schechter.[3]

For purposes of this study, I would like to epitomize the question of the legal relationship between husband and wife among the Jews under Islam with two words: property or partnership? The truth, I think we will discover, lies somewhere between these extremes.

According to earlier rabbinic practice, the formal relationship between husband and wife was contracted by the preliminary stage of the *shiddukh* (match agreement) and the *'erusin* (bethrothal). Islamic law has no parallel to *'erusin*, and Jews who spoke Arabic referred to both Jewish procedures by the same term, namely, *milāk or imlāk*, literally a property conveyance.[4] Does this term indicate that marriage itself was seen as a conveyance in which the husband takes possession of his wife? The question is a rather complex one, and a proper understanding of this issue would require an investigation on several different levels, including one of the possible relationship of the Arabic term with the Syriac *mekhirutha* (as suggested by Goitein),[5] the Hebrew *kinyan*, and similar terms in the Bible and the Talmud, and of the nature of marriage as purchase in the Bible, the Talmud, Christianity, and Islam. But even if apparent relationships were discovered, caution would still be necessary. As Goitein has noted, borrowed legal nomenclature does not necessarily indicate adoption of institutions. Jews who spoke Arabic would naturally use the corresponding Islamic term. Nomenclature is not to be ignored, but the study of the institutions themselves and their functioning is more to the point.[6]

An important factor in contracting a marriage was the financial arrangements made between the two families. Early Israelite marriage was based on a *mohar* payment by the groom (or his family) to the bride's father. Some students of the *mohar* have suggested that it originally served as purchase money for the bride. In certain societies, such as that of ancient Greece, effecting the marriage required a payment by the bride's family to the groom (or his family), the dowry. Few, if any, scholars have interpreted this as a purchase of the groom, which in itself is a cogent argument against identifying the *mohar* as purchase money. Whatever the original purpose of these payments, as time passed, a complexity of forces interacted in establishing the varying practices involved in these marriage payments: tradition, local custom, changing socioeconomic conditions, and individual circumstances. In postbiblical times more and more emphasis was placed on the dowry; the (prepaid) *mohar*, was, in effect, abrogated and replaced by a debt, the ketubah (marriage contract) obligation, collected by the wife at the dissolution of the marriage. The genizah period (tenth to thirteenth centuries) attests a certain revival of the ancient *mohar* payment. The groom's payment was normally divided into two portions. The first, usually designated *mohar muqdam* (early *mohar*), was paid when the marriage was contracted, like the biblical *mohar*; the latter (the *me'uḥar*) remained a delayed payment, like the talmudic ketubah.[7] But there is no suggestion in our sources that the Jews under medieval Islam thought of the early *mohar* as purchase money. In fact, the genizah documents prove that the dowry was almost always many times larger than the money given by the groom or promised by him. Besides clothing and home furnishings, the dowry frequently included items of considerable economic value. This gave the wife's family significant leverage in finding her a suitable match and insuring her proper treatment during marriage.

In accordance with talmudic law the husband did acquire some property rights over his wife's possessions and, to a certain degree, over her person. An example of the latter as practiced in the genizah period are the restrictions placed by a man on his wife's freedom of movement outside the home. We do hear of some seclusion of women in the Talmud. The rabbis opposed what they considered to be excesses in these matters, and locking a wife in or denying her reasonable freedom of movement was grounds for divorce.[8] But attitudes on what is considered reasonable in such matters vary considerably. We are dealing with questions of degree and emphasis. Goitein has suggested that these restrictions became more pronounced under Islam because of Iranian influence.[9] Be that as it may, from its inception Islam has encouraged the seclusion of women.[10] And as we have already noted, Jewish women in Arabia covered their faces hundreds of years before Islam.

Several documents from the genizah suggest that elements within Jewish society as well considered it meritorious to seclude women. Some men demanded that their wives not leave the home without their consent. Others were more specific and insisted that their wives be allowed outdoors only to those places permitted to upright, decent Jewish women, "namely, to go to the synagogue, to the bathhouse, to social visits occasioned by joyous celebrations, or to pay condolence calls and for buying and selling flax." The particular document here quoted, an agreement that averted an impending divorce, includes the interesting datum that women did attend synagogue services and engaged in certain business activities outside of the home.[11] Restrictions on the wife's freedom of movement was sometimes written into betrothal and marriage contracts. Some of these documents emanated from the lower strata of society or reflect special circumstances, and we are still unable to ascertain how prevalent this attitude was.[12] But there can be little doubt as to Maimonides' attitude (Ishut 13:11): "For every woman has the right to go out to her parents' home and to a house of mourning and celebration . . . For she is not in prison to be prevented from coming and going. However, it is disgraceful for a woman always to be going out . . . A husband has the right to prevent his wife from doing this. He should not permit her to go out except about once or twice a month, as may be required, for there is nothing more beautiful for a wife than sitting in the corner of her house." Parenthetically, we remember another infamous ruling of Maimonides (Ishut 21:10), namely, that a wife who refuses to perform any of her obligatory chores "may be beaten even with a whip until she does it."

The genizah documents imply that these actions were exceptional rather than the norm; they were probably usually undertaken as the last, desperate resort at the breakdown of the marriage relationship. As repulsive as they are to us, it would be wrong, I believe, to conclude that a woman was generally thought of as her husband's chattel, to be locked in or beaten at will. When a woman was mistreated by her husband, she petitioned the courts and communal authorities and demanded their protection. The information on wife beating certainly reflects such circumstances.[13]

Life is rarely logical and consistent. There is overwhelming evidence, found in extant Jewish marriage contracts, that points to a very different attitude toward the marriage relationship among the Jews living under Islam. The ketubah written according to the Palestinian custom was not, as in Babylonia, a unilateral document issued in the husband's name. In Eretz Israel, when the groom committed himself to serve, support, and honor his wife, she responded and undertook to serve and esteem him. These mutual obligations (recently found in a newly discovered ketubah written on papyrus in fifth-century C.E. Antinoopolis, Egypt) are richly documented in the genizah fragments from the tenth and eleventh centuries and became one of the distinctive characteristics of the Palestinian-style ketuboth.[14] Moreover, the marriage was defined in these documents as a *shutafut*, a partnership. This usage already occurs in a citation of the ketubah in the Palestinian Talmud. Its retention in medieval Palestine was not simply a case of conservatism in nomenclature but a matter of some consequence. In the clause in which this term appears, the wife was promised the right to initiate divorce proceedings against her husband if for no other reason than gratuitous hatred of him. If she did so, the courts would compel him to issue her a bill of divorce.[15] Iraqi Jews practiced essentially the same divorce procedure, though identifying it with an enactment of the geonim. Goitein cites a genizah letter that states that "living together without mutual consent is like prostitution."[16] And Maimonides himself ruled, on the basis of his understanding of the Babylonian Talmud, that, if a wife despised her husband, she could demand that he be compelled to divorce her immediately because she is "not like a captive to be forced to engage in sex with a man whom she hates (Ishut 14:8)."

We thus see a unique amalgam of elements, some traceable to ancient Jewish antecedents and others comparable to the mores of the surrounding society. Among Jews living under Islam we find excessive restrictions placed on a wife's personal freedom, if not examples of outright physical abuse. On the other hand, our sources attest a noble concept of marriage as partnership, highlighted by the liberality of enabling a woman to obtain a divorce at will. Both extremes are unparalleled in Jewish communities living in Christian countries.

The respective obligations and rights of husband and wife were essentially the same as those fixed by talmudic law. Most of these could be waived or modified with the consent of both parties according to the principle of freedom of contract for monetary matters. Such agreements frequently involved the dowry. This investment normally served to cement the marital relationship. Sometimes it had the opposite effect. The dowry items listed in the marriage contract theoretically enter the husband's jurisdiction. He is obligated to return them to his wife at the dissolution of the marriage or to compensate her for them. Some wives were dissatisfied with leaving their families' wealth in the hands of strangers, that is, their husbands. In many cases matrimonial harmony was not restored until a husband waived his rights over part or all of his wife's dowry. She released him of his responsibility over it and assumed full control to buy or sell, to use it for her own business activities, if she had any, or to use it for any other purpose she desired.[17]

The Talmud assigns a wife's earnings to her husband. The sages considered this benefit to be balanced by his obligation to provide her with food (*mezonot*).[18] The matching of the two has certain legal consequences: A wife may demand to keep her earnings and purchase her own food; such arrangements are mentioned in several Talmudic passages.

Stipulations concerning the wife's earnings begin to appear in the genizah documents toward the beginning of the twelfth century. They follow three essential variations:

1. Her earnings belong to her husband, and he must supply her with clothing.
2. She keeps her earnings and provides her own clothing.
3. She keeps her earnings, and he clothes her.[19]

The first version reaffirms the standard talmudic law; the other two reflect the peculiar socioeconomic circumstances and the relative willingness of the parties to make concessions.

Coupling the wife's earnings with her clothing (*kesut*)—rather than food (*mezonot*), as in the Talmud—is remarkable. Tentatively I suggest that this change may have been made for the protection of women. Were a woman with a large income able to keep it for herself, she would be more than willing to forgo her husband's food allowance. But unforeseen developments could prove her contractual undertaking to support herself impracticable. When R. Akiba's son, R. Joshua, married, his bride agreed not only to release him from his obligation to feed and support her, but she undertook to feed and support him as well, while he studied Torah. After a famine struck, she appealed her case to the sages; they upheld her husband's claim that the stipulation was still binding.[20] In general, we find that the sages considered a husband's requirement to provide his wife with food as self-evident because her very life could depend on it (*qiyyum nefesh*).[21] Posttalmudic authorities may have instructed scribes to exclude food from these contractual arrangements made between husband and wife and restrict the stipulation to clothing.[22] Goitein has further suggested that the change in the stipulation was due to new socioeconomic conditions. In late antiquity a Jewish woman had wider options for making a living and was able to sustain herself and provide her own nourishment. In Islamic times, on the other hand, she was more confined to her home, where she occupied herself with needlework and dyeing textiles. Whereas she was often unable to support herself, providing clothing was relatively easy.[23]

In the preceding remarks I have touched on how marriage institutions reflected in the genizah documents differed from those of talmudic Judaism. To what extent can this be attributed to Islamic influence?

The Jews represented by the genizah papers belonged to communities that had existed continuously since antiquity, and Goitein emphasized repeatedly that they may be assumed to have faithfully preserved ancient patterns of life. At the same time, in matters of commerce, Judaism did adapt itself extensively to Muslim practice (*ʿāda*) because of the aforementioned principle of freedom of contract in monetary matters. This principle could not be applied in most areas of family law, which in any event tended to be more conservative. But changes have always occurred, and Jewish society was bound to have been influenced by the predominant Islamic environment.[24]

This issue has some larger ramifications. The genizah is a unique hoard of documents, and there is nothing comparable from contemporary Islam. One of the basic theses of Goitein's *A Mediterranean Society* and of his Geniza research in general is that these documents depict not only the Jewish communities with which they deal directly but, to a large extent, the surrounding Islamic society. Although Goitein's view has been accepted by most in the scholarly community, it has been challenged by some. E. Ashtor, for example, rejects the tendency to draw comparisons with Muslim society and suggests that Jewish life in medieval Egypt should be compared with other contemporary Jewish communities outside the realm of Islam.[25]

The genizah demonstrates again and again both continuity and adaption in Jewish marriage and family law. Difficulties arise, however, when we attempt to establish criteria for defining these processes. Rarely are we dealing with abrupt revisions of legal practice that may have been the result of Islamic influence. In the majority of cases we must decide whether the practices that we are studying reflect Jewish tradition (or rather *a* Jewish tradition) or change, and if they do reflect change, we must ask how much this is the result of the influence of Islam or of internal Jewish developments or other circumstances. The absence of an "Islamic genizah" means that regrettably, more often than not, comparisons are based on suppositions or implications from literary sources. This obviously means that there is a large realm of subjectivity. The complexity of multiple forces reflected in our sources and the inherent limitations of our attempts to interpret them preclude simple answers and explanations, no matter how tempting these may be.

I illustrate this difficulty with a central issue of marriage, viz. monogamy vs. polygamy—or polygyny, to use the more precise term. The Jews who lived in Islamic countries did not accept the ban attributed to R. Gershom (late tenth to early eleventh centuries) and remained, in theory, polygynous. But how polygynous in practice were the Jews who lived under Islam during the High Middle Ages? A generation ago genizah scholars had not identified any documents that attested polygyny, and they asserted that this society was virtually monogamous.[26] When Goitein began his genizah research, he described having found one case of bigamy from among hundreds of relevant documents. This was from the provincial Egyptian town of Bilbeis, and it reflected special circumstances: The first wife was incapacitated and unable to care for her daughter.[27] In his early genizah studies, Goitein confirms the basically monogamous nature of the genizah Jews, but, in support of his general theory concering these communities' representative nature, he suggests that the same may have been the case in Muslim society:

> When we find that the Geniza society was practically monogamous, although ancient Jewish (like Muslim) law permitted polygamy, this practice was more characteristic of a progressive middle class than of a specific religious community. It is not excluded that the same practice prevailed at the same time in the corresponding layers of Muslim society. We shall get clarity in this point only if and when we shall have documents dealing with Muslims for this period similar in character and number to those provided to us by the Geniza.[28]

When Goitein wrote these lines, he probably was already familiar with a number of documents dealing with polygyny. But the question of numbers is exactly one of the issues that we must address in assessing our sources. The genizah, as we know, is not an archive but a random collection of fragments. When do we say that a specific number of items are exceptions to the rule, and when do we begin to see them as representative of a wide practice? This question remains unanswered today.[29] As Goitein's genizah research progressed, more documents concerning polygyny came to light, but he continued to see this as "a minor social evil."[30] According to him, "Unlike absenteeism, polygyny or its threat was not a major trouble for wives. By custom, albeit not by law, the Geniza society was essentially monogamous . . . Threats to the effect that a husband might take another wife were not entirely absent, but they were rare, and, one has the impression, not taken too seriously."[31] On the other hand, Goitein reconsidered his earlier suggested comparison with Islamic society and concluded that the evidence seemed "to indicate that polygyny was more generally condemned in the Jewish community than in its environement."[32]

E. Ashtor, in his review of the third volume of *A Mediterranean Society*, cites Goitein's findings on polygyny to support his own approach concerning the dissimilarity between Jewish and Muslim societies: "The clear prevalence (if not exclusiveness) of monogamy (also excluding the concubinate with slave girls), on which Goitein rightly dwells . . . , meant certainly a great difference between the family life of Jews and Moslems."[33]

Successive genizah research enables us to examine this question from a fresh perspective. Over the past years I have collected documents dealing with polygyny, adding many newly discovered texts. These include dozens of fragments describing actual or purported cases of polygyny as well as numerous incidents of illicit concubinage with slave girls.[34] Phenomena represented by much less documentation have been described by genizah research as common. A review of the abundant evidence now available suggests that whereas most marriages certainly were monogamous (as is the case in almost all polygynous societies), polygyny and concubinage with slave girls were far from rare occurrences, and the Jewish community frequently occupied itself with the problems associated with these phenomena. The aforementioned absence of comparable Muslim documentary sources precludes drawing any definite conclusions, but on the basis of the genizah fragments I am inclined to surmise that the similarities between the communities concerning polygyny and the slave girl syndrome were considerable.

Propinquity fostered similarities but did not eradicate distinctions. The different social and religious traditions in Judaism and Islam continued to influence the attitudes of the everyday person and had a significant effect on the religious leaders. Defining the elements of continuity and adaption concerning polygyny and the slave girl syndrome within the Jewish community requires a detailed study of talmudic Jewry, an investigation that involves methodological problems of its own that cannot be undertaken here. I briefly note that classical Judaism had certain monogamous trends. This was especially the case in Palestine, where a woman had the right to demand a divorce with full ketubah payments if her husband took another wife, and this legal tradition continued to exert its influence on medieval Egyptian Jewry.[35] As far as concubinage with slave girls is concerned, talmudic law—in contrast with Islam—clearly forbade this, but this did not eradicate the problem of illicit affairs.

Emulation of their Muslim neighbors can be assumed to have resulted in an increase in polygyny and the slave girl syndrome among the genizah Jews. It also left its traces on customary law as well as on the rulings of the religious authorities. An example of the former is the agreements frequently found in genizah texts to grant equal rights to the wives in a polygynous family and, especially, the undertaking to alternate nights with them. R. Solomon Duran of fifteenth-century Algeria correctly surmised that this reflected Islamic influence.[36] As far as the rulings of religious authorities are concerned, we note that, in contradiction to talmudic law, such scholars as the Palestinian gaon Elijah and Maimonides encouraged a man who had an affair with a slave girl to marry her after she was emancipated.[37]

Perhaps the most perplexing question we might consider in this context is whether the marriage institution can be seen as a religious or a political statement.[38] The prophetic description of marriage as a covenant between a man and a woman, entered by the recitation of mutual *verba solemnia* and consecrated by an oath to which God Himself served as witness (Hos. 2:17, Ezek. 16:8, Mal. 2:14, Prov. 2:17), epitomizes the religious nature of marriage in the Bible.[39] The rabbinic marriage ceremony does not contain any of these elements, and statements in the talmudic literature on the sacredness of marriage pale in comparison to the prophetic image. Marriage is certainly a religious duty, and there are elements in the marriage institution of an unquestionably religious nature, primarily the benedictions recited at the betrothal and wedding ceremonies. (I, for one, tend to discount the religious overtones attributed to the word *kiddushin*.[40]) Other elements concerning the institution and its legal structure, how it is effected or dissolved, and the relationship of husband and wife are all sanctioned and regulated by religious laws and traditions, but, in essence, they are of a secular, or perhaps a political, nature. Though the relative weight of the different factors must be assessed in a way that will minimalize the realm of subjectivity, in the final analysis we must speak in relative terms rather than absolutes. Attitudes toward these matters among Jews under Islam probably did not differ much from the talmudic period, but such questions as the religious implications of divorce and the facility of effecting it require further investigation.

I conclude with some brief remarks on the common superscription in Palestinian-style marriage contracts of the tenth to eleventh centuries: "In the name of our Creator." It has been suggested that writing this indicates an appreciation of the religious nature of marriage, and its absence in Babylonian-style ketuboth has been discussed as a possible sign of a secularization of that bond.[41] But the phrase really has nothing to do with marriage as a religious institution. Fifty years ago Professor Lieberman identified this phrase in an obscure passage in the Palestinian Talmud, where a proselytized astrologer recited, "In the name of our Creator," before setting out on a (business) journey. As Lieberman explained, this was a fixed formula recited by Jews before undertaking a difficult venture.[42] Further evidence for this can be adduced from a passage in the midrash that comments on Ps. 65:6 ("Answer us with victory through awesome deeds, O God, our deliverer, in whom all the ends of the earth and distant seas put their trust."): "You are the trust of wrestlers—in Your name do they trust; those who embark on journeys—in Your name do they trust; those who set sail to sea—in Your name do they trust; those who travel in the wilderness by caravan—all of them do trust in Your name."[43]

The religious man and woman always trust in the name of the Lord. It is only fitting that they invoke His blessings by reciting "In Your name (i.e., In Your name do we trust), our Creator" when, full of hopes and prayers, they embark on what for most is life's greatest adventure into the unknown—marriage.[44] Jews in the Talmudic period and under Islam felt the same closeness to, and trust in, their Creator. (So did Muslims; compare the writing and recitation of the bismillah.) To what extent Jews conceived of marriage itself as a religious institution requires further clarification.

NOTES

1. Veils: m. Shabbat 6:6 (on Jewish women wearing veils, see the literature and sources cited by M. A. Friedman, *Jewish Marriage in Palestine: A Cairo Geniza Study* (Tel Aviv and New York, 1980–81), II, 225–26 (hereafter referred to as *JMP*). Cf. Maimonides, Ishut 25:2. Spices and camels: (p. Ketubot X.3, 33d; b. Ket. 67a. (On p. Ket. VI.4, 30d, see the emendation suggested by S. Lieberman, *Tosefta Ki-Fshuṭah* (New York, 1967), VI, 277, n. 26. If Lieberman is correct, it can be assumed that the error resulted from a misunderstanding of the following "'aririn" as "barren" rather than "challenging.")

2. Goitein wrote of the Jewish-Arab symbiosis on several occasions. See, e.g., his *Jews and Arabs*, 3d ed. (New York, 1974), p. 262 (index).

3. Little attention was paid during the first several decades of genizah research to letters, contracts, and court records that deal with marriage and the family. This situation was reversed by Goitein's epoch-making studies, to be found primarily in his *A Mediterranean Society: The Jewish Communities of the Arab World as Portrayed in the Documents of the Cairo Geniza*, 4 vols. (Berkeley and Los Angeles, 1967–83), III: *The Family*. See my review of the third volume of *A Mediterranean Society* in *JAOS* 100 (1980), 128–31. Cf. M. A. Friedman, "On S. D. Goitein's Contributions to Judaeo-Arabic Studies" in *Proceedings of the Second Conference of the Society for Judaeo-Arabic Studies* [in Hebrew], forthcoming.

4. See Goitein, *A Mediterranean Society*, III, 69ff.; M. A. Friedman, "Matchmaking and Betrothal Agreements in the Cairo Geniza" [in Hebrew], *Proceedings of the Seventh World Congress of Jewish Studies: Studies in the Talmud, Halacha, and Midrash* (Jerusalem, 1981), pp. 158ff.

5. *A Mediterranean Society*, III, 95.

6. See S. D. Goitein, "Maimonides as Chief Justice," *Jewish Quarterly Review* 49 (1959), 198, n. 25. Cf. M. A. Friedman, "The Ransom-Divorce: Divorce Proceedings Initiated by the Wife in Mediaeval Jewish Practice," *Israel Oriental Studies* 6 (1976), 298–302.

7. See M. A. Friedman, "Marriage and the Family in the Talmud—Selected Chapter (From *Mohar* to *Ketubba*)" in E. E. Urbach, ed., *Yad la-Talmud: Selected Chapters* (Israel, 1983), pp. 29–36, 99–100; idem, "The Minimum *Mohar* Payment as Reflected in the Geniza Documents: Marriage Gift or Endowment Pledge?" *PAAJR* 43 (1976), 15–47; idem, "Division of the Marriage Gift into Immediate and Postponed Payments in the Geniza Documents" [Hebrew], *Proceedings of the Sixth World Congress of Jewish Studies*, III (1977), 377–87; idem, *JMP*, I, 257–62, 271–88; Goitein, *A Mediterranean Society*, III, 517 (index).

8. E.g., m. Ketubot 7:5. See M. A. Friedman, "The Ethics of Medieval Jewish Marriage" in S. D. Goitein, ed., *Religion in a Religious Age* (Cambridge, Mass., 1974), pp. 87ff.

9. Goitein, *Religion in a Religious Age*, p. 102 (where he speaks of regional differences within Islam, calling attention not only to the severe Iranian seclusion of women but also to the possible influence of the fanatical Muslim West on Maimonides; see infra.); idem, *A Mediterrianean Society*, III, 153ff.; idem, "Human Rights in Jewish Thought and Life in the Middle Ages" in D. Sidorsky, ed., *Essays on Human Rights* (Philadelphia, 1979), pp. 259–60.

10. For the expression *Waqarna fī buyūtikunna* in Qur'an 33:33, where Muhammad's wives are told to stay at home, cf. Prov. 25:17 and II Kings 14:10.

11. Cambridge University Library (CUL), Taylor-Schechter Collection (TS) 8 J 29.13. (I would like to thank Dr. Stefan Reif and the CUL staff for their kind assistance.) See Friedman, "Ethics," p. 90, p. 100, n. 36 where "222" in

the reference to G. Weiss's Ph.D. dissertation is a misprint for "123" (it appears on p. 222 of vol. 2). Cf. MS. Mosseri L 197, ed. S. D. Goitein, "A Maghrebi Living in Cairo Implores his Karaite Wife to Return to Him," *JQR* 73 (1982), 138–45, where a wife is warned that in the future she should be careful not to leave the house except to go to the Karaite synagogue and the bathhouse; see also M. A. Friedman, "Divorce upon the Wife's Demand as Reflected in Manuscripts from the Cairo Geniza," *Jewish Law Annual* 4 (1981), 121, n. 62. Also see MS. Vienna, Papyrus Erzherzog Rainer *1 (S. Shaked, *A Tentative Bibliography of Geniza Documents* [Paris and the Hague, 1964], p. 234), ed. S. Assaf, "Pitom and Damsīs," in *Sefer ha-Yovel . . . Marx* (New York, 1943), p. 75, l. 13: "And she will not leave his house except with his permission."

12. See Goitein, *A Mediterranean Society*, III, 154; M. A. Friedman, *JAOS* 100 (1980), 130; E. Ashtor, review of S. D. Goitein, *A Mediterranean Society, Bibliotheca Orientalis* 38 (1981), 425–26. Ashtor takes exception, on methodological grounds, with comparisons made by Goitein between the Jewish and Muslim communities, on the basis of the Geniza documents, and his assumption that the former represents the latter concerning this and other issues; ironically, he sees no such methodological problem in adducing evidence for the restrictions on freedom of movement for women in medieval Islam from his experiences in the 1950s as a train passenger in Spain.

13. See Goitein, *A Mediterranean Society*, III, 157, 184 ff.; idem, "Human Rights," p. 260; Friedman, *JAOS* 100 (1980), 130; idem, *Jewish Polygyny in the Middle Ages—New Documents from the Cairo Geniza* [Hebrew] (Jerusalem and Tel Aviv, 1986), pp. 58–59 (hereafter Friedman, *Polygyny*).

14. Friedman, *JMP*, I, 179–91 (Goitein's comments in *A Mediterranean Society*, III, 51–52, were written before much of the material discussed here came to light; as to his remark on "love" in the marriage contract, see *JMP*, I, 340). The papyrus has now been published in C. Sirat, P. Cauderlier, M. Dukan, and M. A. Friedman, *La Ketouba de Cologne—Un contrat de mariage juif a Antinoopolis (Papyroloqica Coloniensia* XII) (Opladen, Germany, Westdeucher Verlag, 1986).

15. p. Ketubot VII. 7, 31c; Friedman, *JMP*, I, 312–46.

16. *A Mediterranean Society*, III, 263. On the enactment of the geonim, see M. A. Friedman, "Divorce," pp. 103–26 and literature cited there and idem, *Polygyny*, p. 363 (index).

17. See Goitein, *A Mediterranean Society*, III, 128, 181ff.

18. The two are paired in many sources, the most commonly quoted one being b. Ketubot 47b.

19. See the discussion in M. A. Friedman, *Tarbiẓ* 40 (1971), 355, n. 174; idem, *Polygyny*, p. 103, n. 40. Some examples of the wife's earnings being paired with her food were still found, however; so TS Loan 205 (written 1100–1138): "her earnings are hers, and he is responsible for her food."

20. t. Ketubot 4:7 (ed. Lieberman, [New York, 1967], p. 67); cf. Lieberman, *Tosefta Ki-Fshuṭah*, VI, 244.

21. See *Mekhilta d'Rabbi Ishmael*, ed. H. S. Horovitz and I. A. Rabin (Jerusalem, 1960), p. 259.

22. *Mezonot* was usually understood as including both food and clothing; see Friedman, *JMP*, I, 437–38 and references cited there. The insistence that the husband provide his wife with food could further be seen as encouraging marital harmony; see m. Ketubot 5:9.

23. Goitein, *A Mediterranean Society*, III, 134. For an example of a woman supported by her husband to whom she gave her needlework, see TS AS 152.360, ed. Z. W. Falk, "From the Cairo Geniza" [Hebrew], *Sinai* 85 (1979), 147–48; cf. Goitein, *A Mediterranean Society*, IV, 82 (the edition requires some minor revisions. So in l.9 read B'DH for B'DH; 1.10 begins with two words later deleted: T'SH W'TY; in l.22. For HDYYN 'NṬY I read HDYYN 'NṬW[LY], who is probably the Alexandrian judge Antoli b. Joseph, Maimonides's contemporary—correct accordingly the identification suggested by M. Gil, *Palestine During the First Muslim Period* [634–1099] [in Hebrew] [Tel-Aviv, 1983], II, 528). Examples of the coupling of the wife's earnings with her clothing persist in the *ketubah* through modern times: CUL Or. 1080 4.21 (Cairo, 1823): He keeps her earnings and provides her with clothing.

24. See S. D. Goitein, "The Interplay of Jewish and Islamic Laws," in B. S. Jackson, ed., *Jewish Law in Legal History and the Modern World* (Leiden, 1980), pp. 61–77.

25. See Ashtor (n. 12), pp. 425–28.

26. So S. Assaf, *Sefer ha-Yishuv*, II (Jerusalem, 1944), 46; idem, *Tequfat ha-Geonim we-Sifrutah*, ed. M. Margaliot (Jerusalem, 1954–55), p. 95.

27. S. D. Goitein, *Studies in Islamic History and Institutions* (Leiden, 1966), p. 292.

28. Goitein, *A Mediterranean Society*, I, 73–74.

29. In 1971, when my first study on polygyny in the genizah ("Polygamy in the Documents of the Geniza" [in Hebrew], *Tarbiẓ* 40 [1971], 320–59) was published, I knew of eight documents that described polygynous marriages (six are edited in the article; two others are described on pp. 346, 358; most of these were noted in Goitein's files); but, as these represented some 1 percent of the number of documents concerning marriage that I had studied, I still confirmed the essentially monogamous character of the society (p. 322).

30. Goitein, *A Mediterranean Society*, III, 150.

31. Ibid., p. 205.

32. Ibid., p. 150.

33. Ashtor (n. 12), p. 425.

34. Friedman, *Polygyny*. See also Friedman, "Polygyny in Jewish Tradition and Practice: New Sources from the Cairo Geniza," *PAAJR* 49 (1982), 33–68.

35. See Friedman, *PAAJR* 49 (1982), 40ff.

36. Solomon Duran, *Responsa* (Livorno, 1742), no. 624, p. 129a. See Friedman, *PAAJR* 49 (1982), 64–68.

37. TS Misc. 27.4.23 + 29, ed. M. A. Friedman, "Master and Slave Girl: Two Geniza Documents," *Gratz College Annual of Jewish Studies*, I (Philadelphia, 1972), 56–61; Friedman, *Polygyny*, pp. 314–19. R. Moses b. Maimon, *Responsa*, ed. J. Blau, II (Jerusalem, 1960), no. 211, pp. 373–75.

38. See Gafni's discussion of this same question earlier in this volume, p. 00.

39. See M. A. Friedman, "Israel's Response in Hosea 2:17b: 'You Are My Husband,' " *JBL* 99 (1980), 199–204; cf. Friedman, "Ethics," p. 83.

40. See Gafni earlier in this volume, p. 00.

41. See Goitein, *A Mediterranean Society*, III, 52–53.

42. p. Shabbat VI.10, 8d. See S. Lieberman, *Tarbiẓ* (1935), 234–35; idem, *Texts and Studies* (New York, 1974), pp. 21ff.; see S. Lieberman, *Hayerushalmi Kiphsuto* (Jerusalem, 1934), pp. 114–15.

43. *Pesikta de Rav Kahana*, ed. B. Mandelbaum (New York, 1962), pp. 348–49 (see variant readings). This passage, as well as the genizah ketuboth (see Friedman, *JMP*, I, 91–92), suggests that no distinction was made between "By the name of our Creator" (*bishmei*) and "On the name of our Creator" (*ʿal shmei*) (see Lieberman, *Tarbiẓ* 27 [1958], 57–60).

44. These prayers included the supplication that the couple be blessed with children. On the phrase "the mother of children" found in the marriage formula of Palestinian-style marriage contracts, see Friedman, "Ethics," p. 84; idem, *JMP*, I, 159–60; Goitein, *A Mediterranean Society*, III, 49–50. Note p. Ketubot VI.2, 30c: "TNY BR QPR', PWSQ LŠM KTWBH ʿL MNT LBNYM." But as noted by the commentators, the last word is an error for "LKNWS."

3

Jewish Medieval Marriage Customs in Art: Creativity and Adaptation

JOSEPH GUTMANN

The intention of this study is to examine the emergence of such medieval Jewish marriage customs as the portable canopy, the wedding ring, the shattering of the glass cup, and the decorated ketubah. These practices, which are still adhered to today, indisputably reflect the adaptation by Jews of similar customs of their medieval Christian and Muslim neighbors.

Evidence of the development of medieval Jewish marriage customs can sometimes be found in unanticipated sources. This is true in the case of the *Wimpel* custom, a new Jewish family celebration that was instituted in southern Germany around the year 1500. It then became customary to preserve the linen swaddling cloth on which a boy had been circumcised, wash it, cut it generally into four sections, and stitch these sections together lengthwise. Upon this cloth, which was given the name *Wimpel*, was then embroidered the child's Hebrew name, the date of his birth, and a standard pious formula expressing every parent's wish that a son should grow up to study Torah, get married (*"ḥuppah"*) and perform good deeds.[1] On eighteenth-century *Wimpeln*, near the embroidered word *ḥuppah*, we find that a couple is sometimes depicted standing underneath a portable canopy. The four poles of these canopies are frequently held aloft by four youths.[2] The portable canopy so much a part of today's Jewish wedding is, like the *Wimpel* custom, a latecomer into Judaism. It was probably adopted from Catholicism, which had used the portable canopy for Church ritual since the Middle Ages.[3] The pope, for instance, was often borne under a so-called portable heaven (*Traghimmel, mappula,* or *baldacchino*) to the church altar to perform the Mass. The *Traghimmel*, upheld by four staves, was also carried over the Blessed Sacrament and the relics of the Passion during holy processions.[4]

The portable canopy apparently came into Ashkenazi Judaism in the sixteenth century and appears to be first recorded by Moses Isserles (*Shulḥan Arukh, Even ha-Ezer* 55:1), who writes: "Nowadays the custom is widespread to apply the term *ḥuppah* to a place where they spread a cloth over staves and bring the bride and groom under it in public and he pronounces there the marriage formula. . . . "[5] From the sixteenth century on, the portable canopy was usually set up in the courtyard of the Ashkenazi synagogue, where the ceremony was performed. Like the Catholic *Traghimmel*, the Jewish canopy, called *Trauhimmel* or *Brauthimmel*, was also likened to the heavens. At times it was blue and had Hebrew inscriptions and depictions of the sun, moon, and stars, so that it might resemble the heavens and be an omen that the couple's children, in the words of Genesis 26:4, "be as numerous as the stars of heaven."[6]

During the Middle Ages, beginning in the twelfth century and prior to the sixteenth century, the wedding ceremony was usually held inside the European synagogue. There the huppah was simply a cloth, called *sudar* (= sudarium), or a tallith, spread over the bridal couple. This custom is verified in German and Italian Hebrew miniatures dating from the thirteenth to the fifteenth centuries.[7] A similar and related practice existed already in the early medieval church, where during the nuptial Mass a cloth (pallium, *velamen,* or *velum*) was sometimes spread over the bridal couple.[8] It is probably from this Christian source that the custom was adapted by Jews in Spain, Italy, and Franco-Germany. This practice was given religious sanction and explained by reference to such

1. Torah binder. Schmalkalden, Germany, 1762. Linen, embroidered with silk thread. From the collection of The Jewish Museum. Reprinted by permission.

biblical statements as "Spread your robe over your handmaiden" (Ruth 3:9) or "I spread My robe over you" (Ezek. 16:8).

How different these huppah customs are from the practice of the talmudic period, where the couple knew neither the *sudar*-tallith nor the portable canopy but was ceremoniously led *into* the huppah—frequently a special room or a nuptial tent, at times made "of crimson silk embroidered with gold" (b. Bava Batra 146a, b. Kiddushin 50a)—set up at the groom's or his father's house, where the vows of the *nissu'in* (wedding) ceremony were sexually consummated.[9]

Similarly, the present custom of breaking a glass at weddings has no biblical or talmudic precedents; it was unknown to medieval Sephardi (Spanish-Portuguese) Jews. It apparently arose in medieval Germany and is at home in the Rhineland by the twelfth century. Rabbi Eliezer ben Nathan of twelfth-century Mainz mentions the custom of breaking a glass vessel at weddings (*nissu'in*). He wonders about this custom "of desecrating the cup [of wine] over which the benedictions had been recited and dissipating its contents by pouring it out."[10] Early sources indicate that the second cup over which the *birkhot nissu'in* (nuptial benedictions) had been recited was shattered; later the cup over which the bethrothal benediction had been read was broken. Moses Minz, a German rabbi of the fifteenth century, informs us (Responsum no. 109) that in his time it also became customary to shout, "Mazel tov," when the glass was shattered after the betrothal benediction.[11] It was the custom in medieval Germany often to have the bridegroom shatter the glass against the interior northern synagogue wall. By the eighteenth century, when the wedding had been shifted to the exterior, it appears that a stone for these purposes was often affixed to the outside northern wall of the synagogue building. This stone was known as *sigillum Salomonis* or *scutum Davidis*, as well as *Huppastein, Traustein*, or *Ehestein*. It frequently had an octagonal or hexagonal star carved on it and the initial Hebrew letters of the words *mazel tov* and the verse from Jeremiah 7:34: "The sound of mirth and gladness, the voice of bridegroom and bride."[12] The glass was thrown at the stone, usually affixed, as we said, to the northern synagogue wall, since popular belief held that demons and evil spirits resided in that region. The glass, at times filled with wine, was intended as a bribe for the evil forces. In addition, it was hoped that the broken fragments of glass would hurt the demons or that, at least, the noise of the shattering glass would frighten them away.

In medieval Italy, an empty glass cup was sometimes thrown on the ground after the betrothal benediction or after the wedding blessings.

P.IV

J.C.M: inv: et sculp

2. Nuptial ceremony of the German Jews in the Fürth synagogue. Etching by J. C. Müller in J. C. G. Bodenschatz, *Kirchliche Verfassung der heutigen Juden* (Erlangen, 1748). From the collection of the Library of The Jewish Theological Seminary of America. Reprinted by permission.

By the eighteenth century the Ashkenazi custom of shattering glass had been adopted by the Sephardim of Holland and by other Sephardi communities. There, however, the glass was shattered by throwing it against a specially designed silver or pewter plate, placed underneath the huppah at the groom's feet.[13]

Around the fourteenth century, Ashkenazi tradition justified this originally superstitious custom by interpreting the shattered glass as a symbolic remembrance of the destruction of the Jerusalem Temple (*zekher laḥurban*).[14] A seventeenth-century Italian rabbi, Leone da Modena, in his *Historia dei riti hebraici*, understood the custom to recall the fragility of life—it is "a reminder of death, which can break and shatter us like a glass vessel that cannot be repaired."[15] Similar customs of smashing a glass before or at weddings were familiar in medieval Christian Germany, as popular folklore believed that broken glass could smash the power of demons dwelling in the northern region. Ashkenazi Jews probably adopted this custom from the dominant Christian milieu.[16]

Another Jewish marriage custom, adapted from Christianity and at home in medieval Italy, was the *dextrarum iunctio*—the uniting of the right hands of the couple as the groom placed the ring on his bride's finger. In medieval Italy, a separate ring ceremony was initiated that preceded the betrothal and wedding ceremonies. The officiant in many Italian Hebrew miniatures of the fifteenth century is usually shown grasping the arms of the couple and gently bringing their right hands together.[17] The groom held a ring, which, in the process of the union of their hands, would be placed on the bride's finger while he recited the kiddushin formula. Neither the Bible nor the Talmud speaks of a ring as a binding symbol of the kiddushin ceremony. Both the ring and the oral declaration by the groom of the kiddushin formula—"Behold you are consecrated to me with this ring according to the Law of Moses and Israel"—appear to have been introduced in medieval Europe as part of the combined 'erusin-nissu'in ceremony, and they had become established practice in many Jewish communities by the twelfth century.[18]

In medieval Catholic Europe the officiant frequently linked the couple's right hands at betrothal with the utterance that he was joining them to the hands of the Lord while a formula was recited as the groom placed a ring on the bride's finger. In Italy the Christian engagement was called "the day of the ring," and elaborate banquets followed the ceremony.[19]

It is interesting to note that in artistic depictions from the Roman world the personification of Concordia sometimes stands between the bridal couple and unites their right hands (*dextrarum iunctio*) as a secular

3. Nuptial ceremony of the Portuguese Jews. Etching by Bernard Picart, Amsterdam, Holland, 1733. From the collection of the Library of the Jewish Theological Seminary of America. Reprinted by permission.

סדר נשואים חתן וכלה

4. The Italian *dextrarum iunctio* and ring ceremony. Miniature from a *maḥzor*, Italian rite, Pesaro, Italy, 1481. Hungarian Academy of Sciences, Budapest, MS 380/II, fol. 230. From the private collection of J. Gutmann.

betrothal pledge of mutual trust and as a symbol that the bride has been brought under the manus of the husband. At times the bride would also receive a ring (*anulus pronubus*), which she slipped on her index finger.[20] Hence, an ancient Roman betrothal custom continued to live on in Catholicism and was adapted in the Italian Jewish marriage ritual.

Just as the portable canopy, the ring, and the breaking of the glass are still important components of the Jewish wedding, so is the decorated ketubah. Unlike the preceding ceremonies, which were adapted from Christianity, the custom of decorating the ketubah was apparently adapted from the Jewish encounter with Islam. Our earliest surviving examples appear to date from the eleventh through the twelfth centuries in Egypt and Syro-Palestine.[21] The geometrical and floral decorations in the ketuboth tend to follow the patterns established in contemporary illustrated Islamic marriage contracts.[22] The occasional placing of the bismillah (invocation) above the text of the ketubah and the introduction of such practices as the early and delayed installments (*mohar*) of the marriage payments also follow Islamic practices.[23] The custom of illustrating the ketubah perhaps also arose when the ketubah and its lavish dowry provisions were read aloud and displayed in the Islamic world. The purpose was sheer ostentation as families vied to outdo one another in dowries in order to enhance their status and to impress the Jewish community with their weatlh. It was even customary to assign fictitious, highly inflated values to the dowry outfit of the bride.[24] When the centers of Islam declined in the East, the custom of the illustrated ketubah may have spread to Islamic Spain in the West, but there is no evidence to support this contention. We do find decorated ketuboth from the thirteenth through the fifteenth centuries in Christian Spain, and Rabbi Simeon ben Zemah Duran (1361–1444) of Majorca tells us that it was customary to adorn the parchment sheet borders of the ketubah with decorations and biblical verses in order to prevent the insertion into the empty spaces of the ketubah of additional obligations not originally agreed on (*Sefer ha-Tashbetz*, Responsum 6).[25] With the dispersion of the Sephardi Jews the practice of illustrating the ketubah apparently spread to Turkey and Italy. Abraham ben Moses di Boton, a Sefardi rabbi of sixteenth-century Salonika, Turkey (*Lehem Rav*, Responsum 15), reports the contemporary practice of embellishing ketuboth with pictures of the bridegroom and bride and of the sun and moon; it was a practice he objected to, but such depictions are also found in late seventeenth- and eighteenth-century ketuboth from Italy and from Sephardi communities in Hamburg and Amsterdam.[26]

The true home of the decorated ketubah, however, was Italy, where this art form blossomed in the seventeenth and eighteenth centuries. Until the sixteenth century the ketubah was probably not illustrated in Italy, and many Italian communities had not adopted the Ashkenazi custom of reading the ketubah between the *'erusin* and *nissu'in* ceremonies. The two ceremonies, which were separate during the talmudic period, had been combined by the twelfth century in medieval Europe and the reading of the ketubah became an integral part of the combined ceremony. In many Italian communities, as we can see in a 1481 miniature from Pesaro, Italy, the rolled-up ketubah was simply handed to the bride in the presence of two witnesses at the end of the nuptial ceremony, with the Hebrew formula: "Behold, here is your ketubah, according to the Law of Moses and Israel"[27]—an Aramaic formula introduced earlier in the geonic period and recited in many Islamic communities when the ketubah was handed over as part of the betrothal ceremony.[28]

By the sixteenth century many Italian Jewish communities had adopted the Ashkenazi custom of reading the ketubah as a symbolic separation between the *'erusin* and *nissu'in* ceremonies. As in medieval Egypt, the reading prompted not only the display of the document itself, but also, in the case of rich families, the proclamation of its contents—the lavish dowry and tenaim (written conditions of additional financial obligations agreed on prior to the wedding), which were actually incorporated into the Italian ketuboth.[29] In Ashkenazi territories the reading of the ketubah prompted no ostentatious display, as it did in Italy, and the practice of illustrated ketuboth did not take hold (except for one isolated medieval example from Krems, Austria, in 1391–92).[30]

In Italy the display of the ketubah engendered such fierce competition for splendid artistic renderings that the rabbis in *pragmatiche* (sumptuary laws) tried to limit the amount of money that could be spent on ketuboth (*pragmatiche* of Rome [1702] and Ancona [1766]).[31]

Much more could be said regarding practices of decorating the ketubah, but I will confine myself to one or two final examples. Many ketuboth bear fictitious coats of arms of prominent Jewish families.[32] These coats of arms followed a practice adopted by nouveaux riches Italian families but differed, of course, from those of the Christian nobility, for they were neither bestowed nor granted but simply invented.

Finally, one of the most interesting practices reflected in seventeenth- and eighteenth-century Italian ketuboth was to insert biblical scenes alluding to the Hebrew name of the groom though rarely of the bride.[33] This practice is also found in contemporary tombstones (often of marble) of the Sephardim of Holland and the Netherlands Antilles, where the Hebrew name of the deceased and of members of his family is often alluded to in a biblical scene.[34]

There can be little doubt that medieval Christianity exerted a direct

וְהָיָה כְּעֵץ שָׁתוּל עַל מַיִם וְעַל יוּבַל יְשַׁלַּח שָׁרָשָׁיו וְלֹא יִרְאֶה כִּי יָבֹא חֹם
וְהָיָה עָלֵיהוּ רַעֲנָן וּבִשְׁנַת בַּצֹּרֶת לֹא יִרְאָג וְלֹא יָמִישׁ מֵעֲשׂוֹת פֶּרִי ב
בַּעֲלֵי וְעָלֵיהוּ לֹא יִבּוֹל וְכָל אֲשֶׁר יַעֲשֶׂה יַצְלִיחַ ׃
וְנֶאֱמַר שִׁיר הַמַּעֲלוֹת אַשְׁרֵי כָּל יְרֵא יְיָ הַהֹלֵךְ בִּדְרָכָיו ׃ יְגִיעַ כַּפֶּיךָ כִּי תֹאכֵל
אַשְׁרֶיךָ וְטוֹב לָךְ ׃ אֶשְׁתְּךָ כְּגֶפֶן פֹּרִיָּה בְּיַרְכְּתֵי בֵיתֶךָ בָּנֶיךָ כִּשְׁתִלֵי זֵיתִים
סָבִיב לְשֻׁלְחָנֶךָ ׃ הִנֵּה כִי כֵן יְבֹרַךְ גָּבֶר יְרֵא יְיָ ׃ יְבָרֶכְךָ יְיָ מִצִּיּוֹן וּרְאֵה
בְּטוּב יְרוּשָׁלִָם כֹּל יְמֵי חַיֶּיךָ ׃ וּרְאֵה בָנִים לְבָנֶיךָ שָׁלוֹם עַל יִשְׂרָאֵל ׃

וְנֶאֱמַר כִּי תְשִׁיתֵהוּ בְרָכוֹת לָעַד תְּחַדֵּהוּ בְשִׂמְחָה אֶת
פָּנֶיךָ ׃ וְנֶאֱמַר יְהִי מְקוֹרְךָ בָרוּךְ וּשְׂמַח מֵאֵשֶׁת נְעוּרֶךָ ׃
בָּרוּךְ אַתָּה יְיָ מְשַׂמֵּחַ הֶחָתָן עִם הַכַּלָּה ׃

וְשֻׂשְׂתָן הֶחָתָן וְהַכַּלָּה וְשׁוֹכְרִים אֶת הַכֹּלִים ׃

וְכֹאתָן לָהּ כְּתֻבָּתָהּ בְּפֶרֶף שׁוֹכֵס עֲרִיס
וְאֹמַר לָהּ ׃

הֲרֵי לִיךְ כְּתוּבָתֵךְ בַּת מֹשֶׁה

וְיִשְׂרָאֵל ׃

וּמְגַבֵּיהֶן הַשּׁוֹשְׁבִּיכֶן אֶת כֹּלִים וְאוֹמְרִים

פֶּכְי וְיִרְבָּא כְּרַעֲנַנִּים ׃ יְחִדוּ וְיִרְאוּ אֶבֶן בָּנִים ׃

אֶת חָתָן לְיוֹם חֲתֻנָּתוֹ ׃ אֶת חָתָן לְיוֹם חֲתֻנָּתוֹ
אָסִיר חָכְמָה וְרָב בִּינָה ׃
יִשְׂרִין וְיִרְבָּא כְּרַעֲנַנִּים ׃ יְחִאוּ וְיִרְאוּ אֶבֶן בָּנִים ׃

5. Ketubah ceremony in Italy. Miniature from a *maḥzor*, Italian rite, Pesaro, Italy, 1481. Hungarian Academy of Sciences, Budapest, MS A 380/II, fol. 231v. From the private collection of J. Gutmann.

6. Ketubah. Livorno, Italy, 1783. From the collection of the Library of the Jewish Theological Seminary of America. Reprinted by permission.

influence on the development of such novel medieval Ashkenazi wedding customs as the combining of the engagement and wedding ceremonies into one, the employment of a ring, the use of a portable canopy, and the shattering of the glass cup. In a similar fashion, Islam earlier in the Middle Ages had influenced the introduction of the decorated ketubah into the Jewish wedding.

The complex interaction of Judaism with multiple civilizations, cultures, and societies throughout its roughly 3,500 years of history engendered not only constant novelty but also a rich diversity in marriage customs in Jewish communities throughout the world. The picture that emerges, then, is one of great variety rather than one of unity of practice, so frequently stressed in popular books on the subject. Though this outcome is not wholly surprising, it is important nonetheless, for it forces us to recall that the reality of the development of Jewish practices is a multifaceted one indeed.

NOTES

1. J. Gutmann, "Die Mappe Schuletragen: An Unusual Judeo-German Custom," *Visible Religion* 2 (1983), 167–73, idem, *The Jewish Life Cycle* (Leiden, 1987), pp. 6ff.

2. J. Gutmann, "Wedding Customs and Ceremonies in Art," *Beauty in Holiness: Studies in Jewish Customs and Ceremonial Art*, ed. J. Gutmann (New York, 1970), pp. 324–25, n. 36, and p. 329.

3. J. Sauer, *Symbolik des Kirchengebäudes und seiner Ausstattung in der Auffassung des Mittelalters* (Freiburg, 1924), p. 210; A. Rubens, *A History of Jewish Costume* (London, 1982), p. 95, fig. 127.

4. J. B. O'Connell, "Baldachino," *New Catholic Encyclopedia* (New York, 1967), II, 25; J. Braun, "Baldachin," *Reallexikon zur deutschen Kunstgeschichte* (Stuttgart, 1937), I, 1389–94.

5. S. B. Freehof, "The Chuppah," in *In the Time of Harvest: Essays in Honor of Abba Hillel Silver on the Occasion of His 70th Birthday*, ed. D. J. Silver (New York and London, 1963), pp. 187–88. For an early depiction of a portable canopy, see a liturgical manuscript from southern Germany (1589) containing prayers for the Jewish holidays and the life cycle ceremonies (Nuremberg, Germanisches Nationalmuseum, Inv. No. Hs. 7058, fol. 34v).

6. Gutmann, "Wedding Customs," p. 317.

7. J. Gutmann, "Christian Influences on Jewish Customs," *Spirituality and Prayer: Jewish and Christian Understandings*, ed. L. Klenicki and G. Huck (New York, 1983), p. 133 and p. 137, n. 22; Gutmann, *The Jewish Life Cycle*, p. 16. Cf. T. and M. Metzger, *Jewish Life in the Middle Ages* (New York, 1982), fig. 336, p. 224, for an illustration of the *Worms maḥzor* of 1272; fig. 344, p. 230, for the fifteenth-century "Second Nuremberg Haggadah." See also fig. 183, p. 133, for an Italian Jewish marriage ceremony in 1438, and p. 293, nn. 112 ff.

8. K. Ritzer, *Formen, Riten und religiöses Brauchtum der Eheschliessung in den christlichen Kirchen des ersten Jahrtausends* (Münster, 1962), pp. 158ff., 176, 194, 231f.

9. A. Büchler, "The Induction of the Bride and Bridegroom into the *Chuppah* in the First and the Second Centuries in Palestine," in *Livre d'hommage à la mémoire du Dr. Samuel Poznánski* (Warsaw, 1927), pp. 82–132.

10. J. Z. Lauterbach, "The Ceremony of Breaking a Glass at Weddings," in Gutmann, *Beauty in Holiness*, p. 353f.

11. Lauterbach, "The Ceremony of Breaking a Glass," pp. 340–69; Gutmann, "Christian Influences," p. 137, n. 24.

12. See Gutmann, "Wedding Customs," p. 325, n. 40, and pp. 330 and 336 for depictions of *Trausteine*. See also N. Feuchtwanger, "Interrelations between the Jewish and Christian Wedding in Medieval Ashkenaz," *Proceedings of the Ninth World Congress of Jewish Studies*, Division D (Jerusalem, 1986), II, 31–36; S. B. Freehof, "Ceremonial Creativity Among the Ashkenazim," in Gutmann, *Beauty in Holiness*, pp. 491–93. Early medieval sources speak of a cup or glass cup that was thrown against the synagogue wall; sources from the sixteenth century onward also mention the throwing of a flask. This latter practice is illustrated in eighteenth-century prints (cf. fig. 2). See also the interesting article by N. Feuchtwanger on the medieval Jewish custom of crowning the bride: "The Coronation of the Virgin and of the Bride," *Jewish Art* 12–13 (1986–87), 213–24.

13. Gutmann, "Wedding Customs," pp. 318, 337; Gutmann, *The Jewish Life Cycle*, p. 17.

14. Lauterbach, "The Ceremony of Breaking a Glass," pp. 360f. Cf. R. Gladstein-Kestenberg, "Breaking a Glass at Weddings" [in Hebrew], *Studies in the History of the People and the Land of Israel* 4 (1978), 205–8.

15. Leone Modena, *Historia dei riti hebraici (The History of the Rites, Customs, and Manner of Life of the Present Jews Throughout the World)*, trans. E. Chilmead (London, 1650), pp. 178f.

16. Gutmann, "Christian Influences," p. 137, n. 27.

17. See, e.g., the illustrations in Metzger, *Jewish Life in the Middle Ages*, fig. 187, p. 135, fig. 335, p. 224, and p. 293, n. 110. See also Gutmann, *The Jewish Life Cycle*, p. 15.

18. A. H. Freimann, *The Order of the Betrothal and the Wedding After the Conclusion of the Talmud: A Historic-Dogmatic Study of Jewish Law* [in Hebrew] (Jerusalem, 1964), pp. 19ff., 43f.; J. W. Falk, *Jewish Matrimonial Law in the Middle Ages* (London, 1966), pp. 73ff. See also E. Mihaly, *Teshuvot (Responsa) on Jewish Marriage* (Cincinnati, Ohio, 1985), pp. 15ff.; *Maḥzor Vitry*, par. 466; and S. B. Freehof, *Reform Jewish Practice and Its Rabbinic Background* (Cincinnati, Ohio, 1944), I, 91ff. It should be noted that *ketubot* in Palestine sometimes carried the validating formula: "Be you consecrated to me according to the Law of Moses and the Jews." Cf. also the early thirteenth-century custom of the Romaniote Jews to recite the bethrothal and the seven wedding blessings as part of the kiddushin ceremony although the couple had not yet been under the huppah. See S. B. Bowman, *The Jews of Byzantium, 1204–1453* (University, Ala., 1985), pp. 122ff.

19. B. Witthoft, "Marriage Rituals and Marriage Chests in Quattrocento Florence," *Artibus et historiae* 5 (1982), 45f., 56; A. Heimann, "Die Hochzeit von Adam und Eva im Paradies nebst einigen andern Hochzeitbildern," *Wallraf-Richartz-Jahrbuch* 37 (1975), 22–27; Falk, *Jewish Matrimonial Law*, pp. 75, 105ff.

20. L. Reekmans, "La 'dextrarum iunctio' dans l'iconographie romaine et paléochrétienne," *Bulletin de l'Institut Historique Belge de Rome* 31 (1958), 23–95; C. Reinsberg, "Concordia: Die Darstellung von Hochzeit und ehelicher Eintracht in des Spätantike," *Spätantike und frühes Christentum* (Ausstellung im Liebieghaus Museum alter Plastik) (Frankfurt-am-Main, 1984), pp. 312–17.

21. Cf. S. D. Goitein, *A Mediterranean Society* (Berkeley, Calif., 1978), III, 108ff.; M. A. Friedman, *Jewish Marriage in Palestine: A Cairo Geniza Study* (Tel-Aviv and New York, 1980), I, 96f. L. R. K. Avrin, "The Illuminations in the Moshe ben-Asher Codex of 895 c.e.," Ph.D. diss., Univ. of Michigan. 1974, pp. 210, 214.

22. There is an unpublished decorated Fatimid marriage contract, dated 1160, on cotton in the Kuwait National Museum. I am indebted to Mrs. Ghada Hijjawi Qaddumi for sending me a photo and for her gracious help. See also Y. Rāgib, "Un contrat de mariage sur soie d'Egypte Fatimide," *Annales Islamologiques* 16 (1980), 31–37.

23. Friedman, *Jewish Marriage*, I, vii, 92f., 283. See, as well, Friedman's comments on pp. 000–00.

24. Goitein, *A Mediterranean Society*, p. 126.

25. F. Cantera-Burgos, "La 'KETUBA' de D. Davidovitch y las ketubbot españolas," *Sefarad* 33 (1973), 375–86. Cf. also I. Fishof, " 'Jerusalem Above My Chief Joy': Depictions of Jerusalem in Italian Ketubot," *Journal of Jewish Art* 9 (1982), 74.

26. See A. Rubens, *A History of Jewish Costume* (London, 1982), fig, 163, p. 120; Gutmann, "Wedding Customs," p. 327; L. Grassi, ed., *Ketubbot Italiane* (Milan, 1984), pls. 3, 15, 17, 18, 32. On the Sephardi introduction of the dec-

orated ketubah into Italy, see S. Sabar, "The Beginnings of *Ketubbah* Decoration in Italy: Venice in the Late Sixteenth to the Early Seventeenth Centuries," *Jewish Art* 12–13 (1986–87), 96–110.

27. Hungarian Academy of Sciences, Budapest, MS A 380/II, fol. 231v. Cf. Gutmann, *The Jewish Life Cycle*, p. 12.

28. Friedman, *Jewish Marriage*, I, 213ff.; Freimann, *The Order of the Betrothal*, p. 16.

29. Cf. F. Landsberger, "Illuminated Marriage Contracts," in Gutmann, *Beauty in Holiness*, pp. 394, 403, 413; Grassi, *Ketubbot Italiane*, pls. 7, 12, 16, 22, 24, 26, 27, 28. It should be noted that the reading and displaying of the ketubah in medieval Muslim countries served a social function, whereas in Italy it was an intricate part of the legally prescribed ceremony. Cf. Sabar, "The Beginnings of *Ketubbah* Decoration in Italy," p. 100, n. 28.

30. Landsberger, "Illuminated Marriage Contracts," p. 374; Sabar, "The Beginnings of *Ketubbah* Decoration," pp. 101–2.

31. S. Sabar, "The Use and Meaning of Christian Motifs in Illustrations of Jewish Marriage Contracts in Italy," *Journal of Jewish Art* 10 (1984), 63.

32. C. Roth, "Stemmi di famiglie ebraiche italiane," *Scritti in memoria di Leone Carpi*, ed. Alexander Rofé (Jerusalem, 1967), pp. 165–84; H. Lazar, "Jonah, the Tower and the Lions: An Eighteenth-Century Italian Silver Book Binding," *Journal of Jewish Art* 3–4 (1977), 58–73, esp. p. 67; idem, "Coats of Arms of Italian Jews," *Proceedings of the Eighth World Congress of Jewish Studies*, Division D (Jerusalem, 1982), II, 57–62.

33. Gutmann, *The Jewish Life Cycle*, pp. 13ff.; idem, "Wedding Customs," p. 319, and the excellent study by S. Sabar, "The Beginnings and Flourishing of *Ketubbah* Illustration in Italy: A Study in Popular Imagery and Jewish Patronage During the Seventeenth and Eighteenth Centuries," Ph.D. diss., U.C.L.A., 1987.

34. R. Weinstein, "Sepulchral Monuments of the Jews of Amsterdam in the Seventeenth and Eighteenth Centuries," Ph.D. diss., New York Univ., 1979.

PART II
CHILDHOOD AND ADOLESCENCE

4

Images of Childhood and Adolescence in Talmudic Literature

DAVID KRAEMER

The study of the image of children in the literature of the Talmud is an awkward task. When we speak of the study of children, we are interested primarily in the questions posed by psychology and sociology, such as those relating to children's emotional and sexual development, their place in society, and so forth. But psychology and sociology are both modern disciplines, and if the questions that they frame are applied to premodern subjects, we are likely to be faced with a great deal of frustration. Where the evidence provided by the ancients is tactile, as in art, dress, or toys, for example, then we may simply view the subjects through new lenses. But where the evidence is restricted to the literary record, as is overwhelmingly the case for the society of the rabbis, then it is not the whims of history that have determined what has survived, but the minds of people. Under these circumstances the first question we must ask ourselves is why those individuals preserved what they did.

They were the ones, after all, who framed the questions that the literature sought to address. Unfortunately, if those questions do not accord with the ones that we are now interested in asking, there is not much that can be done; our new lenses simply cannot view what is not there to see. What we are left to do, then, is to adjust for the prejudices of the ancient authors and to hope that we might, through very careful examination, see what they perhaps did not intend us to see at all.

Of course, this latter problem is precisely the one with which we are faced when we ask modern questions concerning children in the Talmud and related literature. The vocabulary and questions of this literature are those of "Torah," that is, the terms of the literature are overwhelmingly legal, and even when this is not the case, the exclusive intent is to instruct. If children's games or dress or nature are not the concern of the law, then the literature of the Talmud is unlikely to preserve any observation relating to these things. Yes, this literature contains hundreds of references to "minors," but minors are not children. Minors are a legal category—that category of people (in this case, usually Jewish people) who are exempt from observing commandments and who cannot be held responsible for their actions. In contrast to minors are "adults," again a legally significant category. Adults, according to this usage, are individuals obligated to perform the commandments and legally responsible for their actions. The children whom we are concerned with, however, are those who cry and play and grow and develop. About these children we would like to know a great deal. How were they treated by adults, for example? Did adult society during the time of the Talmud recognize a distinct quality in childhood, or were children merely little, not yet legally responsible adults? More important, did ancient Jewish society recognize childhood to be a developmental continuum, or did children merely become adults in one fell swoop, say, at age thirteen? These children are the concern of modern scholarly disciplines, but these were not generally the children with whom the rabbis were concerned. Their children, as we said, were the children who had to be trained in Torah but were not yet ready to accept its obligations. When asking about that other species of children, then, we have woefully little to work with.

It is for this reason that there is so little modern literature that asks these questions of the traditional literature. I have been able to discover only one book—*The Jewish Child*, by W. M. Feldman (1918)—that speaks of the traditional Jewish attitude toward children at any length.[1] And even there, I might add, the author was forced to pad the book with chapters on such matters as mathematics in the Talmud, presumably because children learned math in school. Despite this, I will make the perhaps foolish attempt to ask the new questions. These questions are primarily those framed in Philippe Ariès's *Centuries of Childhood* (New York, 1962) or in the general psychological literature. I have already alluded to some of them. Ariès points out, for example, that in premodern Europe childhood was not recognized as a distinct stage, with its own unique traits. In terms of their dress and games, children were merely little adults. Was the same true in ancient rabbinic society? Relatedly, Ariès comments that formal education usually began relatively late and that when it did begin, there was no difference, for example, between the education of a ten- and a fifteen-year-old. Again, there was no recognition of a developmental continuum. Development is central, of course, to the psychological understanding of children. Did the rabbis recognize such development? Were they sensitive to the cognitive and sexual development of children? Central, too, to the psychological description of childhood are certain crucial periods of sexuality. Did the rabbis admit such periods of childhood sexual development, and did they recognize childhood sexuality at all? It may be impossible, of course, to offer definitive answers to these questions based on the evidence of the talmudic literature, but we will discover that very definite directions can be suggested.

Before attempting to examine the evidence, however, I must first define what I mean by *childhood*. If I were defining this inquiry as a talmudist, I might be tempted to conclude childhood at age thirteen. At that time, after all, the child becomes a bar mitzvah, commonly understood to be "a man." But were I to do this, I would be defining the scope of my questioning by the ancient answers. Here I would fall into the very trap that I warned against previously. Instead, for purposes of questioning, I will consider childhood anything that comes before adulthood, and I will only consider someone an adult who has attained the age of marriage and family responsibility. It is at this point that people generally establish their own homes, and it is only then that they can be spoken of as being adults in an adult society. This definition is useful for two reasons. First, it enables us to consider the full developmental continuum if there is one. Second, it offers us the opportunity to see whether or not the talmudic literature admitted an adolescence— a period crucial to the discussions of psychology. In this way, I hope, we can ask the questions that we define and not those defined by the rabbis.

As is to be expected, rabbinic literature has very little to say about childhood beyond the legal definition. The one general evaluation of childhood as a period speaks of it as a "garland of roses," apparently a reference to its ease and comfort because it is contrasted in the same context with the "thorns of old age" (b. Shabbat 152a). Elsewhere children are spoken of as being frivolous and irresponsible. They are thought to be easily tempted by gifts and money, for example (b. B.B. 156a), and there is a general desire to restrict their involvment in monetary transactions though exceptions are made in certain circumstances (see b. Gittin 59a). In another context, children are compared to the evil inclination and to women; that is, they are to be "pushed away with the left hand and drawn close with the right" (b. Sanhedrin 107b). Presumably this ambiguous tension is due to their lack of seriousness, a bad influence for responsible adults (see Rashi, ad loc.).

This latter comment necessitates a consideration of the sexuality of children. The parallel between children, on the one hand, and "the evil inclination" (i.e., the sexual urge) and women, on the other, is surely more than coincidental. The rabbis were apparently aware of the sexuality of children, at least in later childhood. R. Nachman b. Isaac (fourth century C.E.) reports that a decree had been issued declaring that non-Jewish children should be considered ritually impure to a severe degree. The purpose of this decree was to help ensure that Jewish children would not engage in sexual experimentation with non-Jews. At what age, it is asked, does this decree take effect? R. Judah the Prince is reported as concluding that for a boy it begins at age nine, and Ravina (or R. Johanan) adds that for a girl it begins at age three, each of these being the age at which sexual intercourse is considered to be legally significant (b. A.Z. 36b–37a, b. Shabbat 17b). Elsewhere the Mishnah comments that a man may sleep naked in the same bed as his daughter until she grows up (either age nine or twelve, according to two views in the Gemara), seemingly oblivious to the sexual awareness of a young girl. But R. Ḥisda limits the permission granted by this Mishnah to a girl who is not embarrassed to stand naked in front of her father. If she is conscious of her sexuality, however, then the leniency of the Mishnah cannot be granted (Kiddushin, Mishnah 4:12 and Gemara 81b). Sexuality is a recognized part of talmudic childhood, then, if only in limited scope. The age at which it becomes emotionally significant is undefined; we know only the age of legally significant sexuality. Still, we know that a girl might become sexually aware prior to age nine, according to the view of R. Ḥisda, and this is certainly long before actual sexual maturity.

Important, too, is the tone of these expressions concerning the sexuality of children. In none of these instances is their sexuality spoken of as being evil or tempting. Concern is expressed for the daughter's sensitivities, not for the father's temptation. Separation from non-Jewish children is declared on the basis of homosexual coupling—a transgression of which idolators are frequently accused—and not for fear of sex as such. Even in the first instance, where children are spoken of in the same breath as the evil inclination, it is not clear that this is the reason children are to be avoided. Rashi makes the not untenable suggestion that the concern is merely for frivolity. But even if sex is the concern, the fear of it is not decisive. We must recognize, after all, that while pushing away with the left hand, we are to draw the child close with the right. The right hand, we must recall, was always considered to be the stronger of the two.

Moreover, this evaluation of a neutral attitude toward sexuality is confirmed by another tradition that speaks of childhood. At b. Sanhedrin 110b the following question is posed: "At what point does a child [begin to merit] enter[ing] into the world to come?" A number of suggestions are offered, ranging from conception to the beginning of speech to birth in between. But nowhere is there thought of a child's sin; nowhere is there original sin. Sexuality, though present, need not be atoned for. Only on reaching legal majority can a person be held liable for the misuse of his or her sexuality.

Naturally, the most effort is expended in rabbinic literature discussing the education of children.[2] Avot (5:21)[3] reports that five is the appropriate age to begin training in Scripture, and ten the age for the study of Mishnah. In somewhat different fashion, Rav reports that general education began at age six or seven (b. B.B. 21a). Regardless of the actual age, it should be noted that children were often spoken of as "reciting their verses" (see, e.g., b. Hagigah 15a and parallels). This, apparently, was what children were commonly found to be doing.

Talmudic literature also reflects extreme sensitivity to informal education and to the pedagogical necessities of the education of children. R. Isaac reports a directive to parents to educate their children with patience and sensitivity (b. Ketubot 40a). Similarly, Rav declares that discipline should not be harsh (b. B.B. 21a). With respect to the way in which children learn, R. Zeira warns that a person should not promise to give a child something and then fail to do so because this will teach the child, too, to be a liar (b. Sukkah 46b). Above all, education should begin early, and repetition and example are its very foundations (b. Sukkah 42a).

Perhaps the most crucial feature of these texts that relate to education is their clear awareness of childhood as a developmental period. Learning at first begins informally, and it requires a special sensitivity. When a child begins speaking, he is encouraged to begin slowly the cognative task of childhood—memorization of Scripture. This task admits the limitations of the child's intellect—at age five (or six or seven) he begins merely to memorize; understanding will come later. Gradual development is assumed throughout, not uniformity and not immobility. Furthermore, the recognition of this process is not limited to education. It extends from intellectual development to sexuality and from a child's earliest years to his more advanced. Permit me to illustrate.

Midrash Kohelet Rabbah 1 (2) records a lengthy description of the stages of human development, a description that we will have occasion to refer to again later. With respect to a child's earliest years, the midrash[4] describes that "at a year old [a child] is like a king seated in a canopied litter, fondled and kissed by all. At two and three he is like a pig, sticking his hands in the gutters." This is, of course, a child whom we would all recognize. At the other end of the spectrum, the Mishnah itself speaks of the couple of years before puberty as a period of significantly improved intellectual comprehension and, therefore, recognizes that oaths taken at this time are at least potentially valid (m. Niddah 5:6). In the same connection, this is also the time when a child is to begin fasting on Yom Kippur (m. Yoma 8:4).

If, on the basis of these sources, we were now to draw a map of childhood, it would look something like this: At one, a child is a king, that is, spoiled and the center of attention; at two and three, he is dirty by virtue of play; at five through seven, he begins his elementary education; at the same point he is considered to be intelligent enough to sell chattels (though this legal concession was only to ensure that he would be able to purchase food if necessary; see b. Gittin 59a). Before age nine the child might become aware of his or her sexuality; at nine, sex for a male becomes a legally significant event; at ten, eleven, or twelve, the child will experience significant cognitive development—and the girl probably before the boy; and finally, at approximately age twelve or thirteen, the girl and then the boy will arrive at puberty. Though we might have focused on different details of some of these stages, still it is the general picture that is significant, not the details. Childhood, we see here, quite clearly, is considered in rabbinic literature to be a period of evolution. It is a process of development that begins in the earliest years and apparently never ceases. Quite unlike the world that Ariès describes, the child in talmudic society was not described merely in adult terms or as the negation of adulthood. Rather, the child demands special sensitivities and considerations, and these change as the child approaches closer and closer to adulthood.

Sexual adulthood, these texts report, is expected to come at around the twelveth or the thirteenth year. Is that the end of childhood, in the rabbinic mind, or is it something else? Is there any recognition of development beyond the bar mitzvah?

What, then, does age thirteen represent, and what does it mean to be a *gadol*, an adult? It has commonly been assumed that at thirteen a child becomes an adult in the literal sense of the word. For this reason the book by Feldman, mentioned earlier, concludes its deliberations at this age. Thereafter a person is an adult and so should not be spoken of in a book on children. This wisdom must be challenged, however, for the evidence does not support this view.

But first it is necessary to say a few words on the nature of boundaries in talmudic literature. The Mishnah and that literature that follows in its path are literally casuistic. This means that, with rare exception, general rules are not stated, but rather specific cases are formed to illustrate those rules. There is no need, however, for such cases ever to have occurred. *Casuistic*, in this context, also does not mean case law; and, in fact, to illustrate certain general rules, it was necessary to formulate cases that could probably never occur.[5] Mishnah should not be considered case evidence, therefore, but conceptual expression. This, of course, affects our whole understanding of the literature.

When stating boundaries, then, as legal systems frequently have to do, this literature will have to compose cases that embody the boundaries. Cases are often chosen, therefore, not because they are common, but precisely because they are uncommon! They illustrate not the case that falls at the center of the bell curve but the far less common one that falls at its edge—that is, the one that defines the limit. Consequently, when the Mishnah speaks of a three-year-old girl as having sex, this is not because such a thing happened frequently, or even that it happened at all (though, unfortunately, it may have), but merely because that is where the system defines the boundary for legally significant sex for a female.

The same must be understood to be the case with respect to the "age thirteen" boundary. Why thirteen was chosen as the boundary is obviously connected with puberty. For some reason the rabbis believed that this was the point that legal responsibility should begin. But this did not mean, as the common wisdom suggests, that they considered thirteen-year-olds to be adults. At most it means that they were viewed as being at the edge of adulthood for certain purposes. But there is far more to consider before we can understand what this means.

The Bible, of course, knows nothing of age thirteen as a boundary. There the age of significant transition is twenty (see, e.g., Exod. 30:14). This was the age at which the census began and the age at which an individual was obligated to participate in military formations (see Num. 1:18 ff.). Though not widely recognized, twenty was also an extremely significant age for the rabbis, a fact that is crucial to our question, When does a child become an adult?

First, to adduce the evidence.[6] The opinion of R. Huna, Rava, and the Tanna of the School of R. Ishmael is well known: If one passes age twenty without taking a wife, he is tantamount to being a sinner (b. Kiddushin 29b). Whether twenty was the last point at which a man should marry, as suggested here, or whether it was merely the point to begin seriously seeking a mate, as we shall consider later on the basis of other sources, it is clear that twenty represents a significant transition with respect to marriage. The same point, perhaps surprisingly, may be crucial to a woman. R. Hisda observes that if a woman marries by age twenty, then her fertility will be long-lived. If she marries after this point, however, her fertility will diminish accordingly (b. B.B. 119b). The same age is crucial in ritual areas. A baraita at Hullin 24b suggests in the name of Rabbi [Judah the Patriarch] that one should not be appointed *shaliah tsibbur* (representative of the congregation in prayer) or perform the priestly blessing unless he is twenty (cf. y. Sukkah chap. 3, end, and Soferim 14:13, Higger, p. 267). According to a prevalent opinion, twenty is the age at which a person may legally begin selling property he inherited from his deceased father (b. B.B. 155b–156a). It is also the age at which the law generally despairs of one developing signs of sexual maturity (b. Yevamot 80a).

Neither is twenty ignored by the longer lists that evaluate the stages of human development. Avot 5:21 considers twenty the age "to pursue." Whether this is the age to begin earning a living, as some commentaries suggest, or the age to begin army service, or even the age of divine accountability—these are unimportant. What is important is that twenty is again a point of significant transition. Incidentally, the suggestion that twenty is an age with divine significance is based on a midrash at b. Shabbat 89b, where it is made clear that, though thirteen may be the age for human accountability, for the court in heaven responsibility begins at age twenty. The list at Kohelet Rabba 1 (2) also notices age twenty, saying that at that point a man "is like a neighing horse, adorning himself and seeking a wife." Significantly, in this latter list twenty appears in a far more select grouping, and it is chosen even in the absence of any mention of age thirteen. We will return to this point later.

Undisputably, then, twenty is a significant age according to a wide selection of rabbinic texts. Why is it significant? The answer seems to be connected to marriage. Several of the texts allude to marriage very strongly, and sometimes even when no such allusion is obvious, the connection to marriage is still the likely one.[7] Kiddushin believes twenty to be the last point at which a man should marry. Avot supports this connection as well, saying that eighteen is the age for huppah and twenty the age for pursuit.

However, the possibility must be considered that twenty was not the last point for marriage, but perhaps the age at which finding a mate should be taken that much more seriously. Midrash Lekach Tov (to Kohelet 1:2) speaks of the "pursuit" of age twenty as the pursuit of a wife. This midrash is parallel to the one from Kohelet Rabba, already quoted, where twenty is the age when a man begins seeking a wife "like a neighing horse." This is the age when urgency begins, not ends. Even in the text at b. Kiddushin 29b–30a, where age twenty for marriage is stated so forcefully, the several years after that seem not yet to be considered full adulthood. There Rava claims that a man has some opportunity for ethical persuasion of his son because he still has some control over him until age twenty-two or, according to another version, until age twenty-four. These ages are supported by an earlier rabbinic text quoted in that context in which the extent of the meaning of the word *youth* is debated, and again the two points that are considered are twenty-two or twenty-four.

It is perhaps not difficult to understand the apparent contradiction between these texts. Avot and the context in b. Kiddushin, which speaks of twenty as the very latest one should marry are both speaking as teachers of religious ethics. This, we know, is the general intent of Avot. In b. Kiddushin, too, this is quite clear—the immediate argument there ends with R. Ḥisda's praise of himself for having married at age sixteen and his addition that fourteen would have been even better, having afforded him the opportunity to spit in the eye of Satan. The point, obviously, is that early marriage will ensure that one avoids sexual temptation. This is an ethical teaching though, not a statement of reality. Though these texts might be stating the ideal, the others mentioned earlier are probably recording what was true in actuality. The rabbis may have felt it to be best that a man (and perhaps even a woman) should marry by age twenty. However, those texts that merely observe the way things are likely to happen apparently believe that marriage might wait several years after that.[8]

At approximately age twenty, then, Jewish men married, began to have families, and began to make a living on their own. This was also the point that they could expect to have achieved full physical maturity. In the fullest sense, then, this is the first point at which they can be spoken of as being fully adults. If they were adults only at age twenty, then what were they in the teenage years? Are those the years of an adolescence, in any sense, or are they merely years of undefined transition?[9]

The best-known statement regarding adolescence is perhaps the tradition in Avot (5:21) that "[f]ifteen [is the appropriate age] for Talmud." "Talmud," in Mishnaic parlance, meant sophisticated deliberation and questioning, and so this should be understood as an evaluation of the intellectual development of adolescents; that is, at fifteen they are able to handle, for the first time, the subtleties of sophisticated reasoning.[10] This is not the only text, however, that connects education to the middle teens. At B.B. 21a, Rav repeats a legend concerning the founding of public education in Israel. Most curiously, we are told that the first unsuccessful attempt at doing so involved the gathering of sixteen- and seventeen-year-olds (!) for primary education. The obvious question here is, why, in constructing such a legend, should its authors have chosen this age for demonstrating the way things should not be done? The failure of this attempt is connected with the rebelliousness of children at this age; that is, if you are going to wait until this point to begin education, there is no way that you are going to succeed, considering the natural "independent spirit" of teenagers. This text is particularly instructive in two ways: first, the middle teens are not considered inappropriate for education as such.[11] In fact, in the mind of the legendary educational pioneer, this is a natural and necessary point to speak of education. Surely, if teenagers were already involved in marriage and making a living, this thought would be absurd. Rather, the teens are appropriate for education so long as that is not the time that education first begins. Second, the text recognizes the independent, rebellious spirit of teenagers and admits that if they have not been socialized earlier, this point is entirely too late. Furthermore, the text later speaks of the beneficial effects of peer pressure, and though the immediate reference is to younger children, connecting peer pressure to unsuccessful educational attempts makes it clear that the same advice would apply to rebellious teenagers. Undoubtedly, this description of the adolescent is one that we all recognize.

In that the sources recognize these years as a time for continuing education, it is not surprising to find that they comment on the form that that education should take. R. Isaac reports a decree of the rabbinical academy at Usha that says that stricter and more emphatic discipline is required after age twelve (b. Ketubot 50a and see Rashi). The same text to which we referred at b. Kiddushin 30a speaks of the later teens as the appropriate time for a certain moral education in that the parent still has some influence over the child. This latter point is crucial for what it again suggests, that is, that even older teenagers are not yet independent of their parents. If the development of a full sense of autonomy is one of the central tasks of adolescence, as these texts readily admit (cf. the references to seeking marriage), then the fact that it has not yet been successfully accomplished supports our suspicion that this is, in fact, an adolescence.

In this connection, the rabbis were fully cognizant of the fact that responsibility for one's own property and family helped to define adulthood and that adolescents, therefore, could not be considered fully adults. That responsibility for children was a crucial factor is demonstrated by the statement of R. Yoḥanan at b. Yevamot 47a. This is one of several occasions on which the rabbis of the Gemara have a hard time accepting the literal meaning of *katan* (minor) or *gadol* (adult). In this particular text, R. Yoḥanan claims that an adult without children is termed a minor. Because adolescents were not yet married and, therefore, did not yet have children, his definition is certain to include at least the teenage years. At another point (b. B.M. 12a–b) R. Yoḥanan says that a "minor" is a legal adult who is still dependent on his parents. Here adulthood is understood to require material independence, and as teenagers were still dependent on their parents, these years cannot yet be considered adulthood. The Gemara at b. Ketubot 18a supports this evaluation by reporting that, with respect to his father's things, an "adult" is still called a minor.

Further information concerning these years can be discovered by referring again to the texts that speak of age twenty and by asking what they thought the case was before that age was reached. Of course, the traditions that connected twenty to marriage knew teenagers to be single.

Those who considered a twenty-year-old man to be "full-bearded" (the texts on ritual performance) knew that, prior to this, a boy was still developing physically. Finally, the tradition that limited property sale, when possible, to a child aged twenty, obviously thought that prior to this a child could not be considered able to handle such sales responsibly. There, in fact, the text says explicitly that teens are likely to be seduced by the offer of money and do not understand, therefore, the responsibility that they are undertaking.

In sum, rabbinic teenagers bear certain very distinct features in common with our own. In practical terms, they are still maturing physically. They are of independent spirit but often irresponsible. In a literal sense, they are generally still dependent on their parents. Their intellects, though now first capable of adult sophistication, are not yet fully accomplished. This is reflected in the importance of advanced education but is complicated by the recognized adolescent propensity for rebelliousness. They are not only subject to peer pressure, but they are also believed still to be subject to parental influence. This latter influence, however, is tenuous, and there is a recognition both that the time to apply it is limited and that certain modes of discipline are necessary for it to be effective.

There is little doubt, then, that rabbinic society recognized an adolescence and that full adulthood was a stage beyond this. It was a period about which we know very little, to be sure, but what we do know supports a picture that has many features in common with modern adolescence. In terms of independence or lack thereof, in terms of intellectual development, in terms of increased but unfulfilled sexuality—in all of these ways, at least, teens in rabbinic society were very much like our own teens. There can be no question, of course, that there were also significant differences, but to establish the differences was never the challenge. Our task, rather, was to determine whether or not there was a recognized developmental stage between puberty and adulthood. What we have discovered is that there was.

Should any question remain concerning this conclusion, more complete reference to the midrash from Kohelet Rabba should help to dispel it. The text there reads as follows:

R. Samuel b. Isaac taught in the name of R. Samuel b. Eleazar: The seven "vanities" mentioned in Kohelet correspond to the seven worlds that a man beholds. At age one he is like a king, seated in a litter while all hug and kiss him. At two and three he is like a pig, sticking his hands

in the gutters. At ten he skips like a kid. At twenty he is like a neighing
horse, adorning himself and seeking a wife. Having married, he is like an
ass [that is, a beast of burden]. When he has had children he becomes
brazen like a dog, in order to bring in bread and food . . .

Clearly, when choosing seven crucial periods of human development,
the author of this tradition had to be quite selective. It is instructive,
then, that, in making his choice, he saw ten and twenty as crucial points
and ignored thirteen. The same is not the case in our other list, at Avot
5:21. We probably would have expected the choice in Avot, and we
should be equally surprised at the selection of Kohelet Rabba. By what
criterion did he make this selection?

The list in Kohelet Rabba seems to be determined by one's mundane
condition, not by the sublime. At one, a baby is dependent and spoiled.
A young child is playful but dirty. At ten, a child is energetic and even
wild. He wanders off on his own, in his grown-up play, running where
his heart desires. The next crucial change comes when he marries and
beings to support the responsibilities of a family. How is this? During
his teen years he continues to play, and continues to avoid responsibilities. Puberty may bring increased sexual awareness, but in rabbinic
society there was no way to act on it. Therefore the irresponsibility of
the early teens continued to marriage. Since in rabbinic times the many
ritual functions that are now connected with bar mitzvah were not yet
related—fringes and *tefillin* were donned earlier, and serving as *shaliah
tsibbur* should ideally have waited to much later (as we saw, age
twenty)—thirteen was not as momentous, in an obvious way, as it has
now become. For them, rather, the teens were understood as a unit,
and only with the approach of marriage did an individual once again
experience radical change.[12]

What we have discovered, then, is that the childhood known to the
rabbis was a developmental continuum. Children were not merely little
adults but individuals with their own preferences and capabilities. When
young, they played and became dirty. Somewhat later, they began their
education, but an education that was carefully attuned to each cognitive
stage. Sexual awareness was admitted during childhood though such
awareness, of course, became more acute at puberty. At that time, too,
tremendous strides were known to have been taken in cognition.

Furthermore, adulthood did not begin at puberty. As we have seen,
there was a transition between child and adult, a transition that we can
properly term adolescence. This was a period of both sophistication and

irresponsibility and also one generally without sexual fulfillment. Adulthood proper began with marriage and family, usually around age twenty.

All this is not to say that rabbinic childhood was identical to ours.
But, like our society, theirs also knew of a developmental spectrum from
infancy to adulthood, and each stage was viewed in accordance with its
capabilities and limitations. This is rather unlike the premodern Europe
described by Ariès, and our conclusions, therefore, should serve as a
caution to those who blithely distinguish between the modern world and
what preceded it; development is not linear. The ancient world was
equally as diverse as the modern.

NOTES

1. Solomon Schechter wrote an article entitled "The Child in Jewish Literature," which appeared in the *Jewish Quarterly Review* (original series) 2
(1890), 1–24. Schechter combines legal and nonlegal sources in an undiscerning
way and includes texts and ceremonies from all periods of Jewish history. Nonetheless, his work is a valuable introduction to this subject, and he adds several
important sources to those which I cite later.

2. Of course, the rabbis were often generally concerned with males and not
females. This is true is their discussions of children as well. Much of the evidence
is limited, therefore, to male children, and it would be foolish to use "nonsexist"
language in this context. Here *nonsexist* would simply be noncorrect.

3. Avot 5:21 is a later addition to the Mishnah and not part of the original
Mishnaic tractate; See J. N. Epstein, *Mavo lenusach ha-mishnah* (Jerusalem,
1948), p. 978. It is, therefore, incorrect to attribute this tradition to Judah b.
Tema, whose name precedes it. For convenience I will merely refer to it as
Avot.

4. It is impossible to know even the assumed author of this tradition; the
several parallels (Yalkut Shimoni and Midrash Lekach Tov, both on the same
verse from Kohelet) are inconsistent in their attribution.

5. For example, a Baraita quoted at b. Niddah 54a teaches that "if a woman
bleeds one day and does not bleed one day [in repeating fashion] then she may
have sex on the eighth day and its eve, and then four days out of the eleven
. . . if she bleeds two days and then does not bleed two days, then she may have
sex on the eighth day and the twelveth and the sixteenth and the twentieth . . .
if she bleeds three days . . . " and so on—all the way up to eight days of bleeding

and eight days not. Obviously, this text is not considering cases that actually occurred. It is not the least bit concerned whether such combinations are possible. Rather, it is attempting to demonstrate the full implications of the cycle of a woman's seven-day period followed by the eleven-day intervening period. This is a theoretical text, not a case study, and it shares this feature with almost all texts of the same genre.

6. Louis Ginzberg supports our evaluation of twenty as being the age of majority; see his book *An Unknown Jewish Sect* (New York, 1976), pp. 45–46. With respect to punishment in the heavenly court, for which we cite b. Shabbat 89b (see later), Ginzberg adds y. Bikkurim II, 64c and y. Sanhedrin XI, 30b. He also makes reference to Jubilees (49:17) and Karaite sources in support of the importance of age twenty. I believe that Ginzberg's conclusion that twenty is a vestige of some "old halakha" does not accurately represent the full picture. I argue later that twenty is a contemporary fact in rabbinic society and that though thirteen may be the halakic definition of majority, it is a definition that needs to be understood in limited terms. Twenty is an important point of transition of far more than vestigial interest.

7. As in the texts that limit the performance of communal ritual duties to age twenty. In order to be a proper representative of the community it was thought best that a man should have the responsibility and accompanying sobriety of one with a wife and family. The reason may simply be, however, that at that point one had the appearance of maturity owing to a full beard.

8. The parallel of classical Greece is informative in this regard, and may support our conclusion. In Athens, the normal age for a man to marry was thirty, for a woman it ranged from sixteen to nineteen, though because of concern for virginity some girls may have married at fourteen. Plato speaks of twenty-five to thirty-five as the age at which men should marry. Notably, the statement that women should marry very early seems to have been a moral instruction owing to "the Greeks' fanatical emphasis on premarital virginity." The evidence does not support that it was universally upheld, however. Plutarch states that the recommended age is too young and says that Spartan girls waited until they were somewhat older. In addition, the record of Greek visual art seems to admit that girls were not married as early as the literature would have liked. Of course, rabbinic society was also "fanatical" for virginity, and so the same dichotomy of ideal and reality is not unexpected. For the Greek materials, see W. K. Lacey, *The Family in Classical Greece* (Ithaca, N.Y., 1968), pp. 106–7, 162, 179, and illus. 35.

9. I am preceded in asking this question by Norman Linzer of the Wurzweiler School of Social Work. See his book *The Jewish Family, Authority and Tradition in Modern Perspective* (New York, 1984), pp. 119–54. His reference to the psychological material is quite extensive, and for this connection I direct the reader to his work. His examination of the rabbinic sources, on the other hand, is far less complete than that found here.

10. Of course, this corresponds precisely to the observations of modern cognitive sciences. Adolescence is known to be the first point at which a person is able to construct contrary-to-fact propositions; see D. Elkind, *Children and Adolescents* (New York, 1974), pp. 102–3. It is also the first time that an individual is able to subordinate "the real to the realm of the possible and . . . link . . . all possibilities to one another by necessary implications . . . "; see P. N. Johnson-Laird and P. C. Wason, eds., *Thinking: Readings in Cognative Science* (New York, 1977), p. 159. Perhaps no better description for the process of *talmud* could be found!

11. Education during this period is supported by the Greeks as well. According to the Gortyn Code, boys aged twelve to sixteen were known as "youths," and it was during this period that they learned writing, basic laws, and "certain forms of music." School scenes on Greek pottery also suggest that this age was a time when youths were educated. See Lacey, *The Family*, p. 211, and illus. 32–33.

12. Though I have attempted to avoid legal definitions, comparison with Roman law and its identification of developmental stages is instructive. In Roman law puberty was assumed to occur at twelve for a female and fourteen for a male. Before this one was an *impubes*, and only beginning at this point did one become a minor. Legal minority then lasted until age twenty-five. See Adolf Berger, "impubes," in the *Encyclopedic Dictionary of Roman Law* (Philadelphia, 1953), p. 495. Boaz Cohen adds that, before age seven, one was considered an infans under Roman law; Cohen also points out that occasional exceptions to the age of majority were found, with a lower limit of age eighteen. See B. Cohen, *Jewish and Roman Law* (New York, 1966), II, Hebrew section, 1–9. These parallels establish that puberty was not identical with adulthood in the classical world and that a variety of developmental stages between early childhood and the early twenties was recognized.

5

Jewish Children and Childhood in Early Modern East Central Europe

GERSHON DAVID HUNDERT

Family history in general and the history of childhood in particular have been in vogue for some time, particularly since the publication in 1960 of the seminal work by Philippe Ariès, *L'Enfant et la vie familiale sous l'ancien régime* (Paris, 1960). There is now a very considerable literature on the subject.[1] Some of it is quite insightful and valuable. Two approaches are characteristic of this field: One studies issues related to household size and structure, that is, generally demographic and sometimes economic problems, whereas the other deals with emotional and political relations among family members. A branch of the second approach uses, or rather attempts to use, psychoanalytic tools in the study of the history of childhood.[2] But despite this wealth of general scholarship, very little has been written on the subject of Jewish children and on childhood in Eastern Europe in particular.[3] We are, therefore, essentially at the beginning of the study of this field.

All the genres of Jewish literature can be mined fruitfully for infor-mation about one or another dimension of the history of childhood: responsa, commentaries, communal and guild minute books, homiletical and ethical works in Hebrew and in Yiddish. Particular attention is paid here to the *Lev ṭov*, a Yiddish work on ethics, which in the seventeenth century was extremely popular in Eastern Europe.[4] Also, archival ma-terial can be used to collect data on household size and other demo-graphic and economic issues. To be sure, in the period that concerns us here, there were no child-rearing manuals as such. Indeed, their ap-pearance in some ways would be an indication of the end of the early modern period. One of the earliest examples of that sort of literature is *Sefer giddul banim*, published in London in 1771.[5]

It is not at all a simple matter to use ethical literature of any era and, in the absence of corroboration, to be able to state with certainty that it actually reflects the conditions of life in the period of composition. The problem is, of course, that people have been giving advice about how to raise children for a very long time. The conventions in the literary expressions of this advice change very slowly indeed, so that it is quite difficult for the historian to discover points of genuine change.

This problem may be illustrated in the following way. Steven Ozment has written "The Family in Reformation Germany."[6] In his work he devotes considerable attention to a book called *Rosengarten*. Published in 1512, it was "the first printed manual for midwives written by an experienced physician."[7] Ozment uses this work to buttress his thesis—undoubtedly correct—that people cared about their children during the Reformation and, indeed, that in the minds of contemporary moralists the problem was that parents were overindulgent.[8] One of the bits of evidence he cites is a list in *Rosengarten* of the six qualifications that a desirable wet nurse must possess, as if it were a novel contribution of the sixteenth-century author.[9] That list, however, conforms with me-dieval literary conventions. It turns out that a very similar list indeed appears in a fourteenth-century work by Menaḥem ben Zoraḥ of Na-varre called *Ṣeda la-derekh*.[10] And both of these may have as their source a thirteenth-century writer known as Aldobrandino of Sienna.[11] The subject of wet nurses will be addressed shortly. First, however, the literary problems should be illustrated further.

The following quotation is found in *Sefer lev ṭov* by Yiṣḥaq ben Eliakim of Poznán, first published in 1620. The author wrote: "Each father and mother must love his children with all his might. But they must not reveal their love in the presence [of the children] because then the children would not fear them and would not obey them. Every man must teach his children to fear him."[12]

This passage is full of interesting implications. The problem is that it is also a conventional passage in the Jewish literature dealing with child-rearing. The same advice is found in the forty-seventh chapter of the *Brantshpigl* by Moshe Ḥenoch Yerushalmi Altschuler, a book published in German territories in the 1590s.[13] This would not present insurmountable difficulties for the historian because the *Brantshpigl* was circulated in Eastern Europe, and both works arose out of the Ashkenazic milieu. Both, however, were following a work called *Sefer ha-mussar* by Yehuda ben Abraham Khalaz, composed in Algeria in the early part of the sixteenth century and published in Constantinople in 1537. *Sefer ha-mussar* in this passage, as in others, was in turn following *Menorat ha-ma'or* by Israel ibn Al-Nakawa, which was written in fourteenth-century Spain.[14] In the eleventh chapter of *Menorat ha-ma'or*, styled *Be-inyan giddul banim* ("On the Matter of Raising Children"), Al-Nakawa wrote that "a man must love his children with all his soul but must not show this love. He should hide it in his heart."[15] Note that in this early version only the father is mentioned, whereas by the time it reached *Sefer lev ṭov* both parents are included. This is important, but one can see the necessity of exploring earlier literature.

Examples of the degree to which there are conventions of advice on child-rearing are numerous. They constitute a serious difficulty and necessitate careful control over the literature of a long period so that the significant variations can be identified and analyzed. Another general issue is the equally basic problem of evaluating normative or prescriptive literature in an effort to judge the degree to which it reflects the ways in which people actually lived or even their own values and ideals. The following remarks are confined to East European Jews during the early modern period, that is, roughly between 1500 and 1800. Addressed first are some issues related to demography and to the problem of generational conflict.

The Polish-Jewish community experienced two periods of rapid demographic expansion during the three centuries between 1500 and 1800. The first occurred roughly between 1525 and 1630, and the second might have begun as early as 1670 or so and continued through the eighteenth century and most of the nineteenth century as well. During the sixteenth-century expansion there were prosperity, increasing opportunities, and social stability.[16] In the eighteenth century, the growth of the Jewish population occurred at a time when the Polish commonwealth, at least until 1740, was experiencing severe economic difficulties. The dimensions and velocity of trade and commerce were reduced. More and more Christian town dwellers turned to agriculture; there is a literature on the "agrarianization" of the Polish towns during this period.[17] At the same time, more and more Jews turned to artisanry. The limited opportunities in the established communities, which were themselves a consequence of burgeoning Jewish numbers and the difficult economic situation, stimulated geographic mobility. Jews appeared in more and smaller settlements. The proportion of Jews living in villages in Eastern Europe was never greater than it was during the second half of the eighteenth century. At the same time centers of Jewish population became more highly differentiated in terms of occupation and income. As the communities grew, the ties between people weakened, as did the compelling power of social sanctions. And, finally, a constantly growing population, attributable probably to a relatively lower infant-mortality rate, must have meant that the proportion of young people within the Jewish population was increasing constantly. Although one might think that early marriage was the main reason for this rapid growth, it seems likely that that practice, by its very nature, was limited to the upper stratum of East European Jewish society. The continuing increase in the proportion of young people has never been taken into consideration in discussion of the revolts of the artisan guilds or in the attempts to account for the rise of Hasidism. Although it is, at this point, only conjecture, surely the following question warrants further study: Is it not likely that there was some connection between the rapidly growing Jewish population, the high rate of unemployment, increasing numbers of young people, and the appearance of a popular revivalist movement in Poland/Lithuania in the middle of the eighteenth century? This movement, after all, was characterized initially by a mocking attitude toward the learned, energetic dancing, singing and drinking, turning somersaults in the streets, and so on. In a word, was Hasidism generational at its inception? Surely it is not accidental that Naḥman Kossover, a companion of the Besht, addressed the young, as Dinur has pointed out, and punned on the passage in Lev. 19:31 "Turn ye not unto the ghosts" reading it "Turn ye not unto the fathers."[18] This is a legitimate question despite the methodological difficulties inherent in the term *generation*; there is, after all, one born every minute. The issue warrants careful analysis.

Another issue related to demography and to generational conflict is the question of living conditions. Houses were frequently crowded and there was definitely a tendency for Jews, unlike their neighbors, to live in multifamily dwellings. For example, in Opatów, in 1755, 448 Jewish families were listed in a sort of census list. Of these, 90 percent lived in houses of two or more families and 44 percent in houses with four or more families. The residential family units were relatively uncomplicated nuclear families. About 12 percent of the families included married sons or sons-in-law in the residential unit and 3 percent included other relatives.[19] According to Mahler, the average size of a Jewish family in Poland in 1764 was 4.4.[20] They tended to live in two or three rooms, in a building that included four or five rooms and at least one other family. These are very close quarters, particularly when one considers the long winters, which made it desirable to stay indoors much of the time. It was necessary that equilibrium be maintained for this reason and also because the family was frequently a primary unit of production. Dispute and disruption were thus extremely serious. One historian has suggested that in such conditions anger is displaced from its true objects within the family onto neighbors or others outside of the family unit.[21] If this hypothesis were applied to Eastern Europe, one would have to investigate the feud and its frequency in Jewish society. Clearly, in this case, the economic conditions would influence heavily the ways in which the tension between generations would be resolved.

From this viewpoint, a comparison of the social consequences of demographic growth in the sixteenth century with those of the population expansion in the eighteenth century reveals important differences. Ben-Sasson, writing about sixteenth-century and early seventeenth-century Polish Jewry, speaks of "an intensification of the will to take pleasure in life and enjoy it." He quotes Ephraim of Lęczyce's description of public parades of young Jews celebrating on Purim and says this was unknown in medieval Ashkenaz and doubtful in Spain. He ascribes this phenomenon to the health of Polish-Jewish society and the strength of numbers.[22] This sort of public or civic ritual celebration is an indication of the channeling of tension in directions that do not threaten the social fabric. In other words, in conditions of rapid demographic growth in the sixteenth and early seventeenth centuries, the tension between generations did not have very serious consequences. Authority and discipline within the family tended to reflect the authority and the stability of broader social institutions. During the sixteenth century, economic, social, and political conditions tended generally to support patterns of deference and respect for authority. During the eighteenth century, economic, social, and political conditions were not nearly as stable or favorable, and the patterns of deference and respect for authority were breaking down.

I should now like to try to follow the life course of the East European Jewish child from conception to the end of the period of minority.

There are two kinds of children, male and female, and, prior to conception, one prays for male children. Listen to a woman praying in Yiddish after emerging from the ritual bath:

> purify my heart and my thoughts that I may think no evil while (my husband) has intercourse with me . . . send me the good angel to wait in the womb to bring the seed before you. Almighty God, that you may pronounce: from this seed will come forth a righteous man and a pious man, a fearer of your holy Name, who will keep your commandments and find favor in your eyes and in the eyes of all people. May he study Torah day and night, never be ashamed in the Yeshiva, and not err in *Halakha*. And if it is destined to be a daughter, grant me that she be tidy and not impudent and that she may learn to accept reproof from all those who wish to instruct her.[23]

A safe birth and the survival of the child and mother could not be controlled and evoked considerable anxiety. This led to all sorts of superstitions and customs intended to assure magically the survival of the mother and child.[24] This is another fascinating area that is complicated by the relative absence of literary sources antedating the nineteenth century and by the frustrating tendency of anthropologists to telescope whole centuries.[25] Similarly, the protection of children and the desire that they grow up to be as their parents desired was beyond the control of the parents, and this too generated a variety of beliefs and customs. Thus, a preacher warned early in the eighteenth century that if a woman exposed her hair in public, her children would be condemned to poverty. Indeed, Lilith would appear in any house where modesty was absent, and she would harm the small children.[26] Somewhat more reasonably, it was believed that a pregnant or nursing woman's diet would influence her child's character.[27]

About wet-nursing very little can be said with any assurance. It is well known that this practice was a major cause of infant mortality. It was convenient for the mother, who was freed by it from her infant's demands for her time and for her presence in the home. It also served the interests of parents who were aware of the contraceptive effect of nursing and wanted more male children. The use of wet nurses by Jews in medieval Ashkenaz is supported in the sources though it is impossible to say anything about how widespread the practice was.[28] As for Eastern Europe in the early modern period, it can be said that the practice was not unknown because ordinances of the Jewish community and of the Polish commonwealth forbade the use by Jews of Christian wet nurses.[29] The rapid demographic expansion in the periods mentioned, however, leads one to think that the use of wet nurses was not widespread. Also, though there were incentives for Christians to use wet nurses, because the Church required sexual abstinence during nursing,[30] no such prohibition existed in Jewish law.

On the treatment of the infant, aside from various superstitions, the general tendency in the ethical literature is that the mother must see to it that the infant lacks nothing. The baby is to be kept clean and well fed.[31] It is to be clothed at all times to protect it from the stings of insects and worms, from cold drafts, as well as from the evil eye, and to let it grow up without shame. The mother is to sing for the child so that it will be happy and fall asleep. She should not, however, sing Gentile songs. *Sefer ḥasidim*, which was widely read in Eastern Europe, on a significant number of occasions refers to the pleasure that the father takes in playing with his children. The context, however, is that this constitutes wasting time that could be devoted to study. It would appear that this attitude took hold among some segments of East European Jewry. By the eighteenth century, Alexander Süsskind ben Moshe of Grodno proudly asserted in his will that he had many children, but he never kissed even one of them, never took them on his knees, and never had a silly conversation with them.[32] This calls to mind a passage in the famous letter of Gaon of Vilna to the effect that there is no use in having children unless they study Torah and do good deeds.[33] There was a convention, then, that study took precedence over playing with children and that children were worthwhile only if they studied.

In the passage cited earlier from the *Lev ṭov* about not displaying one's love for one's children, a somewhat different principle is operative. It relates to a pedagogical theory, which was very widespread, having to do with what is today sometimes called "the critical learning period." Studying began at home between the ages of three and six. The following is a characteristic passage from *Sefer shenei luḥot ha-berit*:

> One must begin to teach the child from age two or three . . . because whatever his soul acquires in childhood will remain with him naturally for all his days; and, further, if the father rebukes his son early in his life with the staff . . . and using fear while he is young . . . then he will be

accustomed to fear his father always ... but if in childhood the father displays great affection ... then later when he matures he will not listen to his father or his mother. . . . Mothers are to rebuke their children like fathers and even more than the fathers. This is because they are free and found at home more. . . . And since women are of a softer nature, they are obliged "to don the garments of men" and to have brave hearts and not to spare the rod but to strike their sons even if they scream . . . women who are compassionate with their children . . . cook them, that is, they murder them.[34]

Very similar sentiments are expressed in the *Brantshpigl* and in other works.

There was also an often repeated motif, which stressed the idea that children must be dealt with on their own level. The classical locus here is Prov. 22:6: "Train a child in the way that he should go." For example, in the *Lev ṭov* there are five stages of learning, the fifth being learning for its own sake.[35] However, in order to bring the child to that level external rewards must be offered at each stage. According to *Lev ṭov*, one begins with sugar and honey cake, followed by fine clothes. The third stage is a large dowry; the fourth is a rabbinical career. A very similar list can be found in the *Brantshpigl* and in *Sefer yosif omeṣ*, and it appears as well in *Menorat ha-ma'or* and *Shev'ilei emunah* of Meir Aldabi. It ultimately goes back to Maimonides's introduction to *Perek Ḥelek* although Maimonides himself seems to have elaborated on an idea found in *Ḥovot ha-levavot*.[36] The addition, which seems to originate with the author of *Sefer lev ṭov*, is the promise of a large dowry. It is noteworthy that the progression is toward less and less tangible rewards. Also, in this particular motif, the rod is absent.

There were other principles for guiding children as well. Rivka Tiktiner emphasized that "all depends on the formation of habits." To this end situations should be created, even artificially, so that the child will experience the fulfillment of the commandments. Furthermore, as the father is often occupied, it is the mother who must educate the children. And no pious woman, she says. will spare the rod. When she speaks to her children, a mother must not cloud their minds with nonsense; this is like dirtying a slate, for afterward it is difficult to write on it. At bedtime she should speak words of Torah, telling them stories that will bring them to the fear of heaven. And she should speak to them particularly about those who died for the sanctification of God's name, like the story of the binding of Isaac and the story of Hananiah, Mishael, and Azariah.[37]

The parent must set an example for the child and should also point out the pious deeds of others. The *Brantshpigl* takes this notion further, saying that "when a man is led out to be punished for his misdeeds, sentenced to be hanged or whipped, show them this and explain how it came about."[38] Similar advice, by the way, is to be found in the writings of an otherwise enlightened Italian humanist, Mafio Vegio, who said "to let them witness a public execution is sometimes not at all a bad thing."[39] There is, then, a clear understanding that the child must be molded when he is young. The ways in which self-image or *mentalité* were formed, if they are investigated further, will provide one key to understanding the shaping of the character of East European Jewry.

One further question that should be raised is the practical age of majority. At what age was a young person considered a fully responsible member of the community? To begin with, majority did not necessarily coincide with marriage. It is true that in the Jewish artisan guilds in the eighteenth century, generally speaking, one could not be a full member unless one was married.[40] Members of that class, though, tended to marry later than wealthier members of society. Early marriage was a religious ideal, but it was expensive, for the young couple had to be supported at least for a year or two. Even in cases when they were not supported, they paid no rent.[41] Thus, early marriage does not indicate that either partner was considered independent or autonomous. Consider the fact that in the seventeenth century if a young man, under eighteen according to the Lithuanian Council, or under twenty according to the Polish Council of the Lands, contracted a marriage without the knowledge of his parents, his actions were considered to have no legal validity.[42]

Furthermore, according to the Council of the Lands, no note signed by a man within two years after his marriage had any validity. This was in 1624, but in 1635 and 1644 the edict was repeated with the period of unreliability extended to three years after marriage.[43] Another enactment of 1624 barred extending a loan to anyone who was under twenty-five or who had not been married at least two years.[44] According to the Cracow constitution of 1595, one had to be at least twenty years old before conducting business independently.[45] Eighteenth-century sources usually use the term *na'ar* to apply to people up to eighteen years of age.[46] Thus, it may be that the age of majority descended slightly between the sixteenth and the eighteenth centuries. If this is correct, it could be a reflection both of the demographic factors mentioned earlier and of a diminution in the authority of the head of family. During the eighteenth century the community of Opatów, for example, does not seem to have hesitated before expelling three young men, each designated *na'ar*, from the town, removing their "right of settlement."[47] Thus, by the eighteenth century, young men, at least, were "growing up" somewhat earlier. On the other hand, we hear about bands of errant youths in Cracow in the early part of the seventeenth century. "This one steals and that one begs to fill their bellies, and they have no inclination to put on tefillin or pray; rather they herd themselves along an evil path. . . . "[48] There are similar indications in the minute book of the Poznan community.[49] Nevertheless, the stresses and strains in Jewish society in the eighteenth century, as well as the demographic pressure, were more serious than in the earlier period.

I have tried to suggest some of the paths that future research needs to explore. Fundamentally, there are two basic problems to solve—one is to gain control over the ethical literature in order to be able to locate the significant deviations from received conventions. The second is the pressing need for research into the demographic history of the Jewish community of Poland/Lithuania. Careful microcosmic studies of individual communities, in which issues like family size and pace of growth can be examined carefully, would be most fruitful.

The specific issues raised—wet-nursing, youth culture, affect within the family, the division or roles between father and mother, the shaping of mentality, and the stages of life—all need further research. There are, of course, many other questions not even mentioned, like sex-role training, children as domestic servants and apprentices, toys,[50] regional differences, and differences between town and village populations. Finally, there must be comparative studies that will place the Jews within the context of Polish society. There can be no doubt that further study of the history of children and childhood along the lines suggested will result in some fundamental revisions in our understanding of the nature of Jewish society in East Central Europe.

NOTES

1. See Gerald L. Soliday, ed. *History of Family and Kinship: A Select International Bibliography* (New York, 1980).

2. For an example of what, to my mind, is a failure in the attempt to apply psychoanalytic techniques to history, see Lloyd de Mause, "The Evolution of Childhood," in *The History of Childhood*, ed. L. de Mause (New York, 1975), pp. 1–73.

3. Earlier literature on Jewish children and childhood includes Solomon Schechter, "The Child in Jewish Literature," *Jewish Quarterly Review* 2 (1890), 1–24, which is based, in part, on Leopold Löw, *Die Lebensalter in der jüdischen Literatur von physiologischen, rechts-,sitten- und religionsgeschichtlichem Standpunkte betrachtet* (Szeging, 1875); W. Feldman, *The Jewish Child: Its History, Folklore, Biology and Sociology* (London, 1917). See also Regina Lilienthal, "Das Kind bei den Juden," *Monatsschrift für Geschichte und Wissenschaft des Judentums* 25 (1908), 1–8; 26 (1908), 1–55. On Jewish children in Eastern Europe, see Jacob Katz, *Masoret u-mashber* (Jerusalem, 1958); idem, *Tradition and Crisis* (New York, 1971); idem, "Marriage and Sexual Life Among the Jews at the End of the Middle Ages" [in Hebrew], *Zion* 10 (1944–45), 21–54; idem, "Family, Kinship and Marriage Among Ashkenazim in the 16th–18th Centuries," *Jewish Journal of Sociology* 1 (1959), 4–22. See also G. D. Hondert, "Approaches to the History of the Jewish Family in Early Modern Poland-Lithuania," in *The Jewish Family: Myth and Reality*, ed. Steven M. Cohen and Paula E. Hyman (New York and London, 1986), 17–28.

4. Yiṣḥaq ben Eliakim of Poznán, *Sefer lev ṭov* (Dyhernfurth, 1808). First published 1620.

5. See Siegfried Stein, " 'Sefer Giddul Banim'; An Anonymous Judaeo-German Tract on the Education of Children, Printed in London in 1771" in *Remember the Days: Essays on Anglo-Jewish History Presented to Cecil Roth*, ed. John M. Shaftesley (London, 1966), pp. 145–79.

6. Stephen Ozment, "The Family in Reformation Germany: The Bearing and Rearing of Children," *Journal of Family History* 8 (1983), 159–76; idem, *When Fathers Ruled: Family Life in Reformation Europe* (Cambridge, Mass., 1983).

7. Ozment, "The Family," p. 151.

8. This is a critique of Lawrence Stone's hypothesis—and those of others—about "low gradient affect" during that period.

9. Ozment, "The Family," p. 164.

10. Benzion Dinur, *Yisra'el ba-golah* (Tel-Aviv, 1961), II, book 5, p. 66.

11. Mary Martin McLaughlin, "Survivors and Surrogates: Children and Par-

ents from the Ninth to the Thirteenth Centuries," in *The History of Childhood*, ed. L. de Mause (New York, 1975), p. 150.

12. *Sefer lev tov*, p. 54b.

13. S. Assaf, *Meqorot le-toledot hè-ḥinukh be-yisrael* (Tel-Aviv, 1954), I, 55, 58.

14. Israel ibn al-Nakawa, *Menorat ha-ma'or*, ed. H. G. Enelow (New York, 1931), III, 57–59.

15. Israel ibn al-Nakawa. *Menorat ha-ma'or*, ed. H. G. Enelow (New York, 1932), IV, 144.

16. Salo W, Baron, *A Social and Religious History of the Jews* (Philadelphia and New York, 1976), XVI, 15–23, 192–211; Bernard B. Weinryb, *The Jews of Poland* (Philadelphia, 1973), pp. 308–20; G. D. Hundert, "On the Jewish Community in Poland during the Seventeenth Century: Some Comparative Perspectives," *Revue des études juives* 142 (1983), 364–65; R. Mahler, *Yidn in amolikn Poyln* (Warsaw, 1958).

17. Jakub Goldberg, *Stosunki agrarne w miastach ziemi wielunskiej* (Łódz, 1960).

18. He equates "*al tifnu el ha-ovos*" with "*al tifnu el ha-avos.*" Quoted in Benzion Dinur, *Be-mifneh ha-dorot* (Jerusalem, 1972), 160. For a survey of the literature on early Hasidism, see G. D. Hundert and G. C. Bacon, *The Jews in Poland and Russia: Bibliographical Essays* (Bloomington, Ind., 1984), pp. 57–61.

19. Warsaw, Archiwum Główne Akt Dawnych, Archiwum Gospodarcze Wilanowskie; Administracja dóbr opatowskich, 1/110, I/69. Cf. Bogdan Baranowski, *Życie codzienne małego miasteczka w xvii i xviii wieku* (Warsaw, 1975), pp. 86–87. Baranowski misstates the statistics of J. Goldberg, "The Jewish Population of Lutomiersk in the Second Half of the Eighteenth Century" [in Polish], *Biuletyn żydowskiego instytutu historycznego* 15–16 (1955), 183–204. Compare also the figures for 1641 in Poznán, Joseph Perles, "Geschichte der Juden in Posen," *Monatsschrift für Geschichte und Wissenschaft des Judentums* 13 (1864), 420.

20. Mahler, *Yidn in amolikn Poyln*. But see M. Horn, *Żydzi na Rusi Czerwonej* (Warsaw, 1975), p. 60.

21. John Demos, *A Little Commonwealth: Family Life in Plymouth Colony* (New York, 1970), pp. 49–50.

22. H. H. Ben-Sasson, *Peraqim be-toledot ha-yehudim bi-mei ha-beinayim* (Tel-Aviv, 1969), pp. 152–55.

23. *Seder teḥinot* (1752), 9b, quoted in Chava Weissler, "The Traditional Piety of Ashkenazic Women," in *History of Jewish Spirituality*, ed. Arthur Green (New York, 1987). The translation is that of Weissler.

24. See the critique of the use of Gentile witches for this purpose in Rivka of Tiktin, *Minekes Rivke*, quoted in Assaf, *Meqorot le-toledot he-ḥinukh* IV, 45. For other sources, see Joshua Trachtenberg, *Jewish Magic and Superstition*

(New York, 1970), p. 169. On Rivka of Tiktin, see Khone Shmeruk, "The First Jewish Authoress in Poland" [in Hebrew], *Gal-Ed* 4–5 (1978), 13–23.

25. For example, Weissler, "Traditional Piety," and Trachtenberg, *Jewish Magic.*

26. Ṣevi Hirsh ben Aaron Shmuel Koidonover, *Kav ha-yashar* (Frankfurt a. M., 1705), p. 100a.

27. See the will of Moshe Yiṣḥaq of Krotoszyn (1790s) quoted in Assaf, *Meqorot le-toledot he-ḥinukh*, I, 271; *Or zarua*, pt. II, *hilkhot shabbat* no. 48, p. 21, quoted in Dinur, *Yisra'el ba-golah*, II, book 5, p. 67; *Brantshpigl*, also quoted in Assaf, *Meqorot le-toledot he-ḥinukh*, I, 54.

28. Dinur, *Yisra'el ba-golah*, II, book 5, p. 67.

29. *Volumina Legum* (rpt., Warsaw, 1981), V, 286, 399; Majer Balaban, "Die Krakauer Judengemeinde-Ordnung von 1595 und ihre Nachträge," *Jahrbuch der jüdisch-literarischen Gesellschaft* 11 (1916), 101; Jan Pęckowski, *Chrzanów: Miasto powiatowe w województwie krakowskiem* (Chrzanów, 1934), p. 147.

30. Ozment, "The Family," p. 164.

31. *Sefer Ḥasidim*, ed. R. Margaliot (Jerusalem, 1957), nos. 14, 123, 154, and so forth; Koidonover, *Kav ha-yashar*, p. 124a; *Brantshpigl*, chap. 47, quoted in Assaf, *Meqorot le-toledot he-ḥinukh*, p. 54; "Epistle of the Gaon of Wilno," in *Hebrew Ethical Wills*, by Israel Abrahams (Philadelphia, 1926), p. 317. Menaḥem ben Zoraḥ of Navarre (1308–1385) *Ṣeda la-derekh*, ma'amar 1, kelal 3, chap. 14, quoted in Dinur, *Yisra'el ba-golah* II, book 5, p. 66. Joel Sirkes often quoted *Ṣeda la-derekh*. See Schochet, *Bach: Rabbi Joel Sirkes, His Life, Works and Times* (Jerusalem and New York, 1971), p. 72.

32. Assaf, *Meqorot le-toledot he-ḥinukh*, I, pp. 270–71.

33. Abrahams, *Hebrew Ethical Wills*, p. 318.

34. Isaiah Horowitz, *Sefer shenei luḥot ha-berit* (Amsterdam, 1698), Ot Dalet, "Derekh ereṣ" p. 62a. And see there *Vavei ha-amudim*, by Shabbetai Horowitz, which forms Part II of the book: "It is proper that I praise my mother, my teacher, my first instructor" (p. 26).

35. Yiṣḥaq b. Eliakim, *Sefer lev ṭov*, chap. 9, p. 54a, chap. 5, p. 31a.

36. The author of the *Brantshpigl* cites the *Shevilei emunah* of Meir Aldabi, p. 58; Yosef Hahn, *Sefer yosif omeṣ* (Frankfurt, 1928), pp. 280–81; Israel ibn al-Nakawa, *Menorat ha-ma'or*, IV, 121; Moshe ben Maimon, *Haqdamot le-feirush ha-mishnah*, ed. M. D. Rabinoviṣ (Jerusalem, 1961), pp. 113–14; Baḥya ben Yosef ibn Pakudah, *Sefer ḥovot ha-levavot*, trans. Yehuda ibn Tibbon, ed. A. Sifroni (Jerusalem, n.d.), Sha'ar 4, Pereq 4, p. 330.

37. Quoted in Assaf, *Meqorot le-toledot he-ḥinukh*, IV, 45. And see n. 34. The question of a unique mother's role in child-rearing in this period awaits exploration.

38. Assaf, *Meqorot le-toledot he-ḥinukh*, I, 58.

39. De Mause, *The History of Childhood*, p. 14.

40. Mojżesz Schorr, "Organizacja Żydów w Polsce," *Kwartalnik historyczny*

13 (1899), 511; idem, *Żydzi w Przemyślu do końca XVIII wieku* (Lwow, 1903), pp. 262, 266; Feivel H. Wettstein, *Qadmoniyot mi-pinqesa'ot yeshanim* (Cracow, 1902), pp. 29–30.

41. See Katz, *Masoret u-mashber*, n. 7; Wettstein, *Qadmoniyot*, pp. 15–16.

42. Shimon Dubnow, ed., *Pinqas ha-mdinah* (Berlin, 1925), no. 32, p. 8 (1623), no. 430, p. 91 (1647); cf. nos. 42, 43, 185, 314, 361, 461, 968, 1003; Israel Halpern, ed., *Pinqas va'ad arba araṣot* (Jerusalem, 1945), no. 165, p. 59 (1634). Cf. Khone Shmeruk, "Young Men from Germany in the Yeshivot of Poland" [in Hebrew], *Yiẓḥak Baer Jubilee Volume*, ed. S. W. Baron et al. (Jerusalem, 1960), pp. 310, 312.

43. Halpern, *Pinqas va'ad*, no. 123, p. 47; no. 167, p. 59; no. 189, p. 70.

44. Halpern, *Pinqas va'ad*, no. 125, p. 48.

45. Balaban, "Die Krakauer Judengeminde-Ordnung," p. 102.

46. Of course, this could refer merely to Mishnah Avot 5:21. Cf. Leopold Löw, *Die Lebensalter*, pp. 31–33; Shlomo Goren, "Gilei ha-bagrut le-aḥrayut ishit u-le-aḥrayut le'umit," *Maḥanayim*, 103 (Shevat, 5726), 13; Ezekiel Landau, *She'e-lot u-teshuvot noda bi-huda*, "kama", *even ha-ezer* (New York, 1958), qu. 41; Gerald Blidstein, *Honor Thy Father and Mother* (New York, 1975), pp. 88, 125–26; Meir ben Isaac Eisenstadt, *She'elot u-teshuvot panim me'irot* (Lemberg, 1899), qu. 53.

47. Azriel Nathan Frank, "Le toledot ha-ḥazaqah," *Ha-shiloaḥ* 2 (1897), 242, 244, 246.

48. Wettstein, *Qadmoniyot*, p. 6.

49. Bernard D. Weinryb, "Studies in the Communal History of Polish Jewry," *Proceedings of the American Academy for Jewish Research* 15 (1945), 58, 59 [Hebrew section].

50. "I carved for my stepson, a boy of six, a wooden sword in the shape of the iron swords of the nobles . . . " (Ber of Bolechow, *The Memoirs*, ed. and trans. M. Wischnitzer [London, 1922], p. 83).

6

Lost Childhood in East European Hebrew Literature

Approaching the study of the theme of childhood in East European Hebrew literature, one is haunted by the question posed by Bialik, the outstanding Hebrew poet of the modern period: "They say that there is youth in the world—where is my youth?"[1] Clearly, Bialik did not mean to imply that he had had no youth, but that his youth had not measured up to his expectations. What, indeed, were the contours of a literary childhood? Did the modern concept of childhood exist in the literary imagination of the period? To what literary uses is childhood put?

Before embarking on this literary journey through childhood in Eastern Europe, let me express a caveat. Literature, by virtue of its fictive nature, obviously cannot be used to construct a sociologically or historically accurate portrait. Robert Alter brilliantly describes the double prismatic refraction of material as it is shaped by both artist and medium.[2] The fiction that emerges from this prism often looks quite different from the life that enters it. At the same time, there is something fascinating about the reconstruction of an author's fictive world—its themes, its raw materials, and the techniques that mold both. Though it sheds little light on the realities themselves, it serves to illuminate their image. That often elusive image is what we are setting out to explore.

To examine images of childhood in Eastern Europe without having to account for enormous variations in context, I have selected the works of two short story writers whose lives were proximate in both time and place.

The short stories of Isaac Dov Berkowitz and Devorah Baron present us with an ample selection of fairly realistic material about growing up in Belorussia around the turn of the century.[3] Each of them writes of characters who are children, and each employs children to serve a literary purpose. Between Berkowitz, who focuses on young men, and Baron, who concentrates primarily on young women, one gets a fairly comprehensive picture of childhood. Although writing of the same time and of adjacent places they present pictures that, despite scattered points of contact, are largely divergent.

Some of the differences are attributable to the fact that Baron writes largely about the shtetl or town whereas Berkowitz writes, for the most part, about the city. Baron presents or represents reality in her stories. Her shtetl, like her prose, seems to be cut from the fabric of eternity. As Gershon Shaked indicates, her stories have an elegiac, idyllic quality to them.[4] There is, as Rivkah Gurfein states, a stability to the life she describes.[5] Berkowitz uses his clear prose to portray a world in the throes of transition, one that is coming apart at the seams. As Avraham Holtz points out, the Berkowitz shtetl is one where tradition is in decline.[6] The root of the problems of his characters lies in their social situation. Baron's emphasis is on what is stable; Berkowitz's, on what is in flux.[7]

Children play a major role in the writings of both Berkowitz and Baron.[8] Each of them presents children of different ages as both central and secondary characters. For both authors, children serve, not unexpectedly, as the link between the past and the future. Baron views this connection in the most cosmic terms. The opening of her story "*Mishpaḥah*" ("Family"), presents the eternal picture of Jewish continuity in this way: "The chain of the generations, how it began and developed, is briefly recounted in the Bible. Here we read of a certain man who lived for so many years and begat so-and-so and then of so-and-so who lived for so many years and begat sons and daughters—link after link in a chain that is never broken for it is ever renewing itself."[9]

An abbreviated version of the traditional genealogy from Adam to the second Enoch follows, concluding with a comparison of the baby Enoch with "the same Enoch in whose lifetime the city was built." From this broad biblical context Baron narrows her focus, concentrating first on the narrator's shtetl and next on the priestly family, functioning as bakers, in which characters named Leizer, Haim, and Meir follow each other in generational sequence. Finally, the reader is brought to the focus of the story, a family of bearded Levites in which Barukhs, Avners, and Zevils follow each other in a chain. The distance from the earliest reaches of the mythic biblical past to the shtetl of the present is covered in a single leap—and each child to be born becomes a link in the unending chain, which is a recurrent Baron metaphor for family.[10]

Berkowitz, too, albeit somewhat less majestically, presents the child as a link with eternity. The child who narrates Berkowitz's "*Be-Erev Yom ha-Kippurim*" ("Yom Kippur Eve") puts it most movingly as he discusses his situation, unique among his classmates in the ḥeder, of being deprived of grandfathers: "Both my grandfathers, on my mother's side and on my father's side, died before I was born, and I was named for both of them, and therefore their memory was dear and holy to me, almost like the memory of the great forefathers of generations past, Abraham, Isaac, and Jacob, for they were the first links in my chain of ancestry, and these—the last."[11] One could almost imagine this contemporary scene illustrated by the December picture from the calendar at the Musée Saint-Raimond at Toulouse, in which, according to Philippe Ariès's description, the little child in the background symbolizes the continuity from his dying grandfather.[12] In Berkowitz, however, it is presented *sub specie aeternitatis Iudaeorum*.

The aspect of stability is emphasized in the works of both authors by the cyclical reappearance of names in a family. The boy named for his grandfathers reminds his mother of those grandfathers. Thus, as K'na'ani claims in an article on Baron, the child is a hedge against mortality. On his deathbed, the father turns his thoughts to continuing the male line by finding a wife for his son.[13] The use of the same family first names in Baron's story "America," names "which repeat and recur throughout the chain of the generations and reach to the ancestors of their first forefathers," is, according to Baron, something that, like the Shabbat candlesticks, links the new settlement with the old.[14]

In addition to forming a tie to the past, both historic and immediate, the birth of a child has great meaning for his or her parents, particularly for the mother. In the traditional Jewish society depicted, albeit somewhat critically, by Baron, a childless woman is incomplete. Dinah, the barren heroine of "Family," imagines that her sister-in-law Mousha, who has six children, might allow her to raise one of them. "Why should Mousha go bowed down with the precious burden too heavy for her to bear while she, Dinah, was condemned to go through life with empty, idle hands, which to many seem to be of no use to the world?"[15] When Fradel, in the story by the same name, seemed unhappy in her loveless marriage to Avraham Noah, "her neighbors felt pity, but the Rabbi's sage wife said: "She is still 'empty.' That's why she's melancholy. When her hands are 'full' she will be at ease."[16] Yet in this case, the facile assumption of the sage woman proves woefully inadequate.

The situation of a childless wife was not only emotionally vulnerable but also legally precarious. A couple that remained childless for ten years was traditionally expected to divorce. To a wife, then, a child has the further advantage of protecting her from the cruel possibility of being forced to accept the termination of an otherwise happy marriage. Dinah, in "Family," barely escapes such a fate when, in the middle of her divorce proceedings, the document is invalidated because one of the letters is malformed. This fortuitous turn of events becomes miraculous when Dinah subsequently becomes pregnant and bears a boy, thus escaping divorce.[17] The fate of Zlotah in the story "*Kritut*" ("Divorce") is quite different. She cannot tolerate seeing her ex-husband's new wife fondling their baby when she comes to the synagogue after the birth. Her heartrending cry and subsequent decline and death lead a neighbor to ask, " 'Why had they not killed her, this woman, then, at the appropriate time, immediately? What purpose did this prolonged death agony serve? If you are removing the head,' she asked in anger, the tears flowing from her eyes, 'then at least cut it off completely all at once.' "[18] Whatever one's emotional stake in children may be, this legal situation, always harder on the wife than on the husband who routinely remarries, puts an enormous value on children.

Though childlessness is not as tragic for men as it is for women, men do, of course, take great joy in having children. Zalman, in Berkowitz's story "*Ben Zakhar*" ("A Male Child") plans a celebration to mark the birth of this ninth child. Though some of his motivation may have been an unsuccessful attempt to draw the leading members of the community to his home, he throws himself into the preparations and even helps with the cooking.[19] He seems genuinely unable to understand the concerns of the older children, particularly of Ephraim, his nineteen-year-old firstborn, that this child will displace them. The joy of the father at the birth of his second daughter, as recorded in Baron's *"Ha-Yom ha-Rishon"* ("The First Day") is so palpable that even his mother, this fearsome mother-in-law who has spent the day denigrating girls, mellows at the sight of his beaming face. Rules and customs notwithstanding, even a newborn girl is a source of great fulfillment to both parents.

There is no doubt, of course, that male children are valued more than females. The midwife announcing the birth of a son to Zalman in Berkowitz's "A Male Child," says, "But see, see how lucky you are, may the evil eye stay away—almost all your children are males, one after the other!" The father concurs: "With this tender newborn, may they all live long lives, their number will now be seven, excepting the two girls."[20] One of Zalman's buddies comments at the celebration. "My old lady . . . God punished her with three daughters."[21] Reb Yonah in Berkowitz's *"Pere Adam"* ("A Barbarian") describes his family as "three brats at home and one, may she be guarded from the evil eye, daughter."[22] As similar phenomena in Baron's stories demonstrate, the lesser valuation of girls does not represent Berkowitz's personal point of view. When Sarah Elke, the cobbler's wife, in *"Ktanot"* ("Trifles"), annually bears a daughter, her husband hauls her before the rabbinic courts to demand a divorce.[23] When, as is told in "The First Day," her daughter-in-law bears a second daughter, the wife of the rabbi of Tohanovka is indignant. Both her other daughters-in-law have also had girls. Furthermore, it will be a source of embarassment among her son's followers at the rabbinic court. She reviews a list of rabbinic statements deprecatory to women, starting "if a son is like wine, a daughter is like nothing other than vinegar."[24] When she calls in a neighbor's son to transcribe a letter to her husband, it is so scorching that the youngster hesitates to take it down. This devaluation of daughters at birth is but the first step in making a distinction in value between boys and girls.

The difference between the welcome accorded newborn boys and girls continues to affect the lives of growing children. Although both boys and girls find time to play, that is not the major task of childhood. A boy's childhood focuses on learning and school, whereas a girl's focuses on informally developing competence in the performance of the wide range of household tasks she will be expected to perform as a grown, married woman. The lives of boys are structured in contrasting periods of study and play; in girls' lives the activities of household tasks and play are not contrasting but seamlessly interwoven.

Of course, Ariès has pointed to the role of school in setting off a period of life as distinctly other than adult. This seventeenth-century development "profited the boys first of all, while the girls persisted much longer in the traditional way of life which confused them with adults."[25] It is sometimes difficult even in the late nineteenth century to determine the limits of these life stages, particularly for girls. The absence of formal schooling is critical here, for it precludes the facile definition of the school years as a time of life that was not adult.

Ariès's description of the salutory effects of school on the lives of boys notwithstanding, one gets the strong impression that the attitude toward school as portrayed in turn-of-the-century Hebrew literature was less than positive. In fact, the best part of school seems to have been the vacations. In the story "*Malkot*" ("Lashes") Berkowitz presents a horrifying picture of school as described by the child-abusing retired teacher. Gedalyah's educational methodology was beating children; his goal, "to make the shegetz [non-Jew] into a kosher Jew."[26] Gedalyah sarcastically describes the new approaches to education that proscribe the whip and strap and permit only a rapping of the fingers with a newfangled device—a ruler. Yet it is the objective voice of the narrator that tells us that Gedalyah had been, in his time, a sought-after teacher, that "every boy he would take into his hands he would make an improved vessel [*kli metukkan*]."[27] The noise and crowding in this room full of boys of various ages and stages of learning would be intolerable even without abusive corporal punishment. If Gedalyah's is the model school, it is clear why time off from school, even if only during or at the end of the day, was crucial.

Any time off from studies was, indeed, appreciated. The autumnal pleasures of the intersession are presented in Berkowitz's "Yom Kippur Eve." The narrator indicates that his father's review of the High Holy Day liturgy "announced to him freedom from the studies at his teacher's school, stolen blasts on the shofar in the women's section of the synagogue, running without restraint over harvested fields and fallen golden leaves in a nearby grove, roasting potatoes with a group of boys in abandoned gardens, making bonfires of dried brush at eventide, and similar stolen pleasures that the Holy One Blessed Be He took out of his good store of treasure for Jewish children in the period 'between the school terms.' "[28] Baron describes Ephraim, who had learned what was to be learned at school and, while the family tried to agree on his future, was left to roam "free as the wind and soon forgot all he had learnt about scriptural intonation and Rashi script. Instead he learnt to distinguish between beet and turnip leaves in the garden and to tell the difference between ears of rye and wheat in the fields."[29] Ephraim spends his time wandering at will and learning about nature, music and other aspects of life that did not constitute part of the heder, or elementary school, curriculum. It is the absence of school that enables him to broaden his horizons. As is indicated by the way the children burst forth from school during breaks in the school day, even a brief respite is appreciated.[30]

In Baron's story "Fradel," Chaim-Raphael would often spend his breaks playing with the title character. "In leisure hours, when he was free from his studies, he would put her into the swing at the edge of the garden and send her flying into the air, or he would take hold of the doll carriage that had been bought for her in the city and send it spinning down the paved garden path, while he and she, her little hand in his, rushed after it laughing. . . . "[31] While a young girl, Fradel is free to swing or play with dolls as part of her daily activities; Chaim Raphael confines his play to the breaks in his studies. There were also some boys who were free because they were not obliged to study—boys like Berkowitz's Misha'el and Faivke, who were not really teachable and therefore had the latitude to develop other interests. Clearly, for these boys, freedom was not worth the price. Indeed they became social outcasts.

Though girls are not excluded entirely either from learning or from play, they are most significantly depicted as sharing in the work of the household. Thus, for example, fifteen-year-old Hershl is reading Smolenskin while, in another room, it is his younger sister who sings their baby brother to sleep while rocking the cradle.[32] In the moving scene where Mousha tries to select a child to lend to her barren sister-in-law, she cannot relinquish Batia, her eldest, because the younger children need her—"she is the one who is bringing them up."[33] Girls also learn other things like knitting, embroidery, scouring a samovar, kindling a stove, laying firewood, and washing laundry.[34] At the same time, the girls are not always uneducated. The narrator of Baron's *"Mah She-Hayah"* ("What Has Been") has been taught by her father not merely to read but also to understand the Pentateuch in Hebrew with a wealth of haggadic interpretations. This she, in turn, imparts to her illiterate friend Minah as she teaches more than the rote reading that was expected of girls. Girls, particularly young ones, have the freedom to allow them to participate in the games Dinah plays with her nieces and to develop friendships like Minah's with the narrator.

In the world of the shtetl boys necessarily come to take their place in the world of work. Poverty-stricken girls often are forced to do the same. Zevil, in "Family," works in his father's smithy from age thirteen and studies at night.[35] Hannah Gitel, the eldest of the cobbler's many daughters in Baron's "Trifles," is sent to work for a family in the city.[36] Minah virtually takes over the family bakery in Baron's "What Has Been." Yet Hershl, the central character in Berkowitz's "A Barbarian," is at fifteen unwilling to take a fairly well-paying job as a tutor and is jealous of his baby brother, who lies back while their sister cares for him.[37] For girls, paid employment represents only an incremental shift from the life of work at home; for boys, it marks a radical break that sometimes engenders opposition.

Although religion with the duties it imposes is important and suffuses all the literature of the period, its impact on children's lives and minds is perceived differently by Baron and Berkowitz. In Berkowitz's stories religion is, as Holtz indicates, one arena in which the class struggle is played out.[38] The father who wants to buy a maftir (honor of being called to read the prophetic portion) for his bar mitzvah boy is too poor to warrant recognition, and his bid would doubtless have been too low even if he had been important enough to be recognized.[39] The father who wants to boast of his son's becoming a purveyor finds that no one in the synagogue cares.[40] The narrator in "On Yom Kippur Eve" describes how he would "stand alone and abandoned, like a living orphan, by our large reading stand, suffering and ignoring our neighbors," while his father sobbed during Yom Kippur prayers.[41] Although the son does acknowledge the beauty of his father's private practicing, the public performance proves mortifying. For Faivke in *"Yom ha-Din Shel Faivke"* ("Faivke's Judgment Day"), however, the problem is both in the form of religious ritual and in its inner meaning. On the Yom Kippur when this nine-year-old boy, living outside a Jewish community, makes his contact with the synagogue, he is upset to witness, as his initial exposure to communal Judaism, the penitential flogging of his father.[42] He turns down the opportunity to be flogged himself but cannot evade the other threat foisted on him—the pervasive smelling salts. When the father bursts into tears at a point in the service where there seems to be nothing to provoke crying, he is taunted by the reaction, a transparent double entendre to the reader, "[N]o one cries at this place."[43] Obviously, a synagogue where no one cries is of dubious merit. Faivke's underlying problem is neither with the synagogue, nor with his fellow Jews, but with God. Faivke really fears God.[44] He is terrified of Him as the source "of the dire punishments in the world to come."[45] He can neither pray nor bring himself to answer, "Amen."[46]

Religion can have overwhelming negative power. Baron's spare style sometimes leads us to learn more from what is implicit than from what is explicit.[47] There is, however, no mistaking the thrust of her description of a girl who, the day before her wedding, "walked out to the fields with her friends and there, among the hills on the *Grafin*'s estate, she wept—as Jephtah's daughters had done—the passing of her youth."[48] After all, Jephtah's daughter went to mourn in the mountains before her death. The comparison is clear. When this girl's hair was cut off, she kept it gently covered in a manner suggestive of the way "in which one covers the body of a dear one."[49] Numerous occasions on which Jewish law conflicts with human happiness are portrayed in Baron's stories, which are almost always narrated by the rabbi's daughter, familiar with what she saw in her home. The onerous obligations of mourning are, in one story, taught to a young boy after his father's death by an older member of the family.[50] Dinah, the childless central character of "Family," stops attending synagogue on Shabbat owing to the cruel remarks she hears there.[51] Religion can serve as a barrier to the enjoyment of simple pleasures like food, as it does when the children are faulted for eating "without making the prescribed benediction, just like the Gentile children."[52] Yet even conflicts between Jewish law and personal happiness are not presented in a manner designed to overturn this stable way of life.[53]

Religion can, however, also be positive. When, for example, Dinah, at home on Passover, hears the children respond, "Amen," to the cantor, it sounds "so sweetly that her heart quivered with emotion."[54] In this way, at least in the eyes of adults, Judaism can be positive for children.

Not unexpectedly, another major concern in these stories is food. Food is an expression of love and caring, as well as a necessity of life. Thus, for example, Misha'el's mother continues to feed him even after his father has evicted him from the house.[55] Mothers are generally responsible for feeding children, but when Dinah, their aunt, is in charge of her nieces, meals are more fun.[56] When Ephraim takes ill in Baron's story "What Has Been," Dr. Pavlovsky declares that the cause is that he does not eat enough. "Later, his sullen mother brought him some chicken soup and fed him with her own hand, as she had done only earlier, in his childhood."[57] The diagnosis of the illness of Shmulik, Nahum Leib's son, is the same, but in this case proves accurate.[59] The father is willing to undertake any task in order to procure the milk, cocoa, and porridge the doctor prescribes. When, indeed, he manages to acquire the requisite milk, sugar, and cocoa, he feeds his son himself.

"In order not to waste a drop, he kept the cup near the boy's chin and carefully fed him with a spoon, smacking his lips coaxingly before each spoonful so as to show the child how sweet and tasty it was."[59] This act emphasizes the importance of the parent-child bond and warmly depicts a nurturing father.

A lot of love for children is expressed through food, but there is a great deal that is not so tangibly expressed. For Nahum Leib the cry that "contained all the love and all the anxious care in the world is 'abba, daddy.' "[60] Even Hirshl's father, who wants to send him off to be a private teacher, loves him, sacrifices for him, and kisses him.[61] Although Minah's mother does not love her, her father does and goes for walks with her.[62] There is concern even for a problematic child like Faivke. Grandparents, too, are usually described as doting caregivers.[63] Parental love is reciprocated by filial love, and siblings, too, often seem to care for each other. When one is not part of this bond of caring, one can, like Dr. Winik in "Severed," feel guilty and depressed.

The large number of children in extended families would seem to argue for a suppression of individuality. The children Baron refers to as "Bible students, Hebrew students, and those learning the alphabet" "filled the lanes like the plenteous grass in the fields, they sprouted like young shoots in the flower beds. . . ."[64] Particularly in "Family," as if seen through the eyes of the painfully childless, masses of children abound—even in cemetery graves.[65] Smaller groups also seem to lose their individuality, like the "three teenage Leibeh's, of the same height and virtually identical figures and features."[66] Yet when, as previously mentioned, Mousha considers relinquishing one of her five daughters, she lingers lovingly over the needs and qualities of each before deciding that each of her children is precious and none can be spared for her sister-in-law.

Indeed, while parents love their children, they take pride in the accomplishments of their sons. Holtz points out that in many of Berkowitz's stories there are children who aspire to professional careers, and, despite their concomitant break with tradition, merit parental encouragement.[67] When in "*Baal Simḥah*" ("A Proud Father") Leizer leaves the world of traditional Jewish values and enters the world of secular studies, the family changes its life-style and even straightens out the house to accommodate the expectations of the secular world. When he qualifies as a purveyor, his father expects the whole world to share his pride. In "*Maftir*" Moshe-Moti, proud of his son's having become bar mitzvah, wants to share the occasion with his fellow congregants. Less remarkable events are also sources of pride. In "On Yom Kippur Eve" the narrator's father is proud of his son's ability to perform the rite of kapparoth (expiation) properly. Even a troublesome child like Mishael becomes a source of pride when he comes into his glory on Hoshanah Rabbah.[68] These sons bring great joy to their parents; their sisters, involved neither in careers nor in public religious accomplishments, do not serve as sources of pride in the same way.

Children function not only as a cause for pride but also as a cause for grave concern. Two children in particular, Faivke in Berkowitz's "Faivke's Judgment Day" and Ephraim in Baron's "What Has Been," fall into the category of what Reinhard Kuhn, in his study of the child in Western literature entitled *Corruption in Paradise*, calls "the enigmatic child." These boys are wise beyond their years.[69] Both of them are wise in the ways of nature. Faivke's interest is in the arcane world of the forest; Ephraim's encompasses all nature and art. Faivke, however, is like a wild animal whereas Ephraim is "a boy poet, whom God had endowed with the soul of his world."[70] Yet each of these children cannot survive. Faivke has confronted the God of his terrors, and Ephraim's poetic soul has rendered him unfit for ordinary life. As often happens with literary enigmatic children, these boys die rather than grow up.[71]

The fate of girls who do not fit in is different. Two of Baron's heroines, Haya-Fruma in "*Shavririm*" ("Sunbeams") and Minah in "What Has Been" are misfits, but they eventually find a niche for themselves. They are both physically disfigured. Haya-Fruma comes to the village as an orphaned five-year-old. Because her face is "devoid of a single endearing feature," she is denied all sympathy.[72] When she was eight, she broke her leg and subsequently developed a limp. She was also heavy. " 'There goes Haya-Fruma!' children at play would call after her; the grown-ups, who appear to ostracize those of unlovely appearance, would not so much as look at her."[73] She is indigent but supports herself by doing housework and then by working in a bakery. Although she eventually marries an old widower, her marriage is brief and childless but results in her finding a companion in the form of a cow. Haya-Fruma's work— her cleaning and polishing—are in a sense a metaphor for the shining of her soul, which is further refined by the acts of charity she performs. Her final justification is that she dies feeling "as though she were becoming enveloped in the golden haze of an unseen sunrise."[74] Minah's problem is that her plain, freckled appearance induces her peers to call her "Spotty" and her mother to treat her like Cinderella. Though her brother and sister are treated with respect and love, she is expected to do all the drudgery. This she does and further helps tend the bodies and souls of the family members. At the same time she runs the family business. Like Haya-Fruma she is a beautiful soul in a damaged body, and her life works out when she marries a childless miller and bears a son, whom she names for her dead brother. Unlike the enigmatic boys, these girls are very much a part of this world and thus conquer it, to a greater or lesser degree.

To this point, we have examined the literary lives of children, but children also function in literature as metaphors. What is probably the most common metaphoric use of children is in comparison with crying adults. Many of Berkowitz's characters cry like babies—each of the parents in "On Yom Kippur Eve"; both Dr. Winik and his aunt in "Severed"; and Misha'el, to cite a few examples.[75] As Holtz points out, "In Western society young children have come to symbolize hope for the future, yet in Berkowitz's tales, children constantly appear in a state of frustration and hopelessness."[76] When adults are compared to children, they take on this infantile despair, which is actually more appropriate to adults, for true despair requires intelligence.

Children often provide more positive metaphors. Even in Berkowitz's work, not all comparisons to children bespeak frustration. When, in "On Yom Kippur Eve," the mother would describe her father, her face would take on a "childish expression": "A smile like the smile of an infant, lying in his crib in his Daddy and Mommy's house hovering over her thin, pale lips."[77] Ephraim, in "What Was Then," when listening to music, "felt as if his body were swaying gently, as if he were being pampered as in those far-off childhood days when his mother, still tender and loving, sat beside his cot rocking him to sleep."[78] This and other similar references project an image of childhood that is both secure and comfortable. Though it does not presage hope for the future, it does imply a childhood that could serve as a strong base for future growth.

Baron uses children and their activities to symbolize the progress of time. "There was something pleasant and soothing in the sounds of prayer in the gentle, waning daylight—sounds that erupted from the ḥadarim (elementary schools) like the rush of water pouring over a dam. . . . Soon the children came surging out to scamper down the lanes . . . "[79] Night, too, has its signal: "At seven o'clock the pupils from ḥeder passed by, the reflected lights from their lanterns flitting across the dark wall like a flock of golden sheep . . . "[80] The season, as well, is marked by children. "Again it was springtime in the lane, and the warm ground, still damp to the touch, swarmed with children. The infants born that winter gazed wide-eyed at the great, wonderful world that had become a new setting for their mothers' shining faces."[81] These repeating metaphors of time emphasize the pervasive presence of children. They help convey an image of stability in which one generation follows another without major disruption. They also represent a cyclical view of life in which the individual is but one of many people in the same situation.[82]

Indeed, it is this view of a stable society that most clearly distinguishes Baron's characters from Berkowitz's. To Berkowitz the class struggle is important.[83] Shaked sees his works as an expression of determinism; his characters, at the mercy of necessary social processes.[84] His heroes are, by and large, young men in revolt against the traditional mores of generations past. Berkowitz's stories focus on a period of crisis within an ongoing, deteriorating, social situation.[85] Baron's goal is to portray, as Keshet puts it, *"nishmat ha-ayarah"* (the soul of the shtetl)."[86] Her characters, though often suffering at the hands of fate or even of traditional Judaism, do not seek to undo its strictures. Her women, particularly, accept whatever life hands them. Clearly, some of this disparity reflects differences in personal philosophy, in style. Another element may be the difference between the shtetl and the town. Yet another factor may be what is best dubbed "social Gilliganism." In her study of the moral development of men and women entitled *In a Different Voice* (Cambridge, Mass., 1982), Carol Gilligan points to the fact that girls, as they grow up, aspire to be like their mothers; whereas boys aspire to be different from them. In these stories, the girls become part of the very fabric of an integrated, stable female society at an early age, but boys separate from the female society of infancy and toddlerhood to join a world sharply divided into the unpleasant realm of school and Jewish tradition, on the one hand, and freedom, nature, and play, on the other. Their reintegration into traditional Jewish society is more tenuous for this reason, and they have more opportunity for rebellion. In any case, Berkowitz's male characters tend not to fit in. Baron's female ones do.

Literature dealing with the theme of childhood tends to reflect one of two goals: It may attempt to recapture the past, collective or personal, or it may, as it supports a point of view, present childhood as a pretext. Berkowitz, in somewhat fulsome style, portrays the children of the past as a vehicle to convey his outlook, his desire to change what in Jewish life and tradition was, to his mind, no longer viable. Baron, however, as Miron claims, never dealt with the problems facing the youth of her generation as it moved away from the experience of an organic community.[87] Avoiding ideological conflict, political or religious, she tries to present a picture of what was. For all the pain, she tries in her stories "to return and to see again, even if but one more time, the ancient house of my birth, the one which modestly leans on its two beams; to go up to the attic and to find the pages of the old Humash with the first alef-bet notebook stuck there among the boards, to climb and reach the small window and to overlook from there at the same time the whole shtetl and finally to come down and eat American potatoes, cooked at the front of the oven on pine needles and after that—what will be will be."[88]

NOTES

I am grateful to my colleague Professor Avraham Holtz for his advice. Naomi Levy, my research assistant, helped in the research for this paper.

1. H. N. Bialik, "Hakhnisini," *Kol Shirei H. N. Bialik* (Tel Aviv, 1962), p. 182.

2. See Robert Alter's essay in this volume, pp. 225–26.

3. Berkowitz was born in Slutsk, Belorussia, in 1885 and remained there until he moved to Lodz in 1903. He acquired his Jewish education largely in heder, but in secular fields he was self-taught. He moved to the United States in 1913. Berkowitz's fame rests not only on his own fiction but also on his Hebrew translations of the works of his father-in-law, Shalom Aleichem. He died in 1967.

Baron was born in Ozdah, Belorussia, in 1887. Though, as a girl, she received little formal education, her father, a rabbi, alllowed her to listen to her brother's lessons. The result was that she is the only woman writer of the period who has any facility with rabbinic sources. In 1911 she settled in Palestine, where she died in 1956. Various systems yield Devorah, Dvorah, and Devora as possible transliterations of Baron's first name. For convenience I have used the *Encyclopedia Judaica* spelling "Devorah" throughout, ignoring variations.

4. Gershon Shaked, *Ha-Sipporet ha-Ivrit* [in Hebrew] (Tel Aviv, 1978), I, 452–53.

5. Rivkah Gurfein, "Devorah Baron vo-Omanut Sippureha" [in Hebrew], in Devorah Baron, *Yalkut Sippurim* (Tel Aviv, 1976), pp. 9, 13.

6. Avraham Holtz, *Isaac Dov Berkowitz: Voice of the Uprooted* (Ithaca, N.Y., 1973), p. 54.

7. In his discussion of Baron's stories, Schweid emphasizes the cyclical view of time inherent in them. "By means of the story Devorah Baron does not seek to emphasize the special nature of moments and the changes among them. To the contrary! She uses changes to emphasize the unchanging, the static element in human existence, society and the universe" (Elizer Schweid, "Ḥidat ha-Retsifut," in *Devorah Baron: A Selection of Critical Essays on Her Literary Prose* [in Hebrew], ed. Ada Pagis [Tel Aviv, 1974], p. 111). [Translation mine.]

8. Although Shaked, when listing the major themes in Baron's stories, does not so indicate, clearly childhood, most often girlhood, plays a major role in her work. Shaked, *Ha-Sipporet ha-Ivrit*, I, 453.

9. Devorah Baron, *The Thorny Path*, trans. Joseph Schachter (Jerusalem, 1969), p. 1; *Parashiyyot* [in Hebrew] (Jerusalem, 1968), p. 11.

10. Shaked cites this as an example of the use of overt and direct biblical analogies as a method of giving the stories an archetypic and archaic dimension. Shaked, *Ha-Sipporet ha-Ivrit*, I, 464–65.

11. Isaac Dov Berkowitz, *Kitvei I. D. Berkowitz* [in Hebrew] (Tel Aviv, 1959), p. 5a. [Translation mine.]

12. Philippe Ariès, *Centuries of Childhood: A Social History of Family Life*, trans. Robert Baldick (New York, 1962), p. 345.

13. K'na'ani emphasizes that the father's concern in *"Mishpaḥah"* is not with offspring, for his daughters have many children, but with maintaining the male line. See David K'na'ani, *Mi-Bayit* (Tel Aviv, 1977), pp. 51–52.

14. Baron, *Parashiyyot*, p. 442. [Translation mine.]

15. Baron, *Thorny Path*, pp. 21–22; *Parashiyyot*, p. 24.

16. Devorah Baron, "Fradel," *Hebrew Short Stories*, ed. S. Y. Penueli and A. Ukhmani (Tel Aviv, 1965), p. 170; Baron, *Parashiyyot*, p. 98.

17. Baron, *Thorny Path*, pp. 36–37; *Parashiyyot*, p. 35. Baron's choice of words here constitutes a fine pun. Old Uncle Shlomo, the first person to be informed of the pregnancy, says *"Veriḥeim otah Elohim"* ["and God has had mercy on her"]. The Hebrew root *RḤM* has the meaning "womb." From that meaning its use as a term for mercy evolved. Clearly, Baron is here playing on the womb/mercy connection. Thus, in a sense, Shlomo says that God has "wombed" her.

18. Baron, *Parashiyyot*, pp. 191–92. [Translation mine.]

19. Berkowitz, *Kitvei I. D. Berkowitz*, p. 24b. Though these actions clearly indicate Zalman's joy, they also, in that social context, mean that he loses status. The declining role of the father is an important element in the dissolution of the family Berkowitz describes. Holtz, *Isaac Dov Berkowitz*, pp. 51, 55; Shaked, *Ha-Sipporet ha-Ivrit*, I, 335.

20. Berkowitz, *Kitvei I. D. Berkowitz*, p. 23a.

21. Berkowitz, *Kitvei I. D. Berkowitz*, p. 26b.

22. Holtz, *Isaac Dov Berkowitz*, p. 162; Berkowitz, *Kitvei I. D. Berkowitz*, p. 46b.

23. Baron, *Thorny Path*, p. 49; *Parashiyyot*, p. 43.

24. Baron, *Thorny Path*, p. 80; *Parashiyyot*, p. 249. This is apparently based on the statement in Midrash Tanḥuma, Ḥayyei Sarah: "There are three things a person would rather not have: grass in the grain, a female among the children, and vinegar in his wine, and all were created to meet a universal need."

25. Ariès, *Centuries of Childhood*, p. 61.

26. *Shegetz* is a deprecatory term for a non-Jew that was often used as an epithet for Jewish boys. Berkowitz, *Kitvei I. D. Berkowitz*, p. 14a. [Translation mine.]

27. Berkowitz, *Kitvei I. D. Berkowitz*, p. 14b.

28. Berkowitz, *Kitvei I. D. Berkowitz*, p. 6b.

29. Baron, *Thorny Path*, pp. 132–33; *Parashiyyot*, p. 166.

30. Baron, *Thorny Path*, p. 16; *Parashiyyot*, , p. 21.

31. Baron, "Fradel," p. 170; *Parashiyyot*, p. 98.

32. Holtz, *Isaac Dov Berkowitz*, p. 161; Berkowitz, *Kitvei I. D. Berkowitz*, p. 46b.

33. Baron, *Thorny Path*, 22; *Parashiyyot*, p. 25. A literal translation would be: "[S]he watches over them and guides them."

34. Baron, *Thorny Path*, pp. 11, 31; *Parashiyyot*, pp. 17, 31.

35. Baron, *Thorny Path*, p. 19; *Parashiyyot*, p. 23.

36. Baron, *Parashiyyot*, pp. 50–1.

37. Holtz, *Isaac Dov Berkowitz*, p. 171; Berkowitz, *Kitvei I. D. Berkowitz*, p. 50a.

38. It is also often an arena where father suffers loss of status. Holtz, *Isaac Dov Berkowitz*, p. 58.

39. Holtz, *Isaac Dov Berkowitz*, p. 58; Berkowitz, *Kitvei I. D. Berkowitz*, pp. 51–53. Moshe Gil points to this scene as an example of the deterioration of the paternal role; see his "Sippurei ha-Ayarah shel I. D. Berkowitz," in Abraham Holtz, ed., *Yitzhak Dov Berkowitz: A Selection of Critical Essays on His Literary Prose* (Tel Aviv, 1976), p. 83.

40. Berkowitz, *Kitvei I. D. Berkowitz*, pp. 20aff.

41. Berkowitz, *Kitvei I. D. Berkowitz*, p. 6a.

42. Holtz, *Isaac Dov Berkowitz*, p. 182; Berkowitz, *Kitvei I. D. Berkowitz*, p. 122a.

43. Holtz, *Isaac Dov Berkowitz*, p. 188; Berkowitz, *Kitvei I. D. Berkowitz*, p. 124a.

44. Shaked points out that while Faivke's experience of Yom Kippur does not fulfill the requirements of Jewish law, it is more a religious experience than that of the Jews of the town who mistreat him. See Gershon Shaked, "Motif Yom-ka-Kippurim ba-Sippur," *Mahanayim* (New York, 1961), p. 133.

45. Holtz, *Isaac Dov Berkowitz*, pp. 175–76; Berkowitz, *Kitvei I. D. Berkowitz*, pp. 119b–20a.

46. Holtz, *Isaac Dov Berkowitz*, p. 180; Berkowitz, *Kitvei I. D. Berkowitz*, p. 121b.

47. Tuvya Rübner, "M'danim u-Fiyyus" in Pagis, ed., *Devorah Baron*, pp. 135–36.

48. Baron, *Thorny Path*, p. 43; *Parashiyyot*, p. 39.

49. Baron, *Thorny Path*, p. 44; *Parashiyyot*, p. 40.

50. Baron, *Thorny Path*, p. 20; *Parashiyyot*, p. 23.

51. Baron, *Thorny Path*, pp. 28–29; *Parashiyyot*, p. 29.

52. Baron, *Thorny Path*, p. 40; *Parashiyyot*, p. 37.

53. Gurfein, "Devorah Baron," p. 13.

54. Baron, *Thorny Path*, p. 29; *Parashiyyot*, p. 29.

55. Berkowitz, *Kitvei I. D. Berkowitz*, p. 10a.

56. Baron, *Thorny Path*, p. 21; *Parashiyyot*, p. 24.

57. Baron, *Thorny Path*, p. 138; *Parashiyyot*, p. 170.

58. Baron, "To Stand Rebuked" [trans. Joseph Schachter], in *Modern Hebrew Literature* 2, no. 1 (1976), 19–21; *Parashiyyot*, pp. 194–97.

59. Baron, "To Stand Rebuked," p. 21; *Parashiyyot*, p. 197.

60. Baron, "To Stand Rebuked," p. 18; *Parashiyyot*, p. 194.

61. Holtz, *Isaac Dov Berkowitz*, p. 168; Berkowitz, *Kitvei I. D. Berkowitz*, p. 49a.

62. Baron, *Thorny Path*, p. 84; *Parashiyyot*, p. 131.

63. Baron, *Thorny Path*, p. 83; *Parashiyyot*, p. 130. See also Baron's "*Ktanot*" and Berkowitz,s "Be-Erev Yom ha-Kippurim."

64. Baron, *Thorny Path*, pp. 9–10; *Parashiyyot*, 16.

65. Baron, *Thorny Path*, pp. 7–13; *Parashiyyot*, pp. 15–18.

66. Baron, *Thorny Path*, p. 30; *Parashiyyot*, p. 30.

67. Holtz, *Isaac Dov Berkowitz*, pp. 6, 54.

68. Berkowitz, *Kitvei I. D. Berkowitz*, pp. 11b–13.

69. Holtz, *Isaac Dov Berkowitz*, p. 63.

70. Baron, *Thorny Path*, p. 139; *Parashiyyot*, pp. 170–71.

71. Reinhard Kuhn, *Corruption in Paradise: The Child in Western Literature* (Hanover and London, 1982), p. 193. Gil points to Faivke's death as an indication that the shtetl cannot sustain healthy growth. Gil, "Sippurei ha-Ayarah," p. 89.

72. Baron, "Sunbeams" [trans. Joseph Schachter], in *Modern Hebrew Literature* 2, no. 1 (1976), 22; *Parashiyyot*, pp. 114–15.

73. Baron, "Sunbeams," p. 23; *Parashiyyot*, p. 116.

74. Baron, "Sunbeams," p. 31; *Parashiyyot*, p. 125.

75. Berkowitz, *Kitvei I. D. Berkowitz*, pp. 12, 24, 40a, 45b.

76. Holtz, *Isaac Dov Berkowitz*, p. 69.

77. Berkowitz, *Kitvei I. D. Berkowitz*, p. 12. [Translation mine.]

78. Baron, *Thorny Path*, p. 135; *Parashiyyot*, p. 168.
79. Baron, *Thorny Path*, p. 9; *Parashiyyot*, p. 16.
80. Baron, *Thorny Path*, p. 12; *Parashiyyot*, p. 18.
81. Baron, *Thorny Path*, p. 29; *Parashiyyot*, pp. 29–30.
82. Gurfein, "Devorah Baron," p. 9.
83. Holtz, *Isaac Dov Berkowitz*, p. 58.
84. Shaked, *Ha-Sipporet ha-Ivrit*, I, 337.
85. Shaked, *Ha-Sipporet ha-Ivrit*, I, 335.
86. Yshurun Keshet, "Al Devorah Baron," in Pagis (ed.), *Devorah Baron*, pp. 82–83.
87. Dan Miron, "Prakim al Ytsiratah shel Devorah Baron," in Pagis (ed.), *Devorah Baron*, p. 127.
88. Baron, *Parashiyyot*, p. 416. [Translation mine.]

PART III

FAMILY AND COMMUNITY

7

From Father to Son: The Inheritance of Spiritual Leadership in Jewish Communities of the Middle Ages

AVRAHAM GROSSMAN

The place of the family in European society has been extensively researched in recent years. In contrast, research on the place of the family in Jewish society is still in its early stages.[1] The reason for this is not a lack of material or historical data. On the contrary, in Jewish society both in Christian Europe and in Moslem countries the family occupied a most important place in communal leadership. In Christian Europe this phenomenon was especially outstanding in Germany before the First Crusade in 1096. The opinion held by some scholars that Jewish society in Germany during the ninth to eleventh centuries was based on essentially democratic foundations is entirely unfounded. Rather, all the leaders of the communities of Mainz, Worms, and Speyer belonged to few eminent families: five in Mainz and two in Worms. It is possible to trace the family trees of those families for five or more generations until 1096. They held a position of decisive influence in various areas of life; all the political, social, cultural, and religious functions were concentrated in their hands, and they served as community leaders and spokespersons to the authorities. We do not find a single leader who represented the communities to the German authorities who was not a scion of one of those families.[2] Political and social power of that kind was not held by the sages in any Diaspora Jewish community of the Middle Ages. In these important communities of Germany, a novelty was to be discerned: Whereas the aristocratic families in Christian society, as well as the Jewish communities in Moslem Spain, attained influence in the spheres of politics and economics, notable Jewish families in Germany achieved great power in the spiritual sphere, too. The heads of the yeshivot (rabbinic academies) of Mainz and Worms and the great sages of the community at the end of the tenth and in the eleventh centuries generally belonged to certain distinguished families.

It is, however, impossible to describe the reality that existed in Germany without first examining the roots of the phenomenon in Babylonia (Iraq) and Palestine in the Middle Ages, when the family began to play an important role in medieval spiritual leadership. The reality in these two centers influenced Germany, too, as we shall see. Because we are dealing with a development that greatly influenced Jewish society in the Middle Ages as well as in modern times, it is fitting that we study its roots.

The phenomenon of sons inheriting the positions held by their fathers in the spiritual leadership of the Jewish community first appeared in the Middle Ages. Sons were regarded as being entitled to inherit the place of their fathers at the head of yeshivoth in Palestine and in Babylonia, and it is possible to discern in both these regions clear traces of such succession.

The inheritability of yeshiva leadership was a new phenomenon and constituted a change from past custom. The right of inheritances was not mentioned in the talmudic sources, nor was it to be found in reality during that period.

In Palestine in the talmudic period the sons of scholars indeed enjoyed an honorable status and, apparently, a special position in the yeshiva.[3] But these sons definitely did not possess the right to inherit their fathers' posts. We have various evidence of talmudic sages who succeeded in attaining the high rank of *Rosh Yeshiva* (head of the academy) in their own right despite the fact that they belonged to the lower stratum of the population. Two of the greatest Mishnaic authorities—Rabbi Akiba and Rabbi Meir—are reputed to have been examples of this phenomenon.

Evidence of the existence of the same phenomenon in Palestine is to be found as far back as the end of the ninth century. It continued to exist with full intensity until the end of the Arabic period and the Crusaders' conquest in 1099, as the post of *Rosh Yeshiva* was the inheritance of only three families (the Ben Meir family and the two Hacohen families). Furthermore, some inherited their fathers' posts as soon as the fathers died. There was even a case in which a gaon (leader of the rabbinic community) appointed his heir as head of the religious court—the second highest position in the hierarchy in Palestine—and other sons to the next two posts (or titles) following in sequence of importance. The yeshiva thus became a sort of family heirloom.[4]

The situation in Babylonia was slightly more flexible. There inheritance began only in the eighth century. Generally, a son did not succeed his father immediately, but some older person (often the brother of the deceased gaon) usually took his place at first. Only some time later was the son himself appointed as head of the yeshiva. The picture that emerges is that the post of gaon was the inheritance of a number of families, and it was from these families only that geonim were appointed. Generally—and especially in the tenth and eleventh centuries—sons inherited the posts of their fathers only a few years later.[5]

However, it would be wrong to regard this phenomenon as being limited to the post of gaon alone. Distinguished birth and the right of sons to succeed their fathers in spiritual leadership were clearly reflected in appointments to other posts, too, and it may be assumed the phenomenon influenced the structure of Jewish society as a whole, as well as the authority of the yeshiva and its impact on Jewish society.

Evidence of this is to be found in the description by Rabbi Natan the Babylonian of the appointment procedures and study in the yeshiva.

> Their custom was as follows: If one of the heads of the assembly of students died and he had a son who filled his post, the latter succeeded his father and inherited his post even if he was a youngster . . . and if one of the members of the seven senior ranks was greater than the son in wisdom, he was not appointed in his place because he did not inherit the post from his father, but he received more money due to his wisdom.[6]

Rabbi Natan actually wrote these words in the middle of the tenth century, when it was the fashion of Moslem historians to insert anecdotes into their writings, but the nature of this item bears witness to its truth and to the fact that it was not written merely for the sake of stylistic effect. The rest of Rabbi Natan's description clearly indicates that this extremely hierarchical structure of the yeshiva also left its mark on its study and discussion procedures (which differed very much from those in Spain and Germany at the time).

Actually, in support of what we have described, it is sufficient to mention one informative detail that Louis Ginzberg has already noted: The Babylonian Talmud mentioned the names of hundreds of sages and their discussions of religious law and legend, yet only a dozen of them served as heads of yeshivoth.[7] On the other hand, in all the literary sources of the Babylonian geonim, including letters and thousands of responsa, one does not find the names of ordinary sages—only those of the geonim themselves. This detail bears the best possible witness to the real significance of the phenomenon.

This having been noted in Palestine and Babylonia, it is appropriate now to ask two additional questions: Where did the phenomenon first begin, in Babylonia or in Palestine? What were the historical factors that led to it and brought about that great change in the structure of the yeshiva—that is, of the spiritual leadership—a change that, as stated, had consequences for the general structure of Jewish society?

Apparently the phenomenon first appeared in Palestine as early as the sixth century. In my opinion, it may be attributed to the nature and essence of the gaonate there. Whereas in Babylonia the exilarch served as the person in charge of the representation of the Jewish community before the authorities,[8] in Palestine this function, too, was carried out by the yeshiva heads after the abolition of the patriarchate in the fifth century.

In fact, the head of the yeshiva in Palestine at the time of the geonim wore two crowns: "that of the Torah and that of the kingdom," whereas in Babylonia the functions remained separate. Institutions of political leadership were characterized by the dynastic inheritance of the fathers' post by their sons, both in the historical heritage of the Jewish people (kingdom and presidency) and in that of the nations among which the Jews lived at the time. The acceptance of this practice in the yeshiva in Palestine thus came to emphasize its status and authority and to make it more honored. It was the change in function and status that led to a change in the hereditary nature of the leadership.

It appears that this change was introduced in Palestine by Mar Zutra and his descendants, who were members of the exilarch's family in

Babylonia and had fled from Babylonia to Palestine around 520 C.E. This is related in *Seder Olam Zuta*, which was apparently written in the ninth century.[9] Among other things, it tells us that Mar Zutra was appointed head of the Sanhedrin (central rabbinic court), which indicated spiritual leadership. It is clear from the aforementioned sources that he continued the dynastic leadership to which he had been accustomed in the home of his father (the exilarch) in Babylonia in Palestine as well.

The adoption of the custom of having sons inherit their fathers' posts in the Babylonian yeshivoth also apparently stemmed from three factors. First, changes occurred in the procedures, authority, and function of the yeshiva compared with those of the Babylonia yeshiva at the time of the Amoraim (sages of the Gemara), which was principally a place of Torah study. In the geonic period, the Babylonian yeshiva gradually became more established and closed, and the functionaries within it, as well as many of its members, supported themselves on it. The Babylonian Talmud does not contain any testimony at all of sages making a living from their teaching or study at the yeshiva. In the period of the geonim, on the other hand, much evidence of this is to be found.

Also influencing the hierarchy of the academies was a change that took place around 825 C.E., at the time of the Caliph al Ma'amum, when the Iraqi communities were divided administratively into three authorities. At that time the geonim began to collect taxes, appointed judges and other men of authority, and dealt with the complex legal problems that arose within them.[10] The yeshiva, in fact, became an institution in which study was accompanied by political power and public leadership. In other words, it developed to a certain extent like the yeshivoth in Palestine (though not with the same intensity).[11]

A second factor was the triangular competition of the Babylonian yeshivoth with the exilarchs, with the other yeshiva (Sura or Pumbedita—the disputes between them were mainly over money), and with the yeshivoth in Palestine—a competition that continued throughout this period. The struggle was for honor and authority both internally (within the Babylonia communities) and, no less, externally—with relation to the communities that supported the yeshivoth. Succession and family lineage as a symbol of status and legitimacy were obviously of great value in those days. They were, in turn, supplemented by a plethora of regal pomp. This is evidenced, in particular, by the ceremony of the coronation of a king as described in the Bible and from the appointment of a Moslem caliph.

It is not a coincidence that in the literature that has come down to us from this period, family lineage occupies such an extensive place, and in the twelfth century the geonim were still careful to stress their family origin, as did the exilarchs. Thus, for example, Rabbi Petahia relates that he met ten of the greatest sages of the yeshiva in Baghdad "and all of them had a letter of lineage going back to the tribes." Benjamin of Tudela gave testimony of similar evidence before him.[12]

The third factor that influenced this change in the procedure of the yeshivoth was the ascent of the family origin factor and of dynastic succession in Moslem society. The caliph Muawiya sought ways of bequeathing his caliphate to his son Yazid, and the custom continued with greater intensity in the Abbasid caliphate even though it was opposed to the ways and teachings of the first caliphs.

The parallel institution in Moslem society (the madrasah) was also connected at first with the religious activity carried out in the mosques. However, its rise and growth were relatively late. Various teachers established their own schools. The modest beginnings of this phenomenon were in the ninth century, and its growth took place in the tenth and eleventh centuries. There is thus no possibility that the madrasah influenced developments in the Babylonian yeshivoth before the eleventh century.[13]

This change in the procedure of the yeshiva had a harmful influence on its development. Rav Sherira stresses this a number of times, and the letters of the geonim mentioned the periods of crisis, the often small number of students, and the service of the geonim who were not worthy of the post of head of the yeshiva. Particularly worthy of mention is the fact that Rav Saadiah Gaon, the greatest of the geonim in terms of the scope and nature of his writings, managed to attain his post almost miraculously (as Rabbi Natan the Babylonian explicitly states) owing to the fact that a suitable successor was not found in Sura and, in particular, that the situation in the yeshiva in general was so desperate. Thus, preference was given to Rav Saadiah, who, unlike his competitor, Tzemach ben Shahin, was not descended from an illustrious family.[14]

The history of this factor in the other Babylonian yeshiva is also instructive. Between the years 761 and 816 no fewer than fourteen yeshiva heads served in office in Pumbedita. The average duration of each term, therefore, was approximately four years. One must bear in mind that these men were usually very old by the time they came to office, and their ability to manage the affairs of the yeshiva was often restricted. Of course, the heirs of the office were not necessarily unsuitable. On the contrary, there are many examples of extremely capable and talented sons who did honor to the title that they inherited.

Spain and North Africa

The social structure of Jewish communities in Spain differed from that in Germany. Courtiers and royal favorites generally fulfilled the political function in Spain: intercession in the royal court. This was the situation already in the Moslem period and even more so after the *reconquista.* This fact also had an impact on the issue of the inheritance of spiritual leadership.

R. Moshe ben R. Hanoch, who came to Spain, and R. Hushiel, who came to North Africa, brought with them the tradition of Italy and bequeathed their offices at the head of the yeshivoth to their sons. However, these cases were exceptional. In Spanish and in North African communities the right of sons to inherit their fathers' positions at the head of yeshivoth was not recognized. This is clear from an examination of the names of the heads of Spanish yeshivoth in the eleventh century and onward. The distinguished families indeed possessed great strength, and R. Avraham Ibn Daud—who serves as one of the most important historical sources for research on such spiritual activity in ancient Spain—saw fit to stress a number of times that the leading sages in that period belonged to distinguished families or married into them. It may be assumed that the power of these families was of assistance to those spiritual leaders. Obviously, the families also served as a sort of natural "hothouse" whose atmosphere facilitated the growth of sages. However, there is absolutely no possibility to speak here of the actual inheritance of spiritual leadership as it existed in Palestine or Babylonia or even as it existed in Italy and Germany. The fact is that, except for R. Hanoch ben R. Moshe, we do not come across sons—or other relatives—inheriting the positions of their fathers in the yeshivoth of either Cordoba or Lucena.

It is also possible that before the arrival of these immigrants from Italy such inheritance was not practiced. This is made apparent in the words of Ibn Daud describing the rise of R. Moshe ben R. Hanoch. According to his report, it was his wisdom, which was revealed during a discussion of a talmudic question, that led the local dayan to give up his position for his sake and not his origins or his lineage. In his description of the struggle between R. Hanoch ben R. Moshe and R.

Yosef ben R. Avitur over the leadership of the Cordoba Yeshivah, Ibn Daud did not include the legal right of inheritance of a father's post among the claims of R. Hanoch's followers. R. Shmuel Hanaggid's rise to greatness—both political and spiritual—is also described by him in similar terms, as one who rose from "the dunghill" to greatness. "He was a peddler, hardly made a living . . . sat in his shop and hawked his wares."[15]

Because of the legendary nature of these texts, it is difficult to rely on them exclusively. It is possible that here, too, there was a trend to insert anecdotes into a description of real events to create a sense of drama. In any case, it is important evidence of the limitations of inheritance at the time of Ibn Daud (mid-twelfth century) and in the next generation. He could not have described such a reality if Jewish society had accepted the concept that there was something sacred in spiritual leadership by distinguished families, that sons had precedence in receiving the positions of their fathers, and that rights were not given to a person by virtue of his qualifications. Even if legendary texts alone cannot serve as authoritative sources, they still reflect the aspirations, the consensus, and the practice of society at the time they were written.

The appointment of R. Yitzhak Alfasi—a resident of North Africa who fled to Spain following persecutions—as rabbi of Lucena following the death of R. Yitzhak ben R. Yehudah Ibn Ghayyat also testifies to the fact that, despite the great power of the distinguished families in Spain, decisive weight was given to a person's qualifications. The fact that R. Yitzhak Alfasi made sure that his talented pupil R. Yosef Ibn Migash would be his heir is also clear evidence of this. The tradition of preference for talented pupils also continued in later generations in Spain, and it is to be regarded as one of the important factors in the development of the spiritual and literary life there. Even if most of them belonged to those families distinguished by their social and economic power, this was not sufficient to cause their promotion or appointment. It was their wisdom that counted for them.

A similar scene characterized the North African communities, where inheritance of spiritual leadership was not practiced at all. True, in the first half of the eleventh century we see pairs of fathers and sons who took part in spiritual leadership (R. Hushiel and R. Hananel, R. Ya'akov and R. Nissim), but the phenomenon did not continue. It is possible that the forefathers of R. Ya'akov also served in the rabbinate. This is supported by Rav Sherira Gaon at the beginning of his famous epistle, where he speaks of Rav Nissim bar R. Ya'akov ben R. Nissim ben R. Yeshayahu Ibn Shahun.[16]

The question of the inheritance of leadership in the academies of North Africa has been studied recently by M. Ben-Sasson. He concludes that in the large Kairouan community there was no automatic inheritance and that the family was not the official source of authority. The fact that this community served as a center for continuous migration and had numerous social and intellectual sources permitted the choice of the most suitable person for the task. In contrast, in Gabes, which had a smaller population, one family clan stood at the head of the academy.[17]

Italy and Germany

Only a few sources refer to the yeshivoth in Italy during the period surveyed herein. Nevertheless there were various hints that support the assumption that the principle of inheritance in spiritual leadership operated there, though only partially. This is apparent from *The Chronicle of Ahimaaz* (written in 1054), which mentions inheritance a number of times. In one place it was even regarded as a natural phenomenon that did not need any explanation.[18]

The same scene is repeated in other families, first and foremost in the distinguished Kalonymos family. This family's roots were in southern Italy, from which it migrated to Lucca, in the north, and to Mainz, in Germany. One of the family's ancestors, R. Moshe Hazaken, is described as an outstanding liturgical poet and spiritual leader of great authority.

His son and his grandson, R. Kalonymos and R. Meshulam, followed in his footsteps and were among the greatest Jewish sages of their time. Questions on Jewish law were referred to them from various Jewish communities although their main sphere of activity was in northern Italy. Other family members who migrated to Germany served as the heads of the Mainz community for a number of generations (until 1096). They also were among the main spokespersons of the community in Speyer.[19]

A second dynasty was that of R. Yehiel of Rome and his family, to which R. Natan, author of the *Aruch*, also belonged. This family guided Rome's Jewry for a number of generations.

A third dynasty was that of the family of Shabbetai ben R. Moshe, which, as far as can be seen, was called by the title "Rosh Kallah" (head of the [study] session). The sons of Shabbetai ben R. Moshe, too, were brilliant scholars, and one of them (R. Kalonymos) left for Worms, in Germany, where he served at the head of the yeshiva together with R. Shlomo ben R. Shimshon.[20]

Other sources contain more than a hint of the centrality of inheritance in the sphere of spiritual life in some of the important Italian communities. Owing to its special political character at that time, it is difficult to regard this country as a single cultural entity. However, as already stated, these hints are not sufficient to establish hard-and-fast rules. One factor causing difficulties is a list of northern Italian sages in the middle of the eleventh century who studied at the yeshiva of Rav Hai Gaon.[21] We have no further information on some of those listed, and it is difficult to trace the roots of their families.

Considering the practice in surrounding Christian society, the ground was fertile for a development of this kind (special privileges for families belonging to the elite). In Italy great weight was given to noble families. This was especially the case in the north. In Lombard the German legacy granting the privileged status of aristocratic families was preserved in a number of spheres even after 1400.[22]

In Germany distinguished families played important roles both in the political and in the spiritual leadership of the community. The Mainz community contained five such distinguished families: the Kalonymos family, of origins in Italy; the Machir family, to which Rabenu Gershom Me'or Hagolah belonged; the Abun family, which originated in France; and the Hacohen and Halevi families. All leaders of German Jewry in the tenth and the eleventh centuries, as well as all its great sages, belonged to these five families. There is only one sage about whose family nothing is known—R. Ya'akov ben Yakar. In the halakhic literature of the period, the "memorbucher" of the Jews slain in the First Crusade in 1096, and even in the titles inscribed on the gravestones in the Jewish cemeteries, these families enjoyed a special status. The expression *notable family* occurs a number of times in the literature of the period. Furthermore, even a sage as great as Rashi, who lived in France, referred with extraordinary respect to members of these distinguished families— even with self-degradation—despite the fact that he was much more learned than they were: "I hasten to answer one of the small ones who sit on the bench at your feet. . . . Who am I to lift my head and disregard him, since I am your pupil? Why did you pay attention to somebody like me who is like a plant that grows in the dirty water of laundry?"[23]

Because we possess much information relating to this phenomenon, encompassing a variety of sources and deriving from a long period (four generations), it cannot be claimed that these testimonies are but incidental. What, then, were the historical factors that led to the emergence of this reality in Germany?

Apparently, several factors accounted for it. First and foremost is the way in which the early communities were established. The first immigrants from Italy and France were wealthy merchants, some of whom were also scholars. They brought with them to their new homes—after being received by local rulers who hoped that they would help to expand commerce—members of their families and others who joined them.[24] Naturally, these families (which received privileges from the rulers) were granted a special status of leadership in their communities.

The smallness of the communities, many consisting of only dozens or hundreds of people, was also a factor. Even the glorious and important community of Mainz numbered only thirteen hundred people at the end of the eleventh century. Obviously, in such small communities the extended family possesses a particularly strong influence. When even some of its children established families in the same locality, the family's influence was greatly strengthened, especially when members of distinguished families married among themselves.

It is interesting that in German Christian society distinguished families had greater influence than in any other European country, although it is difficult to find any direct connection between this reality and the development described in Jewish society. In some cases, such distinguished families were even granted a decisive role by the authorities in municipal leadership. Evidence of this had been preserved in official documents. The Frankish aristocracy in Germany was based on two types of large family clans. The earlier one, the Sippe, frequented the royal court and had no one center in which they dwelt. Around 1000, the second type, called Geschlecht, gradually arose in various regions, including Champagne in northern France. This type concentrated descendants of one family clan in a more defined geographical area, and it possessed greater power. An interesting difference between the two lay in the way in which status was inherited; in the first it was according to the mother; in the second, according to the father.[25] It is probable that this situation made it easier for Jewish society in general to be willing to accept the preference given to its own distinguished families.

How did the other members of the Jewish community regard this phenomenon? Were any attempts made to oppose these special rights and privileged status of the distinguished families, or were they accepted voluntarily?

The sources depict an interesting picture. There is evidence that the other community members did not agree with the special privileges enjoyed by these families in the economic sphere; in other words, they were opposed to the monopoly (which was called *ma'arufia* or clientele) in certain fields of commerce.

However, there is virtually no evidence of opposition to the leadership in the spiritual sphere. One exception may be a piyyut (liturgical poem) of Shimeon ben Abun (eleventh century). In this piyyut, Ben Abun bitterly attacks separatists of the type of Korach (Num. 16), and he obviously refers to a group within the community that rose up against the traditional leadership in the synagogue on the Sabbath. We do not possess sufficient information to decide what the background to this conflict was, but R. Shimeon does accuse them of putting their trust in property, and this may be a hint that he is referring to wealthy families who were sufficiently sure of themselves to oppose the traditional leadership.[26]

It appears that there was generally no objection to the fact that the community's political and spiritual leaders (up to the end of the eleventh century) belonged to the same families of notables. Apparently there were two reasons for this.

First, the same reality existed in European feudal society. Inequality and special rights were accepted as a natural phenomenon. And, second, the leading notable families paid taxes like all other members of the community. Nonpayment of taxes, which led to great tension in the Spanish communities where the courtier families often evaded taxation and even the sages wished to do so, did not exist in Germany. Nevertheless, the preeminent position of these families had no effect on the organization of yeshiva studies there as it had in Babylonia. Even those students whose lineage was not aristocratic argued with their distinguished rabbis, disagreed with them, and sometimes even refused to accept their opinion. The atmosphere of the studies was free and informal.

In the following generations in Germany, a great change took place in the political sphere. Much evidence has been found concerning community leaders and administrators (parnasim) who were not connected with sages' families. There is no doubt that the rise of the urban classes and the guilds, which constituted a counterforce to the aristocracy and the knights, also exercised an influence on Jewish society. Privileges were now granted to communities and not to distinguished individuals. In any case, the sources clearly mention the category of parnasim who were sometimes in opposition to the sages.

In the spiritual sphere a number of families still had an important status. A good illustration of this is how Rashi's family became the senior family among the tosaphists in the course of time.

One other factor that enhanced this phenomenon was the custom of the yeshiva heads to choose sons-in-law from their most talented pupils. Marriages among the sages' families increased the power of these families. However, these families never regained the power and influence of those who had been influential before 1096.

Summary

Even if the sources that we have discussed are insufficient to draw a clear picture regarding the inheritance of spiritual leadership in the various parts of the Diaspora, they clearly reveal the difference between the Ashkenazi (German) and Sephardi (Spanish and North African) traditions. Until the end of the eleventh century—the period surveyed herein—the degree of influence of inheritance in German communities was greater. This development, as already mentioned, was influenced by three principal factors: the small size of the German communities compared with those of Spain, the way in which the communities evolved, and the fact that many German sages also bore the burden of political leadership, a function carried out in Spain mainly by the Jewish courtiership. It is difficult to know whether this development came about under the influence of the Christian environment in which, in the eleventh and twelfth centuries, great scholars arose whose unique qualities transformed them into teachers and guides to whom pupils swarmed from far and wide. There was no place for inheritance in this reality, particularly when some of the flag bearers of the spiritual-literary renaissance of the time were monks. At the same time, this development in the Jewish communities of Germany and Italy might just as easily be attributed to their closer connections with the legacy of Palestine, where spiritual inheritance was practiced in a most exclusive form.

This difference between the Jewish centers of Germany and Spain in the eleventh century left its impression for many years. The German custom by which yeshiva heads and great scholars chose their best pupils as their sons-in-law further increased the impact of this phenomenon in those regions. In this case, the family did not actually serve as the official source of authority, but in practice its weight and power grew nevertheless. In Spain, on the other hand, this phenomenon was much more limited. Family relationships among the Spanish sages in these generations—and even up to the expulsion at the end of the fifteenth century— were rare. True, the development in Germany may simply be a result of the fact that the family served as a natural breeding ground and not a consequence of any sacred concept of it or of inheritance. But it may, nevertheless, be assumed that the tradition of former days, prior to 1096, also left its mark. Furthermore, the family as a source of the authority of spiritual leadership appears at times as an explicit teaching. This was the case with the German Jewish Pietists (Hasidim), whose mystical teachings were based mainly on the value of their sanctified family traditions, which, according to them, originated in ancient Germany. The dynasties of transmission were bound up with genealogical lineages, and most of them are mentioned in their writings.[27] But in other circles, too, clear traces of its existence remained. It is possible that the teachings of the German Jewish Pietists also influenced other sections of Jewish society. Family lineage was also connected with inheritance of spiritual leadership. It is not difficult, for example, to find allusions to it in talmudic sources. The phenomenon is also found in genealogical records preserved from that period.

What was the attitude of society in general toward the phenomenon of inheritance in spiritual leadership, especially in Palestine, Babylonia, and Germany? Until the end of the eleventh century no explicit reservations or indirect criticisms are found in the sources. The phenomenon may be attributed to two main factors: the small number of sages as a whole in Jewish society and the reality in surrounding Gentile society. The small number of sages reduced competition for yeshivà posts and limited the amount of interest in the convention of inherited possession of these positions. One should not make the mistake of anachronism in this matter. The idealized reality pictured in some researches on Jewish society at that time, showing it to be composed mainly of scholars, is without foundation. Rich Jews who rose to greatness in the Abbasid caliphate and acquired power and influence in the caliph's court competed among themselves to gain positions of influence in Jewish society, too, including in the Babylonian yeshivoth, but they found sufficient expression in the economic and political spheres not to be too concerned about matters of religious-spiritual leadership.[28] The fact is that, despite their great power, only one case has been found of a courtier who exploited his wealth and influence to penetrate the world of the yeshivoth. At the same time, surrounding Moslem and Christian societies were founded from the start on the granting of excess privileges to various classes within them. Inequality was conceived by the people as a natural and accepted phenomenon, especially because aristocratic families commonly received special rights and preferential status.

However, it is difficult to assume that no tension arose within the yeshivoth themselves as a consequence of the inheritance of spiritual leadership. Allusions to it have been preserved in the epistle of Rav Sherira Gaon, and it may be assumed that the act of Rav Aḥa of Shabḥa, who left the Yeshiva in protest, was not the only one of its kind.

As regards Germany, it is to be assumed that in principle the acceptance of dynastic inheritance constituted a voluntary act on the part of other sectors of the community, for there was a gradual increase in the number of new families who gained positions of strength owing to their economic status. Through continuous struggles they succeeded in eliminating a considerable part of the discriminatory arrangements that had been accepted in earlier generations. This was especially the case with the right of monopoly that granted economic benefits of great value to first settlers and deprived new immigrants of their rights. Despite these gains, however, we have not found any evidence of tension stemming from the preference for certain families in the spiritual leadership in the communities of Speyer, Worms, and Mainz.

Still, there is a certain element of doubt in our conclusions regarding the reaction of the other strata in Jewish society to the leadership monopolies of certain families. The question of the *argumentum a silentio* arises here with greatest urgency. The sources were, after all, written by the same leadership circles who, as far as this matter is concerned, were interested parties. Even if there were protests against inheritance, it is hard to believe that they would have been put down in writing. However, we would have expected to find in their writings at least some arguments in favor of the phenomenon, as well as indirect defense of it. This was indeed the case in the allusion preserved in the liturgical poems of R. Shimeon ben Yitzhak ben Abun—the greatest liturgical poet of ancient Germany (beginning of the eleventh century)—against those who opposed the traditional leadership of the Mainz community.[29]

By the thirteenth century there were some among the sages who finally opposed the phenomenon of inheritance in spiritual leadership, as is apparent from a source published recently.[30] The undermining of the power of the traditional leadership in Jewish and Christian society at the same time, and even more so in the fourteenth-fifteenth centuries, serves as an appropriate background to this development. It is even possible that this development stemmed from changes that occurred in the overall status of the rabbinate after the black death, changes that included its turning into an essentially "professional" rabbinate, bitter disputes among the sages themselves, and a readiness in general Jewish society to criticize the deeds and the decisions of the sages.

NOTES

This essay is a revised version of an article that originally appeared in Hebrew in *Zion* 50 (1985), 189–220.

1. In spite of its great importance for both the Jewish people's spiritual life and social life in the Middle Ages, this phenomenon has not yet been studied. Of the little that has been written about it, worthy of mention are the writings of Louis Ginzberg, *Geonica*, 2 vols. (New York, 1909) and of S. Assaf, *Tekufat ha-Geonim ve-Sitrutah* (Jerusalem, 1955), and S. W. Baron, *A Social and Religious History of the Jews*, 18 vols. (New York, 1958). In contrast, this subject has occupied a central position in recent years in the study of the history of the European nations from various aspects: social, economic, demographic, and cultural. One of the most instructive findings of these researches is the important place assigned to a number of privileged families in the social and economic life of all European countries, especially in the north and west.

It is difficult to imagine that the granting of excess privileges to a number of distinguished leading families in European society did not leave its marks on the Jewish community. Rather, it is reasonable to assume that the corresponding development of those privileged families in the Jewish community, especially in the economic and political spheres, was influenced to a certain extent by the general environment. Two of the most important works on the family in European society, of consequence for the subject of our discussion, are J. Heers, *Le Clan familial au moyen age* (Paris, 1974) (in English: *Family Clans in the Middle Ages*, trans. Barry Herbert [Amsterdam, 1977]); and G. Duby, *Les Trois ordres: ou, l'imaginaire du féodalisme* (Paris, 1978) (in English: *The Three Orders: Feudal Society Imagined*, trans. Arthur Goldhammer (Chicago, 1980).

2. See A. Grossman, *The Early Sages of Ashkenaz* (Jerusalem, 1981), pp. 400–11.

3. G. Alon, "The Sons of the Sages," in *Jews, Judaism and the Classical World*, trans. Israel Abrahams (Jerusalem, 1977), pp. 436–57.

4. The two exceptions—Shlomo ben Yehuda and Daniel ben Azaria, who did not belong to those illustrious families of geonim and were appointed with the aid of external forces—do not contradict what has been said, but they are the exceptions that prove the rule. Evyatar's bitter struggle against Daniel's family clearly confirms this. See M. Gil, "The Scroll of Evyatar," in *Jerusalem in the Middle Ages*, ed. B. Z. Kedar (Jerusalem, 1979), pp. 39–106.

5. See S. W. Baron, *A Social and Religious History*, V, 22 ff.; S. Assaf, *Tekufat ha-Geonim*, p. 99.

6. A. Neubauer, *Seder hahakhamim v'korot hayamim* (Jerusalem, 1967), II, p. 87.

7. Ginzberg, *Geonica* I, 6.

8. A. Grossman, *The Babylonian Exilarchate in the Gaonic Period* (Jerusalem, 1984), pp. 45–73.

9. Neubauer, *Seder hahakhamim*, p. 76.

10. See Grossman, *The Babylonian Exilarchate*, pp. 53–56, 63–66.

11. Louis Ginzberg already mentioned this in *Geonica*, pp. 1–14.

12. M. N. Adler, *The Itinerary of Benjamin of Tudela* (London, 1901), pp. 38–39.

13. On this matter, see the article "Origin and Spread of the Madrasa," in *Encyclopedia of Islam* (London, 1936), III, 350–71, esp. pp. 353–57. Later in the thirteenth century evidence is found of the existence of inheritance of the posts of the heads of the schools in Moslem society, too. See A. S. Tritton, "Muslim Education in the Middle Ages," *Moslem World* 43 (1953), 91.

14. B. M. Lewin, *Iggeret R. Scherira Gaon* (Haifa, 1921), pp. 116–17.

15. Abraham ibn Daud, *The Book of Tradition*, ed. G. D. Cohen (Philadelphia, 1967), pp. 48, 53–54.

16. Lewin, *Iggeret*, p. 2.

17. See M. Ben-Sasson, *The Jewish Community of Medieval North Africa: Society and Leadership* (Jerusalem, 1983), pp. 104–7.

18. B. Klar, *The Chronicle of Ahimaaz* (Jerusalem, 1974), p. 29.

19. See Grossman, *The Early Sages of Ashkenaz*, pp. 29 ff.

20. Grossman, *The Early Sages of Ashkenaz*, pp. 348 ff.

21. A. Grossman, "From Father to Son: The Inheritance of the Spiritual Leadership of the Jewish Communities in the Early Middle Ages," *Zion* 50 (1985), 207, n. 54.

22. Heers, *Le Clan familial*, pp. 21–22.

23. Grossman, "From Father to Son," p. 213.

24. See A. Grossman, "The Migration of Jews to Germany and Their Settlement There in the 9th–11th Centuries" in A. Shinan, ed., *Migration and Settlement in Jewish and General History* (Jerusalem, 1982), pp. 109–28.

25. See K. Schmid, "Über die Struktur des Adels im früheren Mittelalter,"

Jahrbuch für frankische Landesforschung 19 (1959), 1–23; Heers, *Le Clan familial*, pp. 12–13, 18–21; K. Leyser, "The German Aristocracy from the Ninth to the Early Twelfth Century," *Past and Present* 41 (1968), 25–53.

26. A. M. Habermann, ed., *Liturgical Poems of R. Shim'on bar Yizḥak* (Berlin and Jerusalem, 1938), pp. 162–63.

27. See J. Dan, *The Esoteric Theology of Ashkenazi Hasidism* (Jerusalem, 1968), pp. 9–45; H. Soloveitchik, "Three Themes in the Sefer Hasidim," *AJS Review* 1(1976), 311–57; I. G. Marcus, *Piety and Society: The Jewish Pietists of Medieval Germany* (Leiden, 1981).

28. W. Fischel, *Jews in the Economic and Political Life of Medieval Islam* (London, 1937); Grossman, *The Babylonian Exilarchate*, pp. 129 ff.

29. See n. 26.

30. M. Saperstein, "The Earliest Commentary on the Midrash Rabbah," in I. Twersky, ed., *Studies in Medieval Jewish History and Literature* (Cambridge, Mass., 1982), pp. 288–90.

8

Family and Community in Sephardic North Africa: Historical and Anthropological Perspectives

HARVEY E. GOLDBERG

One of the major spheres in which the Sephardic tradition has developed in a distinctive fashion is in the realm of family life. But we may not, of course, speak of *the* Sephardic tradition; different Sephardic communities developed along different lines, and it is essential in a study of the family—as in any such study—to take into account the historical diversity of the Sephardic Diaspora. The present chapter will address the family and community within North African Jewry as one instance of the development of the Sephardic tradition.

The cultural and social world of North African Jewry reflects a meeting of Spanish traditions with pre-Sephardic North African culture, shaped by both Jewish and non-Jewish social life. This holds true for the realm of the family even though we often view the family as a bastion for the preservation of religious and ethnic lifeways. To appreciate this to the fullest, it is necessary to supplement historical documentation with an

ethnographic dimension. We thus attempt to widen the understanding
of the context of family and community life of the Jews in North Africa
by reference to anthropological work carried out in North Africa and
in Israel.

Accordingly, we will progress in several phases. First, some of the
basic information describing the influence of Sephardic rabbis on North
African Jewish society will be reviewed. Next, I will summarize some
of the findings of a recent book by S. Deshen,[1] which relate directly to
the theme of our concern. Both these discussions will be based on the
time-honored material of which Jewish historiography is made, rabbinic
and community enactments, the responsa literature, and so forth. Finally, in widening the context of the discussion based on written sources,
I will make reference to anthropological fieldwork carried out in the
past two decades, with the assumption that these researches may suggest
ways to "read" documents of earlier periods. Citing studies of Morocco,
as well as of the Jews of Morocco, will show the importance of viewing
Jewish life in its wider social and cultural contexts.

Most of the material cited will relate to Morocco, with references to
the other North African countries. This focus stems from the fact that
Morocco had the largest Jewish population and that we have more
studies from that region than from others. A secondary focus will be
on the Jews of Libya, who have been the subject of my own research.

The Sepharadim in North Africa

Though there had always been contact between the Jewries of Spain
and North Africa, the date 1391 is usually taken as the beginning of
important Sephardic immigration to the region after the riots and killings
that started in Seville and spread to other parts of Spain. These immigrants settled mainly in Algeria and included such luminaries as Yiẓḥaq
ben Sheshet (Perfet) and Shimon ben Ẓemah (Duran), who quickly
moved into positions of leadership in their new communities. The exiles
of 1492 who settled in the Maghreb mainly reached the cities of Morocco,
settling the towns of the north but continuing to expand southward over
the years. It seems that Tunisia and Tripolitania did not receive many
Sephardic immigrants at first, but Tunisian Jewry was later reinforced
by the arrival of the "Livornese" Jews, the *Grana*. These were Spanish
or Portuguese Jews who came to the Italian city in the sixteenth century,
attracted by the active commercial life. The Livornese families later

"sent out" branches, which established themselves in North African towns (particularly Tunisia and Tripoli) to promote their business interests. In each of these instances, the outcome of the Sephardic meeting with the local communities was somewhat different.

The influence of the Spanish rabbis in Algeria was felt rather quickly, and they instituted new rules concerning communal organization and the place of the rabbi. They also introduced certain new traditions and emphasized the importance of Maimonides's *Mishneh Torah* in matters of halakhah (Jewish law). In Morocco, separate subcommunities were established by the new arrivals, known as the *megorashim*. They continued to follow their traditional practices, many of which were summed up in the form of the *taqqanot* (enactments) of Castille, gathered together by Rabbi Ya'aqov ibn Ẓur in 1698.[2] There was a clear process of gradual Sepharadization of the other Moroccan communities, which proceeded without any major communal conflicts. In Tunisia however, a situation developed whereby two separated communities were created, living side by side: the European-based *Grana* and the local *Tuwansa* (Tunisians). The importance of the difference in traditions was formulated in an agreement dated 1741 and was only abolished, in practice, in the present century.

There are several aspects to the question of the distinct communal life of the *Tuwansa* and *Grana*, which has been described in greater detail in a recent study by Abrami.[3] On the one hand, it may be seen as a simple desire of the Jews from Spain/Italy to preserve the way of life they knew and which they considered correct according to Jewish tradition. On the other hand, the Livornese Jews had a clear interest in stressing their distinctiveness, for they sought be be viewed as "citizens" of their Italian town of origin rather than as subjects of the bey of Tunis, which was the status of the local Jews. This suggests a "motive" for the long-standing insistence on the preservation of their own laws and customs. Chouraqui[4] claims that the source of the conflict lay, basically, in the different place accorded to women in the two traditions. Among the *Grana*, who followed the *taqqanot* of Castille, the status of a woman was "incomparably superior" to that of her counterpart among the *Tuwansa*. Sociologically it might be more appropriate to say that the status of the women *symbolized* the difference between the two communities, whose continued distinctiveness is to be explained by a variety of factors.

In Morocco, as we have indicated, the ordinances of Castille came to be accepted widely except for some of the regions in the south (*Tafilalt va-agapeha*). These indeed included major rules concerning women, the family, and inheritance. For example, they guaranteed that a woman benefited from the estate of her husband on his death, along with his parents, brother, and children. The Castillian *taqqanot* also opposed the custom of *kiddushei seter* (secret marriages) whereby men, in front of witnesses, would attempt to marry a girl without the knowledge of her parents or without representatives of communal/Torah authority. This was apparently a relatively common event in North Africa, and examples are known up to the recent past among the Jews of Libya, for example.[5]

The Sephardic tradition did not include formal acceptance of the ban of Rabbeinu Gershom, which had taken root in Ashkenaz, but other means were used to discourage the practice of polygamy. It was often stipulated in the *ketubah* that a man would not take a second wife unless the first consented to this act. This tradition served to limit polygamy in North Africa but did not eliminate it. We learn that at the beginning of the nineteenth century Jews would come from Italy to Tripoli to take a second wife.[6] Instances of bigamy in the recent past are documented both in Tripolitania[7] and Morocco,[8] including the well-known case of the venerated Moroccan zaddik (saint), Rabbi Yisrael abi-Hatzera, who passed away several years ago.

In sum, it is undoubtedly correct to place North Africa within the Sephardic tradition, but it also should be realized that the influence of the Spanish rabbis was not homogeneous throughout the region. In addition, whereas North African Jewry underwent a process of "Castilianization" in terms of formal halakhah, we also should be aware of reciprocal influences, in which traditional North African patterns helped shape the particular form that Sephardic Judaism took in the Maghreb.

Individual, Family, and Community

Earlier, mention was made of Deshen's work on individuals and community. This monograph focuses on Morocco of the eighteenth and nineteenth centuries (up to the time of major French influence) and is based on the writings of Moroccan rabbis who developed the traditions of the Spanish rabbis of the late Middle Ages in the North African context. The theme of the study is the tension between leadership based on the initiative of individuals and claims of the community. Whereas terms like *shiv'ah tovei ha'ir* (the seven notables of the city) appear in some of the documents studied by Deshen, they usually do not reflect an established body responsible for formulating and executing policy. Rather, many issues were dealt with on an ad hoc basis, indicating an ethos of individual responsibility rather than fully institutionalized communal life.

For example, an incident dating from the beginning of the nineteenth century is recorded involving an individual who was a ritual slaughterer cantor, and teacher. Before Passover, members of the community induced him to do his slaughtering work closer to the main market, which was a more convenient location. The Muslim butchers complained to the authorities that this might bring competition, for it was common for Muslims to buy the meat of Jewish butchers that had been declared unfit for consumption by Jews. The slaughterer was fined by the local communal authority and then appealed for a judgment that the Jewish community should reimburse him the costs of the fine. A decision from Meknes stated that the community had no obligation to pay because the slaughterer had moved on his own decision, not as an employee of the community.[9]

This case illustrates a line of thought characteristic of halakhic thinking in the region. It is relevant to our topic for two reasons. First, it illustrates the amorphous and ad hoc nature of the kehillah ("the community") vis-à-vis individuals and, by implication, families (in this society it is taken for granted that an individual is part of a family and that his "individual" actions have implications for that social unit). Secondly, it shows that interaction with the wider Muslim society had direct effects on relationships among Jews. This is a point stressed by Deshen, who shows that Muslim-Jewish interaction could even touch on such sensitive internal matters as family laws.

With regard to the first point, reference may be made to the widespread phenomenon of private synagogues.[10] In such an arrangement an individual takes part of his house and sets it aside as a synagogue. He provides the services of a hazan (cantor and torah reader), and it is understood that the income from the sale of mitzvoth (the normal North African term for aliyoth—the honor of being called to the Torah) and any voluntary contributions go to his "pocket," which is not formally distinguished from the synagogue "treasury." It is also taken for granted (and this I base on my contemporary experience in Israel) that his wife/daughters will be active in caring for the synagogue's physical needs, such as cleaning the room, filling the lamps with oil, or making sure that there are fragrant leaves available for the evening service on Shabbat. Other women in the neighborhood might join in carrying out these tasks in order to merit a mitzvah. Though we are accustomed to the notion that "women had no place" in traditional synagogue life, I must quote a Tripolitanian friend who, when describing activities such as these, said, "Women's thoughts were always on the synagogue." Thus, the private synagogues of traditional Morocco are probably to be seen as family affairs even though this side of synagogue life may not receive much expression in our written sources.

Another aspect of family-community relations involves the concept of *serarah* (religious office).[11] It was common for religious roles to be transferred, as it were, from father to son, and we find "dynasties" of sages. Of course, an individual had to have qualifications to be appointed to, or accepted as filling, a certain role; but the notion of *serarah* meant that "the merit of one's Fathers" was an important element in laying claim to various offices. This could involve a very respected position such as dayan (judge) in a large community, the right to write ketuboth, bills of divorce, or to serve as the assessor of dowries, which were then recorded in the ketubah. The concept of *serarah* intertwines with the notion of private synagogues, as in the judgment that the *serarah* of a certain synagogue still belongs to the son of the original "owner" of the synagogue despite the fact that he has moved to another city.[12]

With regard to the second issue mentioned, concerning relationships between Jews and Muslims, the relative strength given to individuals/ families as over against the community invites the involvement of Muslims in matters that we might think are confined exclusively to the Jewish community. Deshen cites an instance in which one Jew was visiting another, and a powerful Muslim notable was present. The conversation took a light-headed turn and resulted in one man, jokingly, giving his daughter in marriage to the son of the second man. The rabbis then had to deal with the question of whether this was a valid *kiddushin* (betrothal).[13] In another instance, when the payment of a ketubah after divorce was in question, we find a Jew turning for support to an influential Muslim notable to intervene with the process of rabbinic judgment.[14] In general, Deshen states, the fact that dayanim tended to serve in their home communities and that they were related to important families created conflicts with regard to their ability to exercise impartial judgment.[15]

We thus find that when addressing the question of the family and the community, the concept of "the community" cannot be considered in isolation from the personal relations that many Jews had with powerful Muslim patrons. Moreover, we shall argue that this relationship between

Muslim patrons and Jewish clients may have had somewhat of a "familial" quality to it. It is to the development of this line of thought that we now turn.

Patronage and Jews in Morocco

Scholars of North African society have made the general point that relations between Muslims and Jews have to be seen within the general context of how Muslims perceive social relationships among individuals, that is, how they interrelate among themselves.[16] We wish to pursue this point with reference to familial relationships and suggest that, in some instances, Jews may have been viewed as part of "the family" of powerful Muslims. In an effort to pursue this ostensibly preposterous statement, I turn to an old question in the historiography of North African Jewry—"The problem of the Judaized Berbers."

There is an old notion—and one that has achieved a fair amount of popularity among North African Jews themselves—that many of the Jews of the Maghreb are descended from Berbers who converted to Judaism in the period before the spread of Islam in the region. For example, in his autobiographical novel, Memmi mentions how the idea once was important in his sense of identity.[17] Various authors have remarked on the preponderance of Berber patronyms among the Jews of North Africa, and this has sometimes been cited as evidence of the theory of Berber-Jewish descent.[18]

As has been discussed by Hirschberg, there is little solid historical evidence on which to base this theory, and he concludes, "It appears that the proportion of foreign elements in this [North African] group is no greater than in any other Jewish Diaspora." However, this does not offer an explanation of why Berber patronyms are so often attached to Jewish families. Such an explanation must derive from the sociocultural context in which Jews lived in close proximity to Berber tribal groupings.[19]

In various parts of the Maghreb, but particularly in Morocco, Jews lived in mountainous regions under the protection of Berber tribal chieftains. The Jews filled an important economic role in these areas, providing artisanal skills unknown to the local populace and engaging in regional trade. In these tribal areas, order and security were provided by tribal leaders, rather than by the authority of the central government, and every Jew had to have the protection of a powerful Muslim individual (whether Berber or Arab). As a sign of this protection, it was common for a Jew to be known by the name of his patron, particularly when traveling outside the region under the chief's direct control. Even when the system of tribal rule weakened, one author described, for Tripolitania, that the Jews "are still *called by the name of their lord* and treat it respectfully, as it stands by their side to protect them from the other Berbers."[20]

When this sociocultural arrangement is coupled with the historical process whereby many of the Jews of the interior tribal areas migrated to the large cities, it is not surprising to find Jews carrying Berber (Muslim) patronyms throughout the area. For the purpose of the present discussion, however, we wish to emphasize the fact that Jews often came to be placed under the aegis of a *Muslim family name*, thereby becoming, *in a sense*, a "member" of a Muslim family. We wish to refine this claim by reference to recent anthropological work on "the meanings of family ties" in Morocco by Hildred Geertz.[21]

Geertz's study of family ties takes as a starting point the view that one should not approach the study of "the family" or "kinship" as a universal category to be described and analyzed in each society but must discover how a culture *itself* delineates the domains that we roughly call "family," "relatives," and so forth. She asserts that Moroccan views of "family ties" must be set in a semantic context that includes "friendship" and "patronage," even though the latter two domains would be considered nonfamilial in the context of American culture. Her claim is that "all three—family, friendship, and patronage—are ordered by the same cultural principles," and she, as an example, states that even the "economic dependency between son and father is understood, in part, as a patron-client relationship."[22] Only on appreciating how these various meanings are structured in Moroccan culture and how they become relevant in social action can one reach an adequate understanding of "family" in Moroccan life.

It is within such an analytic approach that I wish to place, for a moment, the Jewish family. If the Moroccan Muslim "family" can include clients and other nonkin, then it can also "include" Jews who are under its protection and who carry its name, at least from the point of view of the Muslims. This formulation, as we have hinted, has most relevance to the tribal areas. In southern Morocco strong tribal families were always constructing new adobe houses that, in the words of one of my informants, might be used for a son getting married or might be given to a Jewish family invited to live under the Muslim family's protection. This description implies a certain "equivalence" between actual kin and protected Jews, and another informant told me that Jews would brag among themselves with regard to whose house they lived in. In pre-Protectorate times, powerful Muslim chiefs would restrict the movement of "their Jews" so as to be sure they remained in the territory. One way to do this, while simultaneously allowing Jewish men to trade around the countryside, was to keep a Jew's wife and family at home. We thus find, in the situation of extreme subjugation of Jews to Muslim rule, the extension of Muslim society into the interior of Jewish family life. The threat posed by this situation is reflected in the claim from Tripolitania that "even though the Gentiles ruled over the bodies of the Jews, they did not rule over their wives, and they did not intermarry with one another." We find another example of the strength of the tribal leaders' influence in the custom, reported from Kurdistan, whereby the Aga collected a large part of the bride-price paid for a woman from his territory when she married a Jewish man from a different region.[23]

The claim that the Jews may seen as "part of" a Muslim family, of course, is not to be understood in a legal or strictly institutional manner, but as part of a universe of meanings and associations that inform social life in North Africa. It takes on most significance in the tribal setting where the social life of the Jews was most vulnerable and dependent on individual Muslims. However, it is precisely in situations of social "weakness" that basic *cultural* conceptions come to the fore, and we suggest that the same notions may have operated, to a lesser extent, in urban settings. Thus, we would like to know, in the case of Geertz's study,[24] whether, from the point of view of the Muslims, "patronymic associations" such as "Nas Adlun" might also refer to Jews who had close ties with the Adlun family. More generally, an understanding of this "expansive" side of "the Muslim family" in North Africa helps illuminate the relative weakness of the kehillah among the Jews, stressed in Deshen's analysis.

Given the power of the Muslim patrons with respect to their protected Jews, it is even more striking that the Jews did succeed in maintaining communal life. Again we may turn to the tribal areas, where the Jews were weakest, to highlight the cultural conceptions at work. In an oral document recorded by Schroeter,[25] a story is found of how the mellah (Jewish section) of Illigh, in the Tazerwalt (southwestern Morocco), was established. According to this account, a merchant Jew decided to come and serve a newly powerful chieftain to help develop trade in the area. At first he came alone, but gradually he convinced the cadi to let him *bring other Jewish families with him* to form a community. According to the document, the ruler agreed to this condition despite some religious opposition, and the community was established. Although this oral account purports to describe events that took place in the eighteenth century, it appears to me to be a cultural prototype of events that probably recurred many times. We know of cases in the last century where Jews lived in very small groupings that barely allowed them to have a minyan (quorum) on Shabbat and where the families of several small Jewish hamlets would have to gather together in the central community of a region during the festivals. In other words, the pull of a guaranteed livelihood under the protection of a strong patron was sometimes closely balanced against the ability to maintain a normal Jewish communal life. The insistence of the Jews on being able to establish and maintain their own institutions in this context is not negligible.

It must also be appreciated that it is not a simple decision for a Muslim leader to agree to the establishment of a Jewish community in his region. While he gains prestige as a powerful patron, it also implies the allotment of land for a Jewish cemetery and the providing of a room to be used as a synagogue and as a school for teaching Torah. In brief, it allows a concession to the religion of the dhimmis (those with protected, but subservient status). Perhaps this is made easier for the Muslim by the cultural conception we have been discussing, which equates kinship and patronage and throws light on the widespread metaphor in North African Muslim culture likening a woman to a Jew.[26] Just as, according to Muslim law, a man can marry a woman who is a dhimmi, so too can he take a Jew into his family-patronage network without worrying that the latter will have undue influence. The Jew is thus allowed to set up his own religious and communal institutions and thereby combat the tendency of the Muslim "family-friendship-patronage" constellation to penetrate into the interior of Jewish existence. In the following section, we will discuss another way in which the integrity of Jewish family and communal life in a Muslim environment has been preserved.

The Laws of Family Purity and the Wider Society

The laws of *niddah* (family purity), based on the biblical code (Lev. 15:19–30), have been a central element in traditional Jewish observance. However, they have received less scholarly attention than they might, perhaps because of the "private" nature of the activity that they concern.

In particular, there is a tendency to focus on the laws themselves and not to inquire as to the significance of these laws in the life of individuals, families, and communities. In this context I wish to cite some of the findings of an anthropological field study by R. Rosen,[27] focusing on the definitions and perceptions of womanhood among traditional Moroccan Jewish women. The research was carried out in a moshav (co-operative settlement) in Israel among families who originated mainly from the towns of Fez and Sefrou in Morocco.

In the course of Rosen's inquiry, she found that the discussion of womanhood inevitably led to the topic of *niddah*. The concept of *niddah* in this community, as in many other Jewish communities, embodied the biological fact of menstruation, the laws prohibiting intercourse during the menstrual period and the "clean days" thereafter, and the immersion in a mikvah (ritual bath) at the end of this period. This bundling of several notions into one key cultural concept is, of course, constitutive of a central symbol in Jewish religious culture.

In anthropological fieldwork it is normal for a researcher to seek acceptance within a community by asking questions in a cautious and nonoffensive manner. Rosen took a somewhat different course and confronted the women with whom she worked with such bold questions as "What is a woman?" or "What is *niddah*?" In answer to the second question she sometimes received the reply, explicitly or implicitly, "What, you are not Jewish?" The observance of *niddah* thus appears as basic not only in terms of halakhah, but in terms of *identity*, as signaling inclusion in the Jewish people.

In probing views on this matter, Rosen formulated the following generality: That menstruation *qua* menstruation is significant in defining a woman, as opposed to a girl, and the observance of *niddah* is significant in defining a Jewish woman as opposed to a non-Jewish woman. Some of her informants clearly linked the observance of the family purity laws with a sense of belonging to the Jewish people. It was important to be "pure" so that children born of intercourse would be pure, and *tum'ah* (impurity) would not diffuse among the Jewish people. The observance of *niddah*, then, was one of the main factors that, in the eyes of a Jewish woman (and her family), set her off from her Muslim counterpart in Morocco.

The importance of the link between the observance of *niddah* and "the Jewish people," Rosen suggests, may also be evident in a method of control anchored in the immediate community. In spending time in the houses of the moshav, she noticed that the door to the bedroom of the couple was always ajar—partially opened and partially closed. This half revealed (and half hid) the practice of the couple with regard to sleeping arrangements, whether there was a separate bed on which a woman could sleep during menstruation, a double bed that could be separated when necessary, or no such arrangements at all. Rosen feels that the leaving of the door half open was not accidental, but a purposeful (but feigned casual) message to the community concerning the particular family's observance of the rules (or their nonobservance).

Anthropologists who have described Muslim households in North Africa have emphasized the division of the house (among families comfortable enough to have several rooms) into male and female sections, with rather strict norms concerning the separation of the areas except in the case of male relatives who may mix more casually with the women of the household. Presumably, similar sentiments were held by North African Jews, though perhaps not to the same degree. In descriptions I have received of mikvahs in Tripolitania, it has often been stressed that the ideal mikvah had two doors, an entrance and an exit, so that no person would have to meet another person, and privacy would be complete. Given this set of values, Rosen's analysis of the subtle, but public, demonstration of the observance of the rules of *niddah* is all the more striking. The community is "invited in," so to speak, to witness the family's faithfulness to the rules. We cannot know whether the situation observed on the moshav held true for the original Moroccan situation or whether it is precisely in a situation of social change that the demonstration of one's family's position within the new cultural framework becomes critical. In any event, the link between the family purity laws and participation in a larger collectivity is clearly suggested.

Custom, Family, and Community

One way of discerning the main characteristics of the Jewish family in North Africa in relation to the community is by throwing Jewish life into relief against the background of the Jews' Muslim neighbors. Here, as elsewhere, the work of S. D. Goitein provides a seminal lead. In his *Jews and Arabs* Goitein simply notes that family life among the Jews and Arabs historically has been "extremely different." Among the Jews, he states, the warm, intimate family featuring the husband and the wife has been highlighted whereas among the Arabs, he claims, the clan—with brothers, uncles, and cousins—has been central. Even though he

TABLE 1. Customs Relating to "Candles" Among Tripolitanian
Jewish Communities

Communities	Number of Shabbat "Candles"	Number of Kol Nidre "Candles"
Tripolitanian Mountain Communities		
Yefren	1 (a few lit more)	1 per family
Tighrinna	1 (a few lit more)	1 per family
Beni'abbas	1 olive, 1 neft	1 per family
Mesallata	1	1 per family
Tripolitanian Coastal Communities		
Zawia	1	1 per person
Tripoli	2, 4, or 7	1 per male
Amrus	2 (a few lit more)	1 per male
Tagiura	1	1 per male
Zliten	1 (a few lit more)	1 per male
Misurata	1	1 per family or one per grown child
Southern Tunisia		
Ben Gardane	2 (a few lit more)	1 per family or 1 per male

may later have modified his views somewhat (as in *A Mediterranean Society: The Family*, where he stresses the importance of brother-sister ties as opposed to husband-wife ties), he put his finger, in this brief statement, on a set of crucial questions.[28] In this section I would like to subject sociological questions of this nature to the test of ethnographic data that I have collected among the Jews of Tripolitania.

The Jews of Tripolitania were concentrated in the city of Tripoli and in smaller communities, usually containing less than one thousand people, in the hinterland. These rural communities may be divided roughly into those on the coast, which were influenced by the urban culture of Tripoli, and those that were in the mountain regions to the south, which were smaller and somewhat more isolated from the urban culture. Family and kinship ties were prominent features in the social structure of these small communities. The accompanying table presents information concerning these communities, indicating whether they are mountain or coast communities and giving data regarding two separate customs regarding "candles,"[29] which were intermeshed with family life. The first is the well-known mitzvah of lighting candles to inaugurate the Shabbat, and the second is a practice mentioned in the *Shulḥan Aruch* in which each family brings an oil light (the Sabbath "candle" was also an oil light) to the synagogue on Kol Nidre night (the night of Yom Kippur).

In preelectric times this custom served both symbolic and utilitarian purposes.

We take it for granted that customs such as the lighting of candles are "multivocalic," that they can have several layers of meaning for different participants or even for the same participant (on different occasions or on the same occasion). Here we wish to examine the possible significance of these practices in terms of group belonging and identification. We do this by attending to the number of candles and the category of persons to which the candles are linked, as well as to the site and setting of the ceremony.

With regard to the lighting of the Shabbat light at home, the most common pattern was that a single lamp "stood for" the whole family. However, the possibility existed of lighting more than one light, and I suggest that when this was carried out, it was associated with a sense of the importance of the separate individuals within the family unit. It is not accidental, I think, that the most explicit statement of many lamps being lit comes from the city of Tripoli rather than from the rural communities. One may claim that it was in the city that wealthy families could be found who could afford to light more than one lamp and that the few families in the hinterland who followed the Tripoli practice were the local economic elite. This is certainly possible but would constitute, in my eyes, a correlative aspect of the process of greater emphasis on the individual person rather than an alternative explanation.

Examining the data with regard to the Kol Nidre lamp reveals a clearer pattern of variation. One lamp per family characterized all the mountain communities whereas the salience of the individual male appears in Tripoli and the other communities on the coast. This naturally raises the question of the conceptual importance of women.

The lighting of a lamp linked to a specific person, of course, is well known in Judaism, in the form of a lamp memorializing a deceased relative. It is interesting, in terms of the family/community theme, that even though a lamp is lit at home, memorialization also takes place in the context of the community-synagogue as well. Among the Jews of Tripolitania it was common for a mourner to bring an oil lamp to the synagogue each Shabbat during the year after the death of a relative. When the year was over, the lighting of this lamp (on a weekly basis) normally ceased. In some cases it continued, however, and I have a strong hunch that this took place when the deceased was a prestigious member of the community and/or when his sons (and daughters) were wealthy and prestigious enough to continue to light this lamp on a regular basis. In such a case, the light also becomes a beacon highlighting the importance of a given *family*, but it is significant that this highlighting of status, sometimes relating to rivalries among families, takes place in the synagogue, that is, under communal scrutiny and partial control. Thus, even when there is a private, or family (shall we say "clan"?) synagogue, as was common in North Africa, the community provides the context within which each person and family makes a claim to prominence.[30]

We may try to follow Goitein's lead by comparing Jewish family and Muslim family values as they are expressed in another set of customs, those of the wedding ceremony. Effecting a marriage in Jewish law and in Muslim law is a relatively simple matter in its essentials. As in all traditional societies, however, the celebration of the wedding was elaborated far beyond what is required by religious law to involve a week or longer of conventional festivities. The customs that made up the various phases of these celebrations in Tripolitania show a resemblance to one another, strongly suggesting Muslim influence on Jewish practice. At the same time there are ways in which the practices seem to emphasize and restate, as it were, central concepts related to Jewish life generally.

Space permits only a brief example of the type of comparison that might be instructive where detailed descriptions of Jewish and Muslim customs are available from the same region.[31] Based on data from the Gharian region of Tripolitania, we find that in both the Jewish and Muslim prenuptial celebrations there is ritual exposure of women's hair. The association of hair and sexuality is widespread, of course, and in the Mishnah the testimony that a bride's head was uncovered during her wedding is accepted as evidence that she was a virgin at the time. The form that the public exposure takes in Tripolitania, however, differs in the Jewish and Muslim celebrations.

At one point during the Muslim celebrations a group of young, unmarried males stand in a semicircle, with the groom in the middle, and opposite them is a line of nubile girls who kneel down and let their hair flow in front of their faces. They dance in this fashion moving their hair, waists, and arms. Here the world of masculinity and femininity confront one another, with the kneeling perhaps hinting at the subordinate position of women.

The public appearance of femininity is more restricted in Jewish practice, and only the bride is involved. During an evening known as the "henna" night, the bride's hair is let down while she is in the center of a crowd of women and young girls, and the only other parts of her body that are exposed are her fingers and toes. There is no dancing in front of men although some women may have danced among themselves in the manner described.

As part of the henna night, other people mill about outside the group of women and girls who surround the bride. Prominent here are the young men of marriageable age, including the groom, and some who have recently been married, who form a group on the periphery of the protective circle that encompasses the bride. This is the setting for the practice of "giving money," which takes place in the following manner: One of the young men will take some coins out of his pocket and begin to make his way toward the bride. In doing so, he has to make his way through the circle of girls and women who surround her. On reaching the bride, he touches her henna-covered feet with the coins and then drops them into a basket on her head. At this point the women ululate in joy (*zgharit*). The boy retreats, and the coins are taken out of the basket by an old woman who is the "mistress of ceremonies" for much of the feminine side of the festivities. She is usually a widow and keeps the coins, turning the gesture into an act of charity. The groom participates in this ritual approach and gift giving in a manner that does not distinguish him from his fellows. It is only several days later that, with the formal transference of the *shaveh prutah* (coin of small value) as part of the kiddushin (betrothal), a special relationship between the groom and his bride is established in terms of halakhah. The henna ceremony, however, seems to anticipate the halakhic act. It is as if at first the bride potentially belongs to all the young men who surround her and later is consecrated to the groom, a set of actions that dramatize the talmudic explanation of the term *kiddushin*: that the bride is available sexually only to her husband whereas formerly she was permitted to the "whole world."

One way of stating the difference between the interlaced Jewish and Muslim traditions may be in terms of the relative emphasis placed on different contrasts or oppositions in the structuring of the wedding ritual. The opposition of the world of males and the world of females seems to have central importance in the Muslim ceremony whereas the contrast (and complementarity) of the nascent family to the community is given prominence in the Jewish celebration. Both themes, defined by contrasts and oppositions, are present in both the Jewish and Muslim cases, but their relative emphasis is different. The distinctiveness of the Jewish family in a broader, intermeshing cultural setting is brought out by careful comparative examination of the organization of the marriage ritual.

Conclusion

We have attempted to discuss various aspects of family and community, and of family-community relations, among North African Jewry, by the combined use of historical and anthropological data and analysis. Behind the basic facts of social life revealed by documents lie conceptions and values that sometimes are accessible only through the study of the customs of everyday life and of festive occasions. In focusing on the family and the community, however, we can easily overlook the third factor in the equation: the individual. As historians or anthropologists we know that notions of family and community cannot be taken for granted but must be explored in the particular forms that they take in different periods and places. We do not recognize as readily, however, variation in conceptions of the individual, perhaps because the concept is so much taken for granted in our own way of life. We wish to suggest, therefore, that various notions of community imply different types of individuals constituting it, and different images of the family assume certain kinds of individuals loyal to it. In Deshen's study, he points to the prominence of the active, aggressive individual in Moroccan maraboutic culture generally and claims that this may be the source of the particular kind of "individual" reflected in the documents he studied. This is certainly a different historical source of "the individual" from the one we assume for modern European culture and community. It would seem, then, that a natural epilogue to the study of the family and community would be to examine different conceptions of the individual (in relation to the other two frameworks) that are to be found in different periods of Jewish history, including the present.

NOTES

1. S. Deshen, *Tzibur viyiḥidim bemaroko* (*Individuals and the Community: The Social Life of 18th–19th Century Moroccan Jewry*), (Tel Aviv, 1983).
2. A. Laredo, "Las Taqqanot de los expulsados de Castilla en Marruecos y su regimen matrimonial y successoral," *Sefarad* 8 (1948), 245–76.
3. I. Abrami, "Les 'Grana' à Tunis d'après leur minutes: La Lutte pour

l'autonomie" [Hebrew and French], in M. Abitbol, ed., *Judaïsme d'Afrique du Nord aux XIXê–XXê siècles* (Jerusalem, 1980), pp. 64–95.

4. A. Chouraqui, *Marche vers l'Occident: Les Juives d'Afrique du Nord* (Paris, 1952), pp. 273–74.

5. H. E. Goldberg, "The Jewish Community of Tripoli in Relation to Italian Jewry and Italians in Tripoli," in J.-L. Miège, ed., *Les Relations intercommunautaires juives en Méditérranée Occidentale* (Paris, 1984), pp. 82, 88.

6. M. Ha-Cohen, *Higgid Mordecai: Histoire de la Libye et de ses juifs— lieux d'habitation et coutumes* [in Hebrew] (Jerusalem, 1978), p. 117.

7. H. E. Goldberg, *Cave-Dwellers and Citrus Growers: A Jewish Community in Libya and Israel* (Cambridge, Eng., 1972), pp. 24–25.

8. M. Yosef, "Jews of Morocco" [in Hebrew], *Hamelitz* [Odessa], 183 (1898), 3–4; 143 (1898) 4–5.

9. Deshen, *Tzibur viyihidim*, pp. 44–45.

10. Deshen, *Tzibur viyihidim*, p. 68. The topic has recently been analyzed in detail by S. Bar-Asher, "Private Synagogues and Succession to Religious Office (*serarah*) in Morocco" [in Hebrew] *Tzion* [Jerusalem], 51 (1986), 449–70.

11. Deshen, *Tzibur viyihidim*, p. 57.

12. Deshen, *Tzibur viyihidim*, p. 76.

13. Deshen, *Tzibur viyihidim*, p. 26.

14. Deshen, *Tzibur viyihidim*, pp. 28–29. See also S. Bar-Asher, "The Jewish Community in Morocco in the 18th Century: Studies in the History of the Social Status and Self-Government of the Jews of Fes, Meknes and Sefrou" [Hebrew], Ph.D. diss., The Hebrew University of Jerusalem, 1981, pp. 105–6.

15. Deshen, *Tzibur viyihidim*, p. 48.

16. L. Rosen, "Muslim-Jewish Relations in a Moroccan City," *International Journal of Middle East Studies* 3 (1972), 435–49.

17. A. Memmi, *Pillar of Salt* (New York, 1955), p. 95.

18. H. E. Goldberg, "The Social Context of North African Jewish Patronyms," *Folklore Research Center Studies*, 8 vols. (Jerusalem, 1972), III, 245–58.

19. H. Z. Hirschberg, "The Problem of the Judaized Berbers," *Journal of African History* 4 (1963), 313–34.

20. H. E. Goldberg, trans. and ed., *The Book of Mordechai: Jewish Life in Libya* (Philadelphia, 1980), pp. 74–77. Emphasis added.

21. C. Geertz, H. Geertz, and L. Rosen, *Meaning and Order in Moroccan Society* (Cambridge, Eng., 1979).

22. Geertz et al., *Meaning and Order*, p. 315.

23. C. DeFoucauld, *Reconnaissance au Maroc, 1883–1884* (Paris, 1888); Ha-Cohen, *Higgid Mordecai*, p. 74; E. Brauer, *The Jews of Kurdistan: An Ethnological Study* [Hebrew] ed. R. Patai, (Jerusalem, 1947).

24. Geertz et al., *Meaning and Order*, p. 347.

25. P. Pascon and D. Schroeter, "Le Cimetière juif d'Iligh (1751–1955):

Etude des épitaphes comme documents d'histoire sociale (Tazerwalt, Sud-Ouest Marocain), *"Revue de l'Occident Musulman et de la Méditerranée* 34 (1982), 39–62.

26. N. Stillman, "Muslims and Jews in North Africa: Perceptions, Images, Stereotypes," *Proceedings of the Seminar on Muslim-Jewish Relations in North Africa* (New York, 1975), pp. 13–27; H. E. Goldberg and R. Rosen, "Itinerant Jewish Peddlers at the End of the Ottoman Period and Under Italian Rule," in M. Abitol, ed., *Communautés juives des marges sahariennes* (Jerusalem, 1982), pp. 303–20.

27. R. Rosen, "Le Symbolisme féminin ou la femme dans le système de représentation judéo-marocain dans un mochav en Israel" [Hebrew], M.A. thesis, Dept. of Sociology and Social Anthropology, The Hebrew University of Jerusalem, 1981.

28. S. D. Goitein, *Jews and Arabs* (New York, 1955), p. 147; idem, *A Mediterranean Society: The Jewish Communities of the Arab World as Portrayed in the Documents of the Cairo Genizah*, 4 vols. (Berkeley, 1978), III: *The Family.*

29. A picture of lamps like these may be seen in A. L. Udovitch and L. Valensi, *The Last Arab Jews: The Communities of Jerba Tunisia* (Chur, 1984), p. 68.

30. The analysis of Jewish memorial practices in a comparative perspective is suggested in a brief communication by W. Zenner, "Memorialism—Some Jewish Examples," *American Anthropologist* 67 (1965), 481–83.

31. H. E. Goldberg, "The Jewish Wedding in Tripolitania: A Study in Cultural Sources," *The Maghreb Review*, 3:9 (1978), 1–6.

9

Marriage and Torah Study Among the *Lomdim* in Lithuania in the Nineteenth Century

IMMANUEL ETKES

Among the major expressions of the process of modernization in European Jewry during the nineteenth century was, as is well known, the change in the nature of the family. The traditional family, whose values and characteristics were consolidated and took root during the Middle Ages, gradually gave way to the modern family. Among the Jews of Russia, to whom the process of modernization came markedly later than in Central and Western Europe, the change in the character of the family also came relatively late. Harsh criticism of various aspects of the traditional family can indeed be found in the autobiographical writings of the maskilim of Eastern Europe from the late eighteenth century on.[1] However, actual changes in the nature of the family only began to take place at the end of the nineteenth century.[2]

Yet even before the traditional Jewish family in Eastern Europe was influenced by the trend towards modernization, it was affected by factors immanent in Jewish society: Hasidism, on the one hand, and the trend of the *lomdim* (lit. "learners")[3] in Lithuania, on the other. Regarding Hasidism it is thought that the intense and intimate bond formed between the Hasid and the zaddik (master) weakened the Hasid's responsibility toward his family.[4] The family life of the *lomdim* in Lithuania was also subject to tension, namely, the tension between the ideal of total devotion to Torah study and family responsibilities. This chapter focuses on various manifestations of that tension and its significance for the institution of the family.

A poignant experession of the tension between Torah study and devotion to one's family is found in the Gaon of Vilna's commentary on Proverbs: "True heroes are men of noble heart with the fullest trust in God, constantly doing mitzvoth and meditating on the Torah day and night even though their home be without bread and clothing and their families cry out: 'Bring us something to support and sustain us, some livelihood!' But he pays no attention at all to them nor heeds their voice . . . for he has denied all love except that of the Lord and His Torah."[5] In those lines the Gaon of Vilna describes an elevated man who devotes his whole being to the study of Torah, denying the life of this world. Obviously, the fulfillment of that ideal demanded the overcoming of many obstacles. Thus, it is quite instructive that the difficulty that the Gaon of Vilna chose to bring out was the need to ignore the suffering of one's family, subject to poverty and want. Doubtless very few people actually behaved in accordance with the strict ideal outlined by the Gaon of Vilna.[6] Nevertheless, his remarks reflect a dilemma with which many of the *lomdim* of Lithuania during the nineteenth century had to cope.

Obviously, the difficulty of combining Torah study with married life was not restricted to Lithuanian Jewry of the nineteenth century. Nevertheless, there is good reason to concentrate on that society in that the character and dimensions of the phenomenon were more pronounced there than in any other Jewish society. In nineteenth-century Lithuania, Torah study flourished to an unprecedented extent as we see from the achievements of many of its scholars and the fame of its Torah institutions. Moreover, respect for the Torah and its study was widespread. That respect was expressed in the willingness to provide generous support for Torah scholars, the proliferation of "societies" that set aside fixed times for Torah study, and the relatively large number of talented young people who sought to become *talmidei-ḥakhamim* (talmudic scholars), whose profession was Torah study. Although we have no exact figures, it is likely that the relative number of such *talmidei-ḥakhamim* in Lithuania was unrivaled by other areas of Eastern Europe.[7]

Naturally, the many young men who wished to excel in Torah study had to dedicate their childhood and youth to the Talmud and its commentaries, and of course the problem of supporting those young men during their studies arose. That problem was particularly severe in nineteenth-century Lithuania for two reasons. First, the communal yeshivoth—which had been active among Ashkenazic Jewry at the end of the Middle Ages and which had supplied the basic needs of their students—ceased to exist in Poland and Lithuania in the eighteenth century.[8] Second, many of the young men who aspired to devote themselves to Torah study came from families too poor to support them.[9] For that reason one might have expected that the young *lomdim* would put off marriage until, through their achievements in Torah study, they attained a post from which they could make a living and, in the meantime, the community would support them. However, such a solution, although justifiable by the halakhah,[10] was totally opposed to the traditional custom of early marriage. Therefore, instead of detaching the study of Torah from family life, an effort was made to combine the two: the institution of the family was meant to support the young scholar and permit him to achieve his ambitions.

Matchmaking and marriage among nineteenth-century Lithuanian Jewry were essentially the same as in traditional Ashkenazic society.[11] We shall mention several typical characteristics of those practices here:

In the first half of the nineteenth century it was still considered desirable to marry off boys at thirteen and girls at twelve.[12] In fact, marriages at that age were common mainly among the wealthy and scholarly segments of society whereas young people of the lower classes generally married at a later age. During the second half of the century, particularly toward the end, it became more common for people to marry at a later age.[13]

The authority for making matches and arranging marriages lay with the parents alone. However, in the second half of the century it became more common for parents to stipulate that the match be dependent on the couple's consent.[14]

The marriage market was based on rational criteria and mutuality. The most important values in that market were wealth and lineage. The state of health, appearance, talents, and temperaments of the candidates for marriage also had considerable weight in the bargaining. Particular value was attributed to the prospective groom's talents and achievements in Torah study.[15] One expression of that is the custom of submitting the prospective groom to an examination at the initiative of the bride's father before the betrothal agreement was signed.[16]

During the nineteenth century, especially in the second half, a new dimension was added to the choice of an appropriate candidate for marriage: the degree of his loyalty to the tradition, or, conversely, his deviation from it. Naturally, the importance of that criterion increased as the process of secularization gained momentum in Jewish society.[17]

Given the young age of marriages and because the newly married couple had no independent means of support, it was common for them to spend the first years of their married life in the bride's parents' home. The number of years during which the couple would be entitled to support (*kest* in Yiddish, *mezonot* in Hebrew) at the bride's father's table was determined in the prenuptial bargaining, and it was one of the main clauses of the agreement signed by both sides.[18]

The combination of those patterns of marriage with the admiration accorded by the society to Torah scholars provided a solution to the problem of supporting young men who wished to devote themselves to Torah study. Because the talents and achievements of the groom were accorded great value in the marriage market, it was common for an affluent father who yearned for a scholarly son-in-law to undertake to support the groom's studies. The father would agree to support the couple at his table for a number of years, and, in addition, he would set aside a considerable sum as a dowry. During the *kest* period, the groom could devote all his time and energy to Torah study, and the young couple's financial future was supposed to be assured by the dowry.

According to this setup, the institution of arranged marriages was mobilized to subsidize the studies of young men during the first years after their marriage. Later we shall find that it was expected that the family would continue to maintain the young scholar and permit him to continue to devote himself to his studies after the period of *mezonot* as well. The combination of Torah study and family life offered a solution to the problem of subsidizing the studies of young men who aspired to become *talmidei-ḥakhamim*. However, both studies and the family paid a price for that solution.

Several expressions of that price can be found in the autobiographical writings of the authors of the Haskalah in Eastern Europe. I refer to the memoirs of Maimon,[19] Gottlober,[20] Guenzburg,[21] Lilienblum,[22] and others. In their youth these writers belonged to the circles of *lomdim*, and their married lives took place within the framework described earlier. However, despite the richness of those memoirs as historical sources, one ought not to make them the primary basis of one's inquiry, for the descriptions of family life and marriages contained in them were largely inspired by an ideology that rejected the values and mores of the traditional society. There are thus grounds for suspicion that the authors of the Haskalah tended to overemphasize the weaknesses of the traditional family. It is preferable to use sources that shed light on family life from within. Indeed, the following discussion is based on sources revealing the inner world of these Lithuanian scholars, including several aspects of family life in relation to Torah study. My discussion is primarily based on the following sources: the letters of Rabbi Shmuel of Kelme; the memoirs of Rabbi Eliahu David Rabinowitz Teumim, known as Aderet; and a number of letters of Rabbi Naftali Amsterdam.

Shmuel of Kelme was one of the scholarly elite of Lithuania.[23] He was the brother of Rabbi Eliahu Rogoler, the rabbi of Kalish. In the late 1850s, Rabbi Shmuel moved to Eretz Israel and joined the circle of scholars who led the community of *Prushim* (disciples of the Gaon of Vilna) in Jerusalem. His letters have been preserved in manuscript. They were written during the 1850s and 1860s and mainly addressed to his son, Arieh Leib Frumkin, later famous in his own right, who was a young man at that time, eating at his father-in-law's table and studying Torah. Among other things, Shmuel's letters contain detailed guidance in Torah study and consideration of some aspects of family life.[24]

Rabbi Aderet was a prominent rabbinical figure in Lithuania. For many years he was the rabbi of the community of Ponevezh. His recently published memoirs[25] are exceptional in that it was uncommon for rabbis of the older generation to write memoirs. Moreover, whereas the biographies of rabbis of the nineteenth century, generally written by their sons or disciples, tend to idealize their subjects, the Aderet is not reluctant to reveal the human weaknesses of the rabbis and scholars whom he encountered.

Rabbi Naftali Amsterdam[26] was one of the closest disciples of Rabbi Israel Salanter, the founder of the Musar movement. In the 1860s and 1870s he corresponded with Rabbi Yitzhak Blazer, also one of Salanter's closest disciples. In those letters Naftali reveals the difficulties and doubts he experienced as a result of the tension between his desire to study Torah and his family obligations.

It goes without saying that the extent of the material at our disposition does not allow us to make statistical generalizations or demographic

analyses. Nevertheless, it seems to me that on the basis of the sources
mentioned thus far, as well as additional sources both from traditional
and Haskalah literature, one can sketch a valid picture going beyond
individual cases and characterizing scholarly circles in general. This picture is particularly characteristic of the fifth, sixth, and seventh decades
of the nineteenth century, to which the aforementioned sources refer.

At this point let us take up the various manifestations of tension between
Torah study and the institution of family in the order in which they
occur in a person's life.

The period of *kest,* that is, the years when the couple eats at the table
of the bride's father, were meant to be a time when the groom devoted
himself to Torah study in hopes of becoming a renowned scholar. It is
only natural that in Shmuel of Kelme's letters to his son we find repeated
urgings in that matter. Thus, for example, in 1865, Shmuel writes: "Beloved son, while you are eating manna, supported by *kest,* and you have
no other worry, thank God, be diligent in your studies and make them
bear fruit, be expert in your studies."[27] Shmuel's remarks and similar
ones[28] express more than a single father's concern for his son's future.
They also express the view common among *lomdim* circles of the purpose
of the *kest.* That period was viewed as a unique opportunity for Torah
study in that the young scholar was entirely freed from concern for his
livelihood. Since the *kest* period was determined and limited in advance,
mere diligence in studies was insufficient. One had to obtain objective
achievements. Generally speaking, while the young groom was eating
at his father-in-law's table, he was supposed to fulfill his parents' expectations and those of his in-laws, who wanted a return on their financial
investment—as well as his wife's and his own expectations of himself.

However, the assumption that the *kest* period was an ideal opportunity
to fulfill those expectations ignores the delicate and complex character
of the process by which the young husband was accepted into his wife's
home, a process that was also meant to take place during the *kest* period.
Anyone who has read the memoirs of Haskalah writers knows that this
process was often attended by tension and controversy. We also read
of such a controversy in the letters of Shmuel of Kelme. In 1864 he
wrote these lines to his son: "My son, beloved of my soul! . . . I heard
a rumor, and my stomach was upset, that your father- and mother-in-
law (perhaps your spouse as well) and your father-in-law's whole household are at odds with you, and you never mentioned it to us, . . . and
you did not tell us that you are belittled in your father-in-law's house,

and they do not pay attention to you."[29] Neither that letter nor others concerning the same matter[30] explain the roots of the controversy that had erupted between Arieh Leib and his wife's family. Nevertheless the letters do contain some information that permits an approximate reconstruction of the course of events: Even before the wedding the bride's family had shown some signs of regret at the match. Those signs appeared again after the wedding and aroused tension with the groom. The mother-in-law played a major role in the deterioration of their relations. She insulted Arieh Leib by casting doubts on his scholarly abilities in comparison with those of her sons. Her invidious attitude toward Arieh Leib disrupted relations between herself and her daughter, who had a miscarriage. Shmuel suggested that it might have happened because of the sorrow provoked by her mother. Of course, that misfortune made matters worse between Arieh Leib and his wife's family.

That controversy was, of course, an individual instance. Nevertheless, it illustrates the difficulties generally encountered by young grooms in fitting into their wives' families. That process was probably difficult for both sides. The groom was a boy of thirteen to fifteen who was forced to leave his parents' home after his marriage. In many cases that separation was a cause of suffering and pain.[31] On leaving his parents' home the young groom had to get used simultaneously to the intimate bonds of matrimony and to his wife's parents' way of life. Moreover, the groom usually moved to a strange city, thus being deprived of the encouragement and support of close contact with his parents.

The bride, too, was faced with a difficult dilemma: To what degree ought the increasingly close ties between herself and her husband develop at the expense of her bonds of fidelity to her parents? Of course, that question became more difficult if there was tension between the bride's parents and the groom. Shmuel's letters show that his daughter-in-law chose to support her husband as opposed to her parents. But that individual case does not justify a generalization. In any case, the issue of the daughter's position in the event of tension between her husband and her parents certainly added another dimension to the complexity of the situation.

The bride's parents also had to devote no small effort to the absorption and adaptation of the strange young man in their midst. However, it would appear that the main difficulty lay in marking out the borders of the young couple's independence. Naturally, the groom sought a certain degree of self-definition in his wife's family home. At the same time he was dependent on her parents economically and subject to their authority in other respects. Clearly, the groom's aspirations for independence and his dependence on his wife's parents were an inexhaustible source of conflict.

In the light of Arieh Leib's case, one can point to two other factors liable to provoke tension between the groom and his wife's family. First, it sometimes happened after the marriage that the wife's family was not fully satisfied with the match. Feelings of that sort could develop from the disparity between the image of the groom as it appeared before the wedding and his actual appearance afterward.[32] It must be recalled that until the wedding the bride's family would have very little real contact with the groom during his brief, formal visits. The groom's image, upon which the decision to arrange the match was based, was created during the bargaining preceding the signing of the prenuptial agreement, when both the matchmaker and the groom's relatives exaggerated his virtues.[33] Moreover, in many cases the bride's father would make the decision on his own without awaiting his wife's approval. She would be likely to express her bitterness at her husband's choice by unmasking her son-in-law's weaknesses.[34]

Another possible source of tension between the groom and his in-laws was the difficulty they had in fulfilling their obligations to the young couple. In Gottlober's memoirs he recounts that matchmakers would make exaggerated financial promises without the knowledge of those whom they represented.[35] From various other sources we learn that the parties themselves, the groom's parents, but especially the bride's parents, sometimes tended to promise more than they could deliver. Their motivation for doing so was essentially quite simple: According to the rules of bargaining in the marriage market, whoever offered the most could expect to get the most in return.

The writers of the Haskalah recount several cases in which the wife's parents violated their promises. Maimon tells that the inn belonging to his mother-in-law—and promised to him as a dowry—proved to be pledged to a creditor. In Lilienblum's case it was the mother-in-law herself who made the match and negotiated the prenuptial agreement. She promised three hundred silver rubles to Lilienblum as a dowry and six years of *kest*. When her husband heard this, he got angry and demanded a change in the agreement. The dowry was reduced to two hundred silver rubles; and the *kest*, to five years. When his five years of support were over, Lilienblum demanded the two hundred rubles promised to him, and his father-in-law tried to sell his house to pay his debt. However, the mother-in-law contrived to drive away potential buyers and steal the prenuptial contract from Lilienblum.[36]

Perhaps the Haskalah authors exaggerated intentionally in order to strike out at the traditional institution of arranged marriages. Nonetheless, the existence of the phenomenon is not in doubt. In Shmuel's letters to his son, we see that both Shmuel and the father-in-law found it difficult to fulfill their promises regarding the dowry, and the payment was therefore delayed.[37] Shmuel urged his son not to worry or be distracted from his studies. Ultimately, both sides kept their promises. In time Shmuel and his wife sank into debt, borrowing money from their son and daughter-in-law, that is, from the dowry they were holding. In a letter to his daughter-in-law, Shmuel thanks her for the loan and begs her not to be concerned, for he would repay the debt, which indeed he did.[38]

On the other hand, fate was not so kind to the Aderet. He tells us that at the end of his six years of *kest*, he left his father-in-law's house naked and bereft of the six hundred rubles he had received for a dowry. His father-in-law, whose business was in very bad straits, had taken that sum from him as a loan but was unable to repay it.[39] In his memoirs the Aderet also tells of a case of intentional fraud. His nephew was engaged to the daughter of a rabbi. During the negotiations the bride's brothers promised both support at their father's table and a thousand silver rubles in dowry. As a guarantee they gave the groom a list of their father's books. After the prenuptial agreement was signed, it turned out that the bride's father was on his deathbed and could not support his son-in-law. As for the books, they had already been pledged in another matter.[40] Thus, one finds that the violation of promises given in prenuptial agreements was a rather common phenomenon. It seems likely that in such cases not only was the couple's economic future jeopardized, but the groom's ability to concentrate on his studies also suffered severely.

Whatever may have been the reason why a groom quarreled with his wife's family, without doubt whenever such a quarrel erupted, the young man was in an unenviable situation. In the case discussed earlier, Shmuel showed himself to be a sensitive and loving father who empathized with his son's suffering and tried to support him. Shmuel intended to visit him for that purpose. But that plan was never carried out, apparently because of the distance and the expense of the journey. In the meanwhile, Shmuel tried to act through his letters. Among the things that he wrote to his son was advice to ignore the insults, not to neglect his health, and under no condition to leave his father-in-law's house and give up his right to support.[41] At the same time, Shmuel urges his son and daughter-in-law to honor her parents and refrain from any friction with them. He also urged his son's parents-in-law to treat the young couple with moderation and indulgence. In so doing, Shmuel adds a sentence indicating that it was rather common for a groom to have trouble accommodating himself to his wife's parents' home: "For, thank the Lord, I myself understand the bridegroom's broken heart . . . and the bridegrooms whom I support at my table, thank the Lord, I and all the members of my household always are cordial to them, and they never hear any bad word from us, perish the thought."[42]

Both in his letters to his son and in those to his son's parents-in-law, Shmuel offers a pragmatic plan: Arieh Leib will leave his wife in her father's home and go to study Torah in another city. His living expenses during his absence will be provided by his father-in-law in the form of a weekly allowance. Although not stated explicitly, Shmuel clearly sought to free his son from his entanglement with his in-laws. At the same time, a young man's departure from his father-in-law's home to study Torah in another city was not deviant behavior but rather a common practice. It is in that spirit that Shmuel argues in favor of his proposal to the in-laws of his son: "Doubtless the greatest success in Torah study results from wandering to places of Torah . . . for in truth Torah cannot be acquired at home so well as in another city . . . As we have seen, the great scholars of our time grew and prospered by wandering."[43]

The pattern of moving from place to place to study Torah was not a nineteenth-century innovation. In the Middle Ages it was common for young men to travel far and wide in order to study in yeshivoth.[44] Another pattern of wandering was called galuth (exile), wherein some men left their families and social lives and took it on themselves to study Torah under conditions of economic deprivation. "Exile" of that kind was viewed as an effort at moral purification, and it is thus no coincidence that it embellishes the biographies of saintly men.[45] Although the phenomenon of wandering during the nineteenth century was evidently influenced by earlier patterns, it was not identical with them. In many cases, the wanderers did not make their way to yeshivoth or Torah centers. Similarly, they did not take "exile" on themselves combined with strict asceticism. The main motivation for leaving was the wish to remove the young scholar from influences that might interfere with his concentration on his studies. It was in that spirit that Rabbi Haim of Volozhin offered the following counsel to his disciples: "Study in a distant place to avoid the impediments and interference of one's household."[46] The length of time a scholar was absent from his home would vary from instance to instance. Some young men spent a year or two away from home, and others wandered for five years or more.[47] During that period the young husband would visit his home on the holidays.[48]

Near the end of the *kest* period, the young *lomdim* stood at a crossroads in life: Should they be satisfied with the years of study already accumulated and turn their attention to economic activity, or should they remain faithful to the ideal of Torah study and earn a living from it? Those who chose the second option had to deal with the issue of supporting their families. The practical alternatives available to such men were rather limited. Teaching young pupils in a heder was a profession that provided a meager livelihood, was of dubious prestige, and left the scholar little time or energy for high-level Torah study. Posts such as *Rosh Yeshiva* (head of the academy) were quite rare. The most acceptable solution was the office of the rabbinate. However, the path to such a position was by no means easy.

First, many scholars recoiled from the very decision to serve as rabbis, for it appeared to contradict the ideal of Torah study for its own sake.[49] Second, even a young scholar who overcame that hesitation was certainly given to doubting whether he had reached a sufficiently high level of Talmudic scholarship to turn to the study of those tractates and *poskim* (in this case: law codes) that he had to master for ordination. Naturally, no objective answer could be given to such a question, and everyone chose his own path according to the level of demands he made on himself.[50] Some men began to prepare for rabbinical ordination from the start, and others decided to devote several more years to the study of the Talmud. In any case, many of them faced the problem of supporting their families until they were fit to serve as rabbis and until a rabbinical post in some community was actually offered to them.

The doubts typical of that stage in the life of a young scholar are manifest in the letters of Shmuel of Kelme to his son. Even before Arieh Leib's period of *kest* was over, his father urged him to study the halakhic literature necessary for ordination.[51] In a rather late letter, Shmuel chides his son because his program of study was not effective enough and he was not yet ready to receive rabbinical ordination. At the same time, he warns him not to join his wife in the management of the store lest he forget all his learning. As a temporary solution to the problem of making a living, Shmuel suggests that his son take on two students and teach them Talmud.[52]

Shmuel's suggestion to his son demonstrates a common pattern among the *lomdim* of Lithuania.[53] Although sometimes such a tutor was called a melamed, that term must not be confused with the melamed of a heder. Here the term refers to a recognized scholar who met with a young man or a small group of young men for a few hours every week and taught them. The students had already finished their studies at the heder and were nearly able to study on their own. However, they still required the guidance and assistance of a more experienced scholar. From the scholar's point of view that profession had several advantages. First, he still had time for his own independent studies. Second, study with his students afforded the teacher an opportunity for reviewing and deepening his knowledge. Sometimes the teacher used that opportunity to test his new insights regarding the passages being studied. Finally, there was the monetary consideration although the income from such private lessons was rather small and not enough to support a family. In fact, it merely provided additional income to the mainstay of the family's livelihood, the store run by the wife.

The occupation that Shmuel recommended to his son as a transitional stage was his own principal occupation. Because he was reluctant to accept a rabbinical post, for many years Shmuel taught boys as described earlier. His pupils were the sons of wealthy householders living in communities distant from Kelme. Thus, Shmuel remained away from home for extensive periods. During all those years his wife ran a store that provided the main source of the family's livelihood.

Teaching Talmud to advanced students was a temporary measure commonly resorted to by scholars who had finished their years of *kest* but had not yet established themselves in a rabbinical post. Not everyone took that path, however. A different course that could be taken after the end of the *kest* is described in Rabbi Aderet's autobiography: "After Shemini Atzeret [5627 = 1866],when the six years of *kest* promised by my father-in-law were finished . . . I headed for exile in a place of Torah to cling to the profession of my fathers, may they rest in peace."[54]

Leaving home after the end of the *kest* is presented here as a natural step and a tradition extending from generation to generation in learned families. First the Aderet went to Vilna, and there he obtained a letter of recommendation for acceptance in the yeshiva of Volozhin. For reasons that are unclear, he changed his mind about that plan and settled in a town called Lipnishak. That town was not a Torah center, nor did it offer a rabbi or teacher with whom the Aderet was interested in being associated. The town seems to have been chosen because of other considerations. First, at that time the Aderet's brother was there with another of his friends, and he found them suitable study partners. Second, in that town there were burghers willing to support Torah scholars. Thus the Aderet and his comrades spent most of their days in the *beit midrash* (house of study), and their meals were brought to them there. On the Sabbath they ate with communal notables.[55]

In the Aderet's case, dedicating himself to Torah study far from home and the disturbances associated with it bore excellent fruit. Here is his description of his daily routine and his accomplishments during his studies at Lipnishak:

> There I saw good results from my studies . . . I gained many new insights [*ḥiddushim*] and wrote them down in a notebook, until I did not have enough time to write them all down. At that time all my concerns and thoughts were only for the Torah, and I had almost no distractions from my studies, and also in my conversations with people my heart always dwelt on some matter from the Torah, and I said then that perhaps that was the meaning of the verse, "and thou shalt meditate on it day and night," that one's reason and thoughts be only concerned with Torah. . . . At that time I studied with my late brother, may he rest in peace. . . . We studied the Order of *Kodashim* from the time of our evening prayers until one or two in the morning without interruption, and we ate supper and slept till the morning. After morning prayers we studied until noon and ate breakfast. Then we slept for half an hour and studied until afternoon prayers.[56]

In 1870, Aderet returned to his home and family after an absence of about four years. Five more years passed during which he studied Torah at home until he was offered the rabbinate of Ponevezh (Panevezys). During that whole time his wife bore the burden of supporting the family, running her father's store.[57]

Thus, the phenomenon of leaving one's family in order to sojourn in a place of Torah learning, which we first saw in the case of Arieh Leib, the son of Shmuel of Kelme, also played a major role in the life of the young Aderet. Common to both cases is, of course, the effort to permit the scholar to devote himself to his studies in peace and concentration, free of the disturbances associated with close and continuous contact with the members of his family. At the same time, the "exile" of Arieh

Leib, which took place in the beginning of his *kest* period, was unlike that of the Aderet, which lasted four years after the end of his *kest*. In the former case and ones like it, the adverse effect on the family was probably less severe, for close bonds between the couple had not yet been formed, and they had not yet had children. Moreover, sometimes such a period of "exile" could improve troubled relations between the groom and his wife's parents, also alleviating the tension arising from the necessity of having sexual relations at too early an age. Despite these mitigating circumstances, Shmuel was apprehensive that his daughter-in-law might be offended by Arieh Leib's desire to leave for another city to study Torah there. Therefore, he made a special effort to placate his daughter-in-law and win her support for his proposed plan.[58]

In the case of the Aderet, in contrast, it seems likely that his prolonged absence after the *kest* period placed a heavy burden, both physical and emotional, on his wife, who had to support the family and raise her child by herself. Although in the Aderet's memoirs there are explicit statements of a deep spiritual bond with his family, it is difficult to find any feeling of guilt for his long absence from home. The Aderet probably considered that the supreme value of Torah study justified the high price paid by the members of his family.

The Jewish woman, working hard at running a store to support her scholarly husband and their children, is a familiar figure in the literature of the Enlightenment. Some Haskalah writers portrayed her with the aim of bringing out what seemed to them to be a flaw in traditional family life. However, it must be emphasized that this was not merely a literary stereotype, but actually a widespread phenomenon. Moreover, we are not referring to cases where the woman was forced to support her family only after the fact, when there was no other alternative, but rather to a social pattern that was considered fitting and proper from the start.

In his memoirs, Gottlober tells how in the marriage market it was common to attribute high values to the girls' ability to carry on a conversation in Polish, for that skill was useful in managing a business.[59] His remark, which apparently refers to the first half of the nineteenth century, is confirmed by internal sources both from the middle and the end of that century. In 1848, Shmuel of Kelme is asked to help find an appropriate match for his brother's daughters. Shmuel's nephew, who wrote to him about the matter, saw fit to emphasize that his younger sister "is educated in reading Hebrew, Polish, German . . . and also the Russian alphabet is not unfamiliar to her."[60] Shmuel himself did the same in 1865, when he proposed a match for the son of his son's parents-in-law. Among the girl's other virtues, Shmuel emphasized that she had a modern education and knew European languages.[61] In general then, the expectation that the woman play an active role in supporting the family was taken into account during the prenuptial bargaining, and it also dictated the character of the education considered suitable for one's daughters. Needless to say, regarding the education of sons, the study of European languages was seen as unnecessary and even dangerous. It is also true that the woman's involvement in the support of her family was not limited, in the time and place under discussion, only to the families of scholars. However, in those families the wife's contribution was decisive in that she was the principal, often the only, breadwinner. Moreover, in families where the husband was the main breadwinner, the wife worked because of economic necessity. But in the families of the *lomdim*, the wife's contribution to the family's living was considered the price she was called on to pay so her husband could devote himself to Torah.

Up to this point we have discussed the economic role played by the wife during the years between the end of the *kest* until the husband was settled in a rabbinical post. However, we find, too, in many sources that the wife's contribution to the family's livelihood was also necessary after the husband began to serve as a rabbi. One individual case illustrating that phenomenon is found in the life of Rabbi Naftali Amsterdam. In 1867 he wrote to his friend Rabbi Yitzhak Blazer, who was then the rabbi of the community of Petersburg, asking for his help in finding a rabbinical post. In his letter[62] Naftali tells that for years his wife has been supporting the family by running a bakery. The work was exhausting and beyond the strength of a woman without her husband's help. Moreover, the needs of the family had grown recently. For that reason, Naftali intended to join his wife and help her in the bakery. But Rabbi Israel Salanter, the teacher and mentor of both Naftali Amsterdam and Yitzhak Blazer, was opposed to that solution, which would prevent Naftali from studying Torah. The plan proposed by Salanter, which Naftali sought to carry out, was to separate from his wife and children, who lived in Kovno, and to go to some community where a rabbinical post could be found for him. Naftali emphasized that he did not seek a post with a high salary, for the family would continue to depend on the bakery run by his wife. He only wanted enough salary for his own needs and to help his family a little.

Naftali's efforts bore fruit and he obtained a rabbinical post in Novgorod. In 1872 he was the rabbi of the community of Helsinki in Finland. In a letter dated Kislev of that year, Naftali complains about his own suffering and that of his family because they are apart.[63] In a letter written a few weeks later Naftali mentions that his wife is about to visit him in Helsinki "for a short time."[64] In a letter of Iyar of that year[65] he tells that he intends to go to Kovno for two months because he has to take care of his older children's future. In that letter Naftali tells Blazer that he is secretly entertaining the thought that if he travels to Kovno he might not return to Helsinki, for the burden of the rabbinate is heavy, and he and his family suffer from the distance between them.

The pangs of loneliness and the difficulties of daily life led Naftali to make a new plan: His wife and children would leave Kovno and join him in Helsinki. Naftali mentions that his wife also supports that plan, but she makes it conditional on finding some business for her in Helsinki that would bring in between ten and fifteen silver rubles weekly. Naftali tells that he has consulted with local people on that matter and discovered that it is extremely difficult to find a business suitable for his wife.[66] The various efforts he made to find an alternative source of income to the bakery managed by his wife in Kovno were unsuccessful, and in the end his wife and children remained where they were. We do not know exactly when Naftali left the rabbinical post in Helsinki. In any case, in the summer of 1874 we find him in Kovno again, upset, anguished, and facing his old dilemma: the need to help his wife support the family versus the ardent desire to be alone and devote himself to the study of Torah and his moral improvement.[67]

Perhaps the case of Naftali Amsterdam is exceptional in the sense that he served as a rabbi in small communities, so that his salary was particularly low. However, we know that the rabbis in large and well-established communities also needed their wives' help to support their families. Rabbi Aderet may be numbered among those. During the many years he served as the rabbi of Ponevezh, the Aderet and his family suffered from severe want, and his wife had to run a store. When he was offered the rabbinate of Wilkomierz in 1883, he made his acceptance conditional on permission to run a shop in that community as well.[68] Another instructive example is that of Rabbi Meyer Yonah Barentski. He served as the rabbi of a small community called Swislocz until he was invited to assume the rabbinate of the community Brisk in Lithuania in 1872. For a year and a half Rabbi Meyer Yonah lived in Brisk by himself because his wife was a merchant and not prepared to abandon her store and be dependent on a Rabbi's salary. For that reason Rabbi Meyer ultimately had to decline the prestigious post in Brisk and go back to serve as rabbi in the small town from which he had come.[69] In general, it would seem that the involvement of rabbis' wives in the support of their families was a very widespread phenomenon, and it goes without saying that wives played a decisive role in the support of their families when their scholarly husbands were either unwilling to serve as rabbis or unsuccessful in finding posts.[70]

Another aspect of the tension between the ideal of Torah study and the institution of the family comes to the fore when *lomdim* whose profession was Torah study wished to marry their daughters to young men who were also *bnei Torah* (students of Torah). At that stage in their lives the *lomdim* faced the necessity of offering their future sons-in-law the conditions that they themselves had sought in their youth. Thus, these *lomdim* were forced to accept financial obligations that, on the one hand, were burdensome to their wives, who labored to support the family, and, on the other, made it difficult for them to study Torah in peace and quiet. Three examples of this dilemma follow.

Rabbi Eliahu Rogoler, the older brother of Rabbi Shmuel of Kelme, at that time the rabbi of Kalish, frequently complains in his letters that he wishes to abandon his post because the duties of the rabbinate interfere with his Torah studies. However, he continues to serve as a rabbi in order to provide a dowry for his two daughters.[71]

Rabbi Simcha Zissel Ziv of Kelme, one of the most important of Rabbi Israel Salanter's disciples and one of the prominent leaders of the Musar movement, writes to his friend, Rabbi Yitzhak Blazer, that his daughter is running a store to earn her dowry. Until recently his wife had also kept a store to support the family. Because his wife's store was no longer profitable, he and his family were supported by his daughter's store. Now the daughter is going to marry, and he obligated himself to feed the groom at his table. Consequently, Rabbi Simcha Zissel Ziv's daughter would have to support both her husband and her parents with the store she was running.[72]

In his memoirs, the Aderet says that in 1884 his elder daughter Alta began to be spoken highly of: "Many people proposed to marry her and I greatly wished to marry her to a God-fearing scholar, though my situation was not prosperous." Finally the Aderet chose a "superior young man whose parents are not overflowing with money, but a God-fearing scholar." The Aderet's young son-in-law was later to become the famous Rabbi Yitzhak Hacohen Kook. In the nuptial agreement signed in Elul in 1884, the Aderet agreed to pay eight hundred silver rubles as a dowry and three years of *kest*. Until the wedding date the young man studied in Volozhin and the Aderet sent him a silver ruble every week and also bought his clothing. At the end of 5645 (1885) the Aderet wrote in his memoirs: "The year has passed, bringing nothing new, only my hope to marry my daughter. And, I am a poor man . . . " Apparently the wedding date was put off because the Aderet found it difficult to raise the sum he had agreed to pay. His hope to receive that sum from the community he served was disappointed, and what he received from the community and from individuals within it was far less than what was needed. Finally, the wedding took place at the end of Nissan, 5646 (1886). The financial plight of the Aderet's household was so severe that in 1888 the son-in-law decided to leave the house and accept a rabbinical post. On that development, the Aderet wrote: "I wept in the bitterness of my heart that my sins forced him to become a rabbi in the springtime of his years, because of my pressure and urging, that I could not support them in my home."[73]

In light of the sources so far quoted and examined, it would appear that one might speak of the phenomenon of the "scholarly family." Though this type of family depends on the patterns of the traditional family, it is also different from it. The main difference is in the division of roles between the husband and the wife: The husband was freed from concern for making a living for years, and in the case in which he remained away from home for extended periods he was also free of any direct concern for household matters and the education of his children. Instead, he was supposed to study diligently during those years in order to become a great scholar. Even when he succeeded in attaining a high level of Torah studies, if he decided to make a career out of them, he could not be the sole supporter of his family, and his wife had to continue bearing the burden. Sometimes the wife remained the main breadwinner. The role occupied by the wife as the supporter of the family was not the result of unexpected misfortune but rather of her mission, for she was married to a *ben Torah*.

The two partners in the scholarly family were supposed to be content with the division of labor described earlier. The woman accepted her fate as a vocation, for she had to provide emotional support for her husband and find personal satisfaction in his achievements in Torah studies. In that spirit Rabbi Shmuel of Kelme offers guidance to his young daughter-in-law,[74] and that expectation can also be read between the lines written by the Aderet about his sister. The Aderet's brother-in-law remained away from his home for five years in succession to study

Torah. "And my sister, the rabbi's wife," recounts the Aderet, "supported herself with great labor and in great poverty and oppression, feeding her children, and she was always happy with her lot, and on his return he was stuffed full with Torah."[75]

The scholarly husband was also supposed to be content with that exceptional division of labor between himself and his wife. In the beginning of this chapter, the Gaon of Vilna was quoted as saying that the ability of the scholar to deny the urgent needs of his family, while he himself withdrew for the study of Torah, is a great virtue. Indeed, what the Gaon of Vilna prescribes in connection with the interpretation of a verse from Proverbs is what he himself practiced regarding his own family, as we see from admiring remarks that the Gaon of Vilna's sons wrote about him:

> How devoted he was in his soul to avoid the company of his household and his sons and daughters. He sought only to dwell in the pure fear of God . . . so that he never asked his sons and daughters about their livelihoods or their situations. In his life he never wrote them a letter to ask their health. If one of his sons came to visit him, even though he was very happy—for he had not seen him for a year or two—nevertheless he would never ask them about the situation of their sons and their wives or their livelihood, and when the son had rested for an hour or so, he would urge him to return to his studies.[76]

The sons of the Gaon of Vilna go on to praise their father for not hesitating to leave home to study Torah in isolation although his then only son, the infant Shlomo Zalman, was lying ill. Moreover, the Gaon of Vilna was so steeped in his studies that only after a month did he recall the sick son and return home to inquire about his health. That event, in his son's opinion, demonstrates the spiritual superiority of those who "leave the paths of this world in order to labor in Torah and mitzvoth . . . They isolate themselves in the ways of God and His Torah, until in the sweetness they find in it they sever the cords of nature and throw off the bonds of love for their children even if they are their only ones."[77]

From the words of the children of the Gaon of Vilna, it would seem that among the *lomdim* there was a sharp awareness of the intensity of the confrontation between the aspiration to give oneself over totally to the study of Torah and the natural feelings of fathers for their children. The Gaon of Vilna's overcoming of his fatherly feelings is described, precisely in light of that awareness, as a great virtue. In this matter, as in regard to other manifestations of withdrawal (*prishut*) for Torah study, the figure of the Gaon of Vilna represents the ideal in its full severity. Though that austere ideal was probably not fulfilled by most *lomdim*, nevertheless its imprint was stamped on them, and it influenced their patterns of behavior.

Did the wives of the *lomdim* actually accept their fate as a mission? It seems that many of them found compensation for their labors and isolation in the common view that it was a high privilege to support a great scholar. Nevertheless, we know of isolated instances in which women sought to break through the limitations imposed on them by the tradition and to study Torah like men.[78] Were those women exceptional in their aspirations or simply the very few who dared express the secret feelings harbored by many other women?

To our great regret we know of no sources that would permit us to give a real answer to those questions. To the extent that our sources show sensitivity to the tension between the study of Torah and family life, they express it only from the man's point of view. In those writings one sometimes finds expressions of guilt toward the family. Those guilt feelings perturb the husbands and interfere with their studies.[79] But the literature makes no similar mention of the feelings of the scholars' wives and children.

One surprising phenomenon is the silence in the sources known to us concerning the husband's duties toward his wife according to the ha-lakahh. I refer to the obligation to support one's wife and the commandment to satisfy her sexual needs. Apparently, the high value given by those circles to Torah study overshadowed those duties. Regarding the commandment of satisfying the wife's sexual needs, perhaps the husband's extended absences from his home was consistent with the tendency to restrict sexual activity to procreation. That assumption must, of course, be verified. Another cause for surprise arises from the behavior and silence of the leaders of the Musar movement regarding the husband's duties toward his wife and children. Naftali Amsterdam was, as noted, a disciple of Rabbi Israel Salanter, the founder and leader of that movement. Salanter himself left his wife and young children in Kovno and wandered among the communities of Germany and Russia for more than twenty years.[80] Some of his disciples and followers were also absent from their homes for long periods when they served as the heads of musar yeshivot.[81] That behavior is particularly surprising in that Salanter and his disciples emphasized and deepened the demand for morality in human relations. Did that imply alienation from one's wife?

The phenomenon of the "scholarly family," as described in this essay, raises a number of questions: What influence did the family's dependence on the wife's work have on the wife's status in the family and on relations between her and her husband? How did the scholarly husband's long absences affect his household, his position in the house, and his relations with his wife and children? Can one say, in general, that the wives of *lomdim*, who bore the burden of earning a livelihood, enjoyed a relatively larger degree of authority in family matters and in the education of their children? It is difficult to offer real responses to these questions and others like them on the basis of the sources we have used.

The historical study of the Jewish family in general, including the specific aspect discussed here, is still in its infancy. It is to be hoped that with the discovery of other sources and the adoption of new research methods, it will be possible to grapple with the questions raised but not answered here. In the meanwhile, we must be satisfied with having brought them up for discussion.

In closing, we should point out that the combination of Torah study with married life, as described earlier, was an arrangement that lasted for generations, permitting many young men to become Torah scholars. The consolidation and functioning of that arrangement are an expression both of the enormous admiration in which nineteenth-century Lithuanian Jewry held the study of Torah and also of the family's willingness to become a means for attaining that ideal.

NOTES

I am grateful to Professor Yakov Katz, Professor Shmuel Ettinger, Dr. Shaul Stampfer, Dr. Richard Cohen, Dr. Michael Silver, and Ms. Nurit Arnon for reading this essay in manuscript and offering constructive criticism.

Abbreviations

Shmuel's Letters = the collected letters of Rabbi Shmuel Ben Yakov of Kelme, mostly addressed to his son Arieh Leib Frumkin. Housed in the Manuscript Collection of the National Library in Jerusalem, no. 8^0 3287.

Seder Eliahu = "Seder Eliahu," the life of the Gaon Rabbi Eliahu David Rabinovitz Teumim (the Aderet), written by himself (in Hebrew), Jerusalem, 1983.

Naftali's Letters = selected letters of Rabbi Naftali Amsterdam, published as the appendix to *Sefer Kokhvei Or* by Rabbi Yitzhak Blazer, Jerusalem, 5734 (1974), pp. 208–48.

Letters of David Hale = letters of Rabbi David Hale of Slobodka, addressed to his uncle, Rabbi Shmuel of Kelme. Housed in the Manuscript Collection of the National Library in Jerusalem. no. 8^0 714.

1. On the autobiographies of Haskalah authors, see Sh. Vilnay (Verses), "Autobiographical Methods in the Haskala Period" [Hebrew], *Gilyonot* 17 (1948), 175–83; A. Mintz, "Guenzburg, Lilienblum, and the Shape of Haskalah Autobiography," *AJS Review* 4 (1979), 71–110. On the attitudes of Haskalah authors to the traditional family, see D. Biale, "Childhood, Marriage and the Family in the Eastern European Jewish Enlightenment," paper presented at the Consultation sponsored by the William Petsekek National Jewish Family Center, March 18, 1982.

2. Biale "Childhood, Marriage, and the Family," shows that the maskilim reverted to traditional patterns when they sought to marry off their own sons and daughters. On changes in the nature of the family toward the end of the nineteenth century and the beginning of this one, see M. Levin, "The Family in Jewish Revolutionary Society: Norms and Customs Among the Members of the 'Bund' " [in Hebrew], *Measef* 13 (1982–83), 109–26; 14 (1984–85), 157–71.

3. The term *lomdim* here is used in reference to young men who devoted their youth to the study of Torah and to mature professional scholars. It goes without saying that from the ideological point of view the *lomdim* of Lithuania were opponents of Hasidism and saw themselves as followers of the Gaon of Vilna and his disciples.

4. J. Katz, *Tradition and Crisis* (New York, 1971), p. 243. The influences of Hasidism on the traditional family still awaits detailed research.

5. Eliahu Ben Shlomo Zalman, *Commentary on the Book of Proverbs* [Hebrew] (Warsaw, 1837), 23:30.

6. The Gaon of Vilna enjoyed considerable financial support from the community of Vilna. Nevertheless, his words could express his experience from an earlier time, before he enjoyed public recognition and support.

7. The statement concerning the status of Torah study in Lithuania during

the nineteenth century is based on an impression gained from many and varied sources that cannot be listed in detail here. We shall merely offer a few examples: Yakov Lifshitz, *Zichron Yakov* (Frankfurt am Main and Kovna, 1924–30); Barukh Epstein, *Mekor Barukh* (Vilna, 1928); A. A. Friedman, *Sefer Hazikhronot* (Tel Aviv, 1926); Yakov Mark, *Bemehitzatam shel Gedolei Hador* (Jerusalem, 1958). On the yeshivoth of Lithuania during the nineteenth century, see Shaul Stampfer, "Three Lithuanian Yeshivot During the Nineteenth Century" [Hebrew] Ph.D., diss., The Hebrew University of Jerusalem, 1981.

8. E. Etkes, "The Thought and Activities of Rabbi Hayim of Volozhyn as a Reaction of 'Mitnagdim' to Hasidism" [Hebrew], *Proceedings of the American Academy for Jewish Research* 38–39 (1972), 16–18.

9. On sons of the poor who studied in the yeshiva of Volozhyn in the early nineteenth century, see, *Sefer tosefet ma'ase rav* (Jerusalem, 1896), in the *Sheiltot*, fol. 16b, par. 52. See also Seder Eliahu, p. 14.

10. b. Kiddushin 29b; Maimonides, *Mishne Torah, Hilkhot Talmud Torah*, 1:5.

11. See Jacob Katz's pioneering article "Marriage and Sexual Life Among the Jews at the Close of the Middle Ages" [in Hebrew] *Zion* 10 (1945), 21–54; see also Yisrael Yakov Yuval, "An Appeal Against the Proliferation of Divorce in Fifteenth-Century Germany [Hebrew], *Zion* 48 (1983), 177–216.

12. Katz, "Marriage and Sexual Life," pp. 22ff.; Yisrael Heilperin, "Hasty Marriages in Eastern Europe" [in Hebrew], *Zion* 27 (1962), esp. pp. 38–39. On the reactions of eighteenth-century Enlightenment figures to the phenomenon of early marriage, see Yakov Goldberg, "Jewish Marriages in Old Poland in Public Opinion During the Enlightenment" [Hebrew], *Galed* 4–5 (1979), 31.

13. On changes in marriage age during the nineteenth century, see the statistics collected and analyzed by Stampfer, *Three Lithuanian Yeshivot*, pp. 223–30.

14. Shmuel's Letters, p. 190; Seder Eliahu, p. 22.

15. Shmuel's Letters, p. 186; Shlomo Maimon, *The Life of Shlomo Maimon* [Hebrew] (Tel Aviv, 1953), pp. 90–91; Mordecai Aharon Guenzburg, *Aviezer* [in Hebrew] (Vilna, 1864), p. 40.

16. Seder Eliahu, pp. 24, 30; also in the works mentioned in the previous note.

17. The following are two examples from the present sources, both spoken of later in this chapter. In 1851, David Hale wrote to his uncle, Rabbi Shmuel of Kelme about arranging a marriage. Among other questions the writer posed regarding the proposed groom was whether the boy was free of "the strange incense of the blasphemous sacrifices of the maskilim of Rossain, may their names be blotted out, because many people here are afraid of Rossain boys" (Letters of David Hale). The first arranged marriage of the Aderet (see n. 32) was called off by his father in 1858, although the nuptial agreement had been signed. That unusual step was taken because he feared lest the Aderet might be adversely influenced by the modern arrangements introduced into the household by the bride's stepmother (Seder Eliahu, p. 23).

be adversely influenced by the modern arrangements introduced into the house-hold by the bride's stepmother (Seder Eliahu, p. 23).

18. Seder Eliahu, pp. 22, 24; see also the sources mentioned in n. 15.

19. See n. 15.

20. Avraham Ber Gottlober, *Memories and Journeys* [Hebrew], vol. 1 (Je-rusalem, 1979).

21. See n. 15.

22. Moshe Leib Lilienblum, *Autobiographical Writings (Hatot neurim)* [He-brew] (Jerusalem, 1970).

23. For a short biography of him written by his son, see Arieh Leib Frumkin, *Toldot Eliahu* (Vilna, 1900), pp. 65–82.

24. Shmuel's Letters to his son are included in MS 8⁰ 3287 in the Manuscript Collection of the National Library in Jerusalem. I intend to publish these letters with an introduction and notes. The references in this essay refer to the man-uscript page numbers.

25. *Seder Eliahu, the life of the Gaon Rabbi Eliahu David Rabinovitz Teumim* (the Aderet), written by himself (Hebrew) (Jerusalem, 1983).

26. D. Katz. *The Musar Movement*, 5 vols. [Hebrew] (Tel Aviv, 1963), II, 274–85.

27. Shmuel's Letters, p. 179.

28. Shmuel's Letters, pp. 183, 186.

29. Shmuel's Letters, p. 154.

30. Shmuel's Letters, pp. 149, 161.

31. Guenzburg, *Aviezer*, p. 67; Gottlober, *Memories and Journeys*, p. 111.

32. On the cancellation of marriage arrangement because of disappointment with the groom, see Seder Eliahu, pp. 35, 37, 39.

33. The extent to which it was common to exaggerate the virtues of the candidates for betrothal can be seen in the letter of David Hale to his uncle, Rabbi Shmuel of Kelme, about an arranged marriage, which said: "Your honor can tell Rabbi Nathan Neta that I am no marriage broker nor the son of a marriage broker and that everything I say is based on firm foundations of truth. I have added nothing in my praise of Rabbi Shakhna and his daughter" (Letters of David Hale).

34. On differences of opinion between the husband and his wife concerning an arranged marriage, see Guenzburg, *Aviezer*, p. 40.

35. Gottlober, *Memoirs and Journeys*, pp. 87–88.

36. Maimon, *Life of Shlomo Maimon*, p. 98; Lilienblum, *Autobiographical Writings*, pp. 89, 92, 127.

37. Shmuel's Letters, p. 171.

38. Shmuel's Letters, p. 179.

39. Seder Eliahu, p. 30.

40. Seder Eliahu, p. 71.

41. Shmuel's Letters, pp. 154–55.

42. Shmuel's Letters, p. 161.

43. Shmuel's Letters, pp. 149, 161.

44. Mordecai Breuer, "The Ashkenazi Yeshiva in the Late Middle Ages" [in Hebrew], Ph.D. diss., The Hebrew University of Jerusalem, 1967.

45. For example, in the biography of the Gaon of Vilna as well. See Yehoshua Heschel Levine, *Sefer Aliot Eliahu* [Hebrew] (Vilna, 1856), pp. 65–67.

46. Asher Hacohen, *Sefer Orḥot Ḥayim*, Keter Rosh, appendix to *Siddur Ishey Yisrael al-pi derekh ha-GRA*, par. 52.

47. Seder Eliahu, p. 20.

48. On married young men who studied in the yeshiva of Volozhyn, see Stampfer, *Three Lithuanian Yeshivot*, pp. 220ff.

49. Yitzhak Blazer, *Sefer Or Israel* (Vilna, 1900), p. 112.

50. See later in this essay on the course chosen by Rabbi Aderet; see also Seder Eliahu, p. 31.

51. Shmuel's Letters, p. 174.

52. Shmuel's Letters, p. 184.

53. See the words of Rabbi Israel Salanter appearing in *Sefer Etz Pri* (Vilna, 1881), p. 23. Sometimes the young scholar gathered a few young men about him, gave them lessons, and thus founded a kind of yeshivah. See Letters of David Hale; see also Lilienblum, *Autobiographical Writings*, pp. 128–29.

54. Seder Eliahu, p. 30.

55. Seder Eliahu, pp. 31–32.

56. Seder Eliahu, pp. 31–32.

57. Seder Eliahu, pp. 32–38, 48–51.

58. Shmuel's Letters, p. 161.

59. Gottlober, *Memories and Journeys*, p. 86.

60. Letters of Rabbi Eliahu Rogoler, *Kovetz Al Yad* [Hebrew], n.s., 6 (1967), 549.

61. Shmuel's Letters, p. 186. Cf. Letters of David Hale; Buki Ben Yogli, *What My Eyes Have Seen and What My Ears Have Heard* [Hebrew] (Jerusalem, 1947), pp. 63–64; Seder Eliahu, p. 72.

62. Naftali's Letters, pp. 209–10.

63. Naftali's Letters, p. 238.

64. Naftali's Letters, p. 212.

65. Naftali's Letters, pp. 235–36.

66. Naftali's Letters, pp. 229–30.

67. Naftali's Letters, p. 243.

68. Seder Eliahu, p. 61.

69. B. M. Levine, ed., *Metivot* (Jerusalem, 1934), p. 157. I am grateful to Dr. D. Rosenthal for calling my attention to this source.

70. That, for example, was the situation in Shmuel of Kelem's family. One of the reasons why his wife refused to join him when he moved to the Land of Israel in the late 1850s was her refusal to be supported from contributions, for

she ran a shop. Rabbi Simcha Zissel Ziv, one of Rabbi Israel Salanter's disciples, was supported by a shop kept by his daughter. See Yitzhak Blazer, *Sefer Kokhvey Or* (Jerusalem, 1974), pp. 189–90.

71. R. Eliahu Rogoler, *Kovetz Al Yad*, pp. 537ff., letters 1, 4, 7.

72. Blazer, *Sefer Kokhvey Or*, p. 189.

73. Seder Eliahu, pp. 63–67.

74. Shmuel's Letters, p. 178.

75. Seder Eliahu, p. 20.

76. This passage is taken from the introduction the Gaon of Vilna's sons wrote to their father's commentary on the *Shulhan Arukh*.

77. See the introduction the Gaon of Vilna's sons wrote to their father's commentary in the *Shulhan Arukh*.

78. A few incidences are described by Barukh Epstein, *Mekor Barukh*, pt. 4, chap. 46.

79. In a sermon Shmuel composed in honor of the founding of a society for the study of *Sefer Ḥayei Adam*, he writes in an ironic vein, among other things, that men who are engaged in commerce can set aside time to study Torah and concentrate in tranquility because they are not distracted by worries about their livelihood. For that reason they are also not afraid to marry and bring children into the world. The lot of professional scholars is different. They are so concerned with the difficulties of supporting their families that they are unable to study the Torah in depth, and thus their study is merely lip service (Shmuel's Letters, p. 141).

80. Immanuel Etkes, *Rabbi Israel Salanter and the Beginning of the Musar Movement* [in Hebrew] (Jerusalem, 1982), pp. 255–56, 337–40.

81. Rabbi Simcha Zissel Ziv, the "Grandfather of Kelme," ran an educational institution in Gerobin, in Kurland, while his family remained behind in Kelme. See Katz, *The Musar Movement*, II, 65–68. Rabbi Nathan Zvi Finkel, the "Grandfather of Slobodka," founded and directed the Slobodka Yeshiva while his family lived in Kelme. See Katz, *The Musar Movement*, III, 37. Rabbi Yosef Yozel Horowitz, the founder and leader of the Novaredok Yeshiva, lived an extremely ascetic life. After his wife's death he sent his children to various families and refrained from taking another wife. See Katz, *The Musar Movement*, IV, 186.

10

The Modern Jewish Family: Image and Reality

PAULA E. HYMAN

Jews entered the modern era with a powerful myth about the strength and stability of the traditional Jewish family throughout the ages. From the period of the Enlightenment to the last third of the nineteenth century, when a vigorous public debate about Jewish emancipation (and hence about the value of Judaism) raged in Western and Central Europe, even critics of Jewish culture and religion acknowledged the admirable qualities of the Jewish home.[1] Because domestic orderliness and serenity within the patriarchal family were central values of the emerging bourgeois culture of the nineteenth century, Jews seeking to acculturate to the standards of the urban middle classes of their societies could, and did, point to their family life as compelling evidence for the worth of Jewish culture and as a sign of their own adherence to bourgeois norms.

Yet the celebration of the virtues of Jewish family life has gone hand in hand in the modern period with caustic criticism by Jewish communal leaders of the Jewish family of their own time. Indeed, I will argue that, by the second half of the nineteenth century and into our own day, the family has become *the* issue on which concern for assimilation has focused within the Jewish community. Emancipation, mass migration, and entry into urban industrial economies promoted relatively rapid social change among Jews and stimulated feelings of discontinuity with the past. Changing roles for women appeared to disrupt the stability of the home. Alert to the decline in Jewish religious practice, Jewish communal leaders blamed contemporary Jewish families for deviating from the standards of a noble past and attributed assimilation to the Jewish family's alleged failure to maintain its traditional strengths. As the guardian of the hearth in the period of bourgeois domesticity, the Jewish woman, in particular, was held responsible for the behavior of her husband and children. These two contradictory though related themes, of nostalgic pride and contemporary anxiety, have coexisted in Jewish portrayals of the family in modern times.

Before we explore the implications of modern images of the Jewish family, it is useful to survey the characteristics of the Jewish family in modern times. It is, of course, impossible to speak about *the* Jewish family. Jewish families have varied in the past two centuries, as previously, according to country of residence, socioeconomic class, and level of acculturation. In my discussion I will focus on the changing patterns of Jewish families in those areas that first experienced emancipation and industrialization—that is, the countries of Western Europe as well as the United States in the century before World War I.

Family historians have characterized the modern family as a small domestic unit, with few obligations to extended kin and strong barriers between itself and the larger community. Unlike its traditional predecessor, its members demonstrate a large measure of affection (or other form of emotional intensity) for each other. Particularly in its bourgeois format, it is primarily a unit of consumption rather than a unit of production. In many ways, the Jewish family of the West modernized early and rapidly. Even before emancipation, traditional Jewish families possessed many of the attributes that family historians label "modern." For example, as the work of S. D. Goitein and a variety of memoirs reveal,[2] premodern Jewish parents displayed considerable affection for their children at a time when, as Philippe Ariès has noted, "indifference to small children [was] characteristic of all traditional societies."[3] Though marriages were arranged, the development of close emotional bonds between husbands and wives was also not uncommon.

The most striking feature of the Jewish family in modern times has been the early reduction of its fertility. Perhaps because of their strong desire to achieve upward social mobility and the relative uselessness of children in commercial enterprise, Jews have been avid and efficient users of birth control. As my work on the nineteenth-century French Jewish population and Steven Lowenstein's on Bavarian Jews of the same period disclosed, by midcentury Jewish women were giving birth to their last child when they were in their early thirties—a clear sign of the use of birth control.[4] By the last third of the nineteenth century Jews were in the vanguard among Central and West European populations in controlling their fertility, and they have maintained that distinction in twentieth-century Europe and America. Whereas the low birthrate that Jews have demonstrated for the past century can be accounted for in part by their social characteristics—their levels of education and urbanization, as well as their professions, for example—numerous studies have indicated that European and American Jews have had lower birthrates than the general populace even when controlling for such characteristics.[5] The causes of the precipitous decline in Jewish fertility are a subject of vigorous debate, and the connection between Jewishness and family size has not yet been fully elucidated. Moreover, the decline in Jewish fertility in the West did not stimulate communal concern as long as the total Jewish population continued to grow through the immigration of large families from the East.

Just as the size of the Jewish family was dramatically reduced in the modern period, so the roles of its members changed as Jews acculturated to the norms of, and were integrated economically into, the local bourgeoisie. Until the last third of the nineteenth century most Jews in Western Europe and America were petit bourgeois, engaged in the traditional Jewish trades of peddling, dealing in old clothes, and small retailing. A sizable minority lived on the edge of poverty. However, rapid social mobility enabled West European and American Jews—and later East European immigrants to America—to achieve solid middle- and upper-middle-class status in one to two generations.

This success story transformed the roles of women and men within the Jewish family. Like their female counterparts in the Gentile bourgeoisie,[6] who were retired from business life as family firms prospered with industrialization, Jewish women also retreated into the home, where they occupied their time with domestic tasks or management of their household staff or both.[7] Though Jewish tradition had always promoted different roles for men and women, economic necessity and social hardship had modified those gender ideals in practice. Now the amenities of middle-class life enabled their realization, reinforcing with a secular ideology women's subordination to their husbands and channeling women's aspirations for meaningful work into the realm of philanthropy. Indeed, Jewish women's organizations, from local ladies' aid societies through such sizable institutions as the National Council for Jewish Women, Hadassah, and the Juedische Frauenbund were all founded before World War I, in the heyday of the bourgeois century.

The role of Jewish men also changed. With their emancipation and acculturation, Jewish men achieved status virtually exclusively through their success in the world of business or the professions. Only in limited circles did the alternate path of mobility through Torah study remain a viable option. This secularization of communal gender ideals and cultural values for males meant that Jewish men experienced a more wrenching discontinuity with the past than did Jewish women and ceded some of their position as transmitters of Jewish tradition within the home to their wives, whose domain bourgeois ideology held the home to be.

By the middle of the nineteenth century the pronouncements of the educated elite of Western Jewish communities articulated a Jewish version of the bourgeois ideal of family life. An 1848 French-language prayerbook, written and edited by the Chief Rabbi of Strasbourg for private prayer, sharply delineated the roles and responsibilities of husbands and wives. The husband's prayer included the following meditation: "May I never forget that if might and reason are the prerequisite of my sex, hers is subject to bodily weakness and to spiritual sensitivity; do not permit me, Oh Lord, to be unjust to her or to demand from her qualities that are not of her nature. May her weakness even serve as a stay against my might; for it would be cruel to abuse a weak and delicate being whom love and law have placed under my protection."[8] The wife, for her part, was to accept her role as domestic angel to her benevolent provider: "Lord, you have given me a husband as the companion of my life, to guide my steps and to share my destiny. It is from him that I receive my subsistence . . . May I never forget that man's work taxes his soul with cares and troubles and that it is his wife's duty . . . to restore calm and serenity to her husband's heart through her obligingness, her submission, her indulgent character."[9] If the prayerbook presented this ideal of husband-wife relations, it also provided a prayer for a less-than-ideal marriage, a prayer for "an unhappy wife:" "Oh my God, enlighten me so that I may judge myself with severity. Perhaps my husband's conduct is the fruit of my faults and defects; for You are just, Lord, and the fate which I am suffering is doubtless a deserved punishment . . . Oh my Father, restore to me the heart of my husband. Preserve me, my God, from all feelings of hatred or bitterness; and if my husband is inaccessible to pity, make my heart never change towards him."[10] Although traditional Judaism had mandated the submission of wives, the emphasis on female weakness (ironically at a time when industrialization was diminishing the importance of physical strength) is a new theme. In general, the tone of these prayers is far more stringent, far more explicit, than most traditional Jewish sources and is a reflection of the acculturation of nineteenth Jewish elites to the middle-class values of their milieu.

The sentiments of Rabbi Aron's prayerbook are echoed in other writings of nineteenth-century Western Jewish communities. In its first year of publication, in 1844, the London *Jewish Chronicle* described the "masculine virtues [as] firmness, seriousness, and self-dependence" while noting that "woman, to whom nature has denied this strength and fixedness of purpose, . . . makes up this deficiency of power, by converting her feebleness into mildness, tenderness, softness, and sincerity."[11] A generation later (1875), in an editorial opposing women's suffrage, the paper commented with approval that "Judaism throughout its whole history makes a well-recognised distinction between the sexes. In family life, where the power finally to decide must reside somewhere, it subordinates woman to man . . . [N]ature by having as a rule with but few exceptions denied to woman that robustness of constitution and that physical strength requisite for self-protection . . . has clearly made her dependent upon the strong arm of her male companion . . . No doubt, woman, like all dependents, is subject to great disadvantages—many more than should have fallen to her lot . . . [S]uffrage would . . . only increase them by taking her out of the sphere which is her natural home—appointed home!"[12] In a gentler tone a bride prays, in an 1858 German prayerbook written by a woman for private devotions, to keep her husband's love by appearing to him "in raiments of virtue and grace" and by performing her duties "with diligence and zeal" and perfectly realizing her pursuits "as an attentive, orderly, prudently managing housewife."[13] Accentuating the positive, the *American Israelite* of April 5, 1861, praised the "exalted position" and utility of the wife and mother whose "noble counsel," "sweet temper," and "good manners" bring "peace and harmony" to the household and make her husband so happy that "he earns abundantly."[14] Though these statements prescribed communal ideals, it is, of course, difficult to ascertain how closely Jewish husbands and wives of the period adhered in their daily behavior to this bourgeois code of domestic felicity.

With all the changes of size and domestic sentiment that accompanied emancipation, acculturation, and social mobility, there were many aspects of continuity in the modern Jewish family of the West. In a pioneering article on European Jewish family life on the threshold of the modern period,[15] Jacob Katz cited as a key aspect of the modernization of the Jewish family the introduction of freedom of choice in the selection of one's spouse. Yet that innovation occurred far later and more gradually than previously thought. As Marian Kaplan's recent significant article, "For Love or Money: The Marriage Strategies of Jews in Imperial Germany,"[16] conclusively demonstrates, as a rule German Jews found the economic foundation of marriage too important to leave the choice of a marriage partner to young people. Only after World War I, when inflation destroyed savings and women's earning potential replaced the formal dowry, did the ideology of romantic love truly supplant the arranged marriage. Along with Aron's prayerbook, several sources on the Jews of Alsace, published in the 1850s, 1860s, and 1870s[17] (two to three generations after emancipation), also attest to the prevalence of arranged marriages, complete with formal *shadkhn* (matchmaker) and dowry. All that had changed was that the parents and couple in such arranged marriages, bowing to the new ideal of love matches, conspired to hide the arranged nature of the match.

Just as the patterns of family formation display continuity in the nineteenth century, so does the age at which Jews in the West married. Whereas a Jewish physician, writing in Lemberg (Lvov) in 1821, exhorted the readers of his bilingual Hebrew/Yiddish child-rearing manual *Giddul Banim* to abandon the custom of adolescent marriages[18]—a cause taken up by later maskilim[19]—Jews in Central and Western Europe had given up that practice by the eighteenth century. In the nineteenth century they generally followed the patterns of the local bourgeoisie in marital timing. Jewish women in Alsace, for example, married for the first time at a mean age of close to twenty-seven from the 1820s through the 1840s, and twenty-eight in the 1860s, at ages approximately the same as Gentile women. Their husbands were, on the average, two to three years older than their brides.[20] Bavarian Jews married even later in the first half of the nineteenth century, largely owing to a combination of economic circumstances and restrictive legislation, and maintained a median of about twenty-five for women and about thirty for men from the 1860s through the 1920s.[21] In Baden, too, throughout the nineteenth and twentieth centuries Jews demonstrated similar patterns of age at marriage.[22] Only in America, among Jews of German origin, was the pattern slightly different. Whereas the men waited to wed until they were financially established, in their late twenties or early thirties, the women, who were in relatively scarce supply, married in their late teens or early twenties.[23]

As age at marriage remained relatively stable for Jews in the century of change associated with emancipation and social mobility, so the family also retained its centrality for Jews seeking the rewards of social mobility. It is true that most modern Jews in the West lived in two-generation nuclear families, but the claims of kin were important. Jewish family firms were often founded by brothers, and family contacts sustained the mercantile success of Jewish entrepreneurs in both Europe and America.[24] Dozens of memoirs reveal that when young Jews from villages in Alsace or Baden or Bavaria set out for the big city or a foreign land to make their fortune or further their education, they turned to their uncles or cousins for lodging.[25] Often these bonds between members of the extended family were nurtured by middle-class women, for whom the cultivation of family contacts was part of their domestic responsibility. Denied higher education and freed from responsibilities for making a living, before marriage, Jewish women of leisure made the rounds of their relatives, enjoying new sights, tending the elderly, and meeting eligible prospects. Later, as housewives, they combined entertainment of kin with celebration of the festivals of the Jewish year.[26]

Although the nuclear family was the predominant form of family structure for Jews in the nineteenth century, the extended family was not only available for support, but it was also often nearby. With all the mobility that characterized the nineteenth century, family ties were not destroyed. My study of the Jews of Alsace, based on manuscript censuses, reveals some interesting phenomena. In Strasbourg at mid-century, for example, 14 percent of the Jewish households were extended families, containing grandparents, unmarried sisters or brothers, or other relatives. Another 20 percent of the households had relatives living in the neighborhood, half of them in the same building. This was the case despite the fact that about two-thirds of Strasbourg's Jewish household heads had not been born in the city.[27] In the three Alsatian villages and towns that I studied the pattern was similar. Ten percent of the households contained extended families whereas almost 30 percent of the Jews had close kin living in the same locale, 18 percent in the same dwelling.[28] If borne out by studies of other Jewish populations, these findings would indicate that kin ties maintained their hold on Jews in the West even in an era that enshrined the nuclear family and offered

unparalleled opportunities for individual advancement. In the nineteenth century, at least, the Jewish family was a stable institution with
important emotional, social, and economic claims on its members.

Despite this stability, the family attracted considerable attention on
the part of Jewish communal figures. This is not surprising, for the family
became an object of fascination in the bourgeois century. As Peter Gay
has noted in his magisterial study of the nineteenth-century bourgeoisie,
"[P]oets and painters idealized [the family], social scientists anatomized
[it], and ideologues put [it] on trial. A handful of emancipated, radical
feminists preferred to do without the family; utopian socialists offered
blueprints for its replacement; the Marxists diagnosed it as transient . . .
and conservatives . . . discerned little but threats to its integrity and decline from its historic eminence."[29] Jewish commentators responded not
only to perceptions of rapid social change shared with non-Jews but also
to the special place of the family in Jewish apologetics and identity. In
taking up the family as an object of both pride and concern, they ham-
mered out their strategies for self-defense and for combating
assimilation.

The dominant theme sounded by Jewish writers, scholars, and artists
who depicted the Jewish family was one of pride. In an age that held
up so many aspects of Jewish experience to criticism or ridicule, they
could point to traditional Jewish family life as a model of noble domestic
behavior and thereby rehabilitate both Judaism and the Jews. Often
they trumpeted the superiority of the Jewish family to that of the surrounding population. "Nowhere is family sentiment more profound than
among the Jews," claimed the *Archives israélites* in 1846. "There, conjugal love and parental love still exist in all their strength. This is not a
privilege of wealth: in the most modest classes, crimes which offend
nature are never committed. One never hears of a depraved father, of
a mother who has antipathy for her children, of a son who refuses
assistance to his elderly parents."[30] In a similar vein, responding to an
anti-Semitic article in the popular *Family Herald*, the London *Jewish
Chronicle* in 1851 and 1852 referred to instances of murder, child aban-
donment, and infanticide, brought on because of ignorance of God's
law, and then asked of the *Family Herald*'s editor "to tell us how many
divorces have been decreed among the Jews of this country within the
last ten years, since divorces are so very easy among them; and how
many women have poisoned their husbands among the professors of
other creeds for want of that humane custom and law."[31] Or, again, in
1875, the *Jewish Chronicle* noted smugly: "The papers have again lately

reported several cases of wife beating. This iniquity, we are happy to see, is very rare in the Jewish community."[32] In addition to praising contemporary Jewish family life, Jewish journals in England, France, Germany, and the United States frequently published articles defending the domestic attitudes and practices of the ancient Hebrews and of the Talmudic rabbis, particularly in contrast with the allegedly immoral and degrading customs of the surrounding peoples.[33]

This effusion of newspaper articles and editorials was accompanied in the nineteenth century by the proliferation of "ghetto tales" and genre paintings celebrating the virtues of traditional Jewish family life. Leopold Kompert, Ludwig Philippson, and Berthold Auerbach in German, and Daniel Stauben, Alexandre Weill, and Léon Cahun in French presented romanticized and sympathetic portrayals of a Jewish way of life now past or fast disappearing.[34] As Ismar Schorsch has persuasively argued with respect to the painter Moritz Oppenheim, whose *Bilder aus dem altjuedischen Familienleben* in portfolio and bound editions enjoyed enormous popularity in Germany, these works provided a powerful refutation of both the Enlightenment and conservative critiques of Judaism as religion and culture.[35] Because so much of Jewish ritual is family-centered, it was simple and authentic to introduce Jewish customs and the rhythm of the Jewish calendar in a family setting.

By anchoring their defense of Judaism in scenes of family life whose warmth, dignity, and moral tone had to resonate with an audience steeped in bourgeois domesticity, these writers and artists were able to transmute admiration for family virtues into respect for the religion in which those virtues were nurtured. Léon Cahun went so far as to find in family the source of Jewish survival and the promise of Jewish good citizenship. "It is neither the rabbis, nor the synagogue, nor the Talmud, nor even the law or persecution which preserved the Jewish religion," he asserted. "It is the love of parents for children, the love of children for parents—it is the family . . . One should not mock this quasi dogma-less religion in which the family is everything, for in giving free rein to the Jew's veneration for his ancestors, it opens the way for his ancient instincts of passionate love for the polity (cité); since the revolution which recognized us as legitimate children of the fatherland, our polity—those of us from Alsace—is the Gallic polity, is France."[36]

This pride in the Jewish family and assertion of its virtues as proof of the moral worth of Judaism was mixed with concern for the survival of those virtues in the absence of traditional Jewish observance. As early as 1859, in a review of a book entitled *L'Amour*, the *Archives israélites* added a cautionary note to the commonplace claim that "this ideal marriage was realized in Israel . . . more frequently than elsewhere . . . May progress and indifference not disturb this cult of the family," it concluded. "Aren't there too many examples that already prove how threatened is this glorious superiority?"[37] This theme of the Jewish family endangered by the new opportunities offered by a more tolerant society appeared ever more frequently, as evidence of radical assimilation—particularly in the form of intermarriage—captured the attention of modern Jewish communities.[38]

Connecting manifestations of assimilation in all its forms with a failure of the family, Jewish leaders laid that failure at the feet of Jewish mothers. This is not surprising, for bourgeois ideology conferred on wives and mothers responsibility for the moral and religious tone of the home. If the family was no longer succeeding in transmitting Jewish knowledge and loyalty to the younger generation, then the guardians of the hearth had fallen down in their task. What was new in these accusations against Jewish mothers was the presumption that all truly significant Jewish education of the young took place within the home and that mothers must be the transmitters of Jewish knowledge and identity to their children. As early as 1844, the London *Jewish Chronicle* called for the religious instruction of females, "for how is a mother enabled to engraft in the heart of her tender offspring dogmas strange to herself? . . . Externally restrained by political hindrance and by allurements of apostasy, . . . these young shoots require especial and particular maternal vigilance and attendance."[39] Similarly, in 1852 the *Archives israélites*, responding to the growing religious indifference it saw in French Jewish society, baldly stated, "[T]he health of our religion depends henceforth above all on the education of girls."[40] Here it presented in full its vision of the postemancipation model of the Jewish family: "Our fathers, absorbed by their business, their commerce, their industry, their travels . . . can not follow with a vigilant eye the physical, moral and intellectual progress of the young family; they abandon that care to maternal solicitude. The woman is the guardian angel of the house; . . . her religiosity, her virtues, are a living example for the children whom she has constantly under her eyes . . . Man exists for public life, woman for domestic life."[41] German-Jewish communal spokespersons concurred that women bore a heavy responsibility for religious survival. "Women are giants who carry the world on their shoulders by caring for the home," wrote one editorialist. "If the religious home falls, so does the world of religion."[42] American Jewish writers, too, drew on sentimental maternal images to enlist women in this new task of Jewish education. As an article in *The American Hebrew* queried in 1895, "Can there be a more beautiful picture than that of the mother resting after a busy day, gathering around her her little ones, and in the warm firelight drawing their thoughts to the Father above[?]"[43] In the same journal, Kaufman Kohler, drawing on more vigorous female role models, reiterated the necessity for Jewish women to become, in his words, "the standard-bearer[s] of religion . . . Will the time not be nigh," he reflected, "when we may again have our Miriams and Deborahs . . . A bread-and-butter Judaism, a soup-kitchen Sisterhood is not enough. We need nurture for the soul. We need Jewesses to give us again Jewish homes, Jewish men, a Judaism spiritualized."[44]

Though the elevation of the Jewish woman to the status of primary religious influence on her home and children made possible her access to Jewish education, much communal ambivalence was attached to this new status. In the first place, Jewish women bore the brunt of communal criticism for the flourishing of assimilation among the younger generation—this despite the fact that throughout the nineteenth and twentieth centuries it is Jewish men who have outpaced Jewish women in both apostasy and intermarriage. Thus, in 1904, while praising bourgeois Jewish mothers with one voice for their maternal devotion and involvement in their children's studies, the *Archives israélites* damned them with another for failing to make them Jews.[45] And in Texas Jewish women were pointedly reminded of their new responsibilities: "You as daughters of Sarah and Rebecca, ought never to forget that it is your sacred duty . . . to instruct your children, to give them a religious and moral training . . . [R]emember that there is a great debt of responsibility resting upon you, and that you are held accountable for the acts of your children."[46] Communal critics were convinced that the ultimate cause of assimilation was the decline in religious observance and sensibility among women. "[P]ossibly there is no feature of the age more dangerous or more distressing than the growing irreligion of women," wailed the *Jewish Chronicle* in 1875. "It was formerly a fact, and it is at present a fancy, that women are more religious . . . than men."[47] The *Archives israélites* also noted with regret in 1889 that Jewish women were not the models of piety they had been just fifty years before: "All the general qualities of the modern woman have developed in her at the expense of the particular qualities of the Jew." And therefore, "she leaves her children, unfortunately, in absolute ignorance of their faith."[48]

For some communal spokespersons the role of domestic educator was so important that it precluded any other role for Jewish women. The London *Jewish Chronicle*, for example, opposed women's suffrage, higher secular education for women, and their employment on the grounds that "the glitter of the world" diverted women from their most solemn, and apparently exclusive, task of guiding the moral and religious development of their children.[49] And the *Archives israélites* contended that women continue to be barred from synagogue administration because the natural forum for their religious influence was the home.[50] At least temporarily, then, the ideology that placed women at the heart of the Jewish identity formation of their children could promote a social conservatism on issues affecting female roles.

By focusing on the failings of Jewish mothers as transmitters of Jewish culture to their children, communal leaders were able to project on women their own guilt over their inability to set limits to assimilation. In doing so, they transformed assimilation from an individual to a familial act, from activity in the public (masculine) sphere to inactivity in the domestic (feminine) sphere. They thereby reshaped communal perceptions and discussion of the Jewish family. Even as the Jewish family remained relatively stable—and perhaps more resistant to change than other aspects of Jewish life—Jewish spokespersons from the end of the last century until our own day have combined the old expressions of pride, increasingly retrojected into the past, with new themes of the decline and crisis of the Jewish family of their own time. The modern Jewish family, as ideological construct, has thus become the symbol for the deleterious consequences of assimilation, for the discontinuities of modern Jewish history. On the threshold of the modern era its idealized image was superior to its social reality; for the past century the reality of Jewish family life has been more favorable than its image.

NOTES

1. For an extended discussion of this point, see my introduction to Steven M. Cohen and Paula E. Hyman, eds., *The Jewish Family: Myths and Reality* (New York, 1986), pp. 3–4.

2. S. D. Goitein, *A Mediterranean Society: The Jewish Communities of the*

Arab World as Portrayed in the Documents of the Cairo Geniza, 4 vols. (Berkeley and Los Angeles, 1978). III: *The Family; The Memoirs of Glueckel of Hameln*, trans. and with notes by Marvin Lowenthal (New York, 1977); *Die Memoiren des Asher Levy aus Reichshofen im Elsass* [in Hebrew and German], trans. and edited by Moses Ginsburger (Berlin, 1913).

3. Philippe Ariès, *The Hour of Our Death*, trans. Helen Weaver (New York, 1981), p. 447. It is important to note that Ariès's claims of the indifference of premodern parents to their children have been challenged.

4. Paula Hyman, "Jewish Fertility in Nineteenth Century France," in *Modern Jewish Fertility*, ed. Paul Ritterband (Leiden, 1981), pp. 82–83, 91; see also Steven M. Lowenstein, "Voluntary and Involuntary Limitation of Fertility in Nineteenth Century Bavarian Jewry," in Ritterband, ed., *Modern Jewish Fertility*, pp. 99–103.

5. See Ritterband, ed., *Modern Jewish Fertility*; John Knodel, *The Decline of Fertility in Germany, 1871–1939* (Princeton, N.J., 1974), pp. 137–38; see also U. O. Schmeltz, *Jewish Population Studies* (Jerusalem, 1970).

6. Bonnie Smith, *Ladies of the Leisure Class: The Bourgeoises of Northern France in the Nineteenth Century* (Princeton, N.J., 1981).

7. See Charlotte Baum, Paula Hyman, and Sonya Michel, *The Jewish Woman in America* (New York, 1976), pp. 26–27; Marion Kaplan, "The Acculturation, Assimilation and Integration of Jews in Imperial Germany: A Gender Analysis," *Leo Baeck Institute Yearbook* 27 (1982), 9–10.

8. Arnaud Aron, *Prières d'un coeur israélite: Recueil de prières et de méditations pour toutes des circonstances de la vie* (Strasbourg, 1848), p. 263.

9. Aron, *Prières d'un coeur israélite*, pp. 264–65.

10. Aron, *Prières d'un coeur israélite*, pp. 266–67.

11. *Jewish Chronicle*, New Series, 1 (1844–45), 54.

12. *Jewish Chronicle*, Dec. 3, 1875, p. 577.

13. Fanny Neuda, *Stunden der Andacht* (Leipzig, 1858), pp. 74, 76.

14. As cited in Baum et al., *The Jewish Woman in America*, p. 29.

15. Jacob Katz, "Marriage and Sexual Life Among the Jews at the End of the Middle Ages" [in Hebrew], *Zion* 10 (1944), 21–54.

16. *Leo Baeck Institute Yearbook* 28 (1983), 263–300.

17. *Prières d'un coeur israélite*, pp. 278–79; Alexandre Weill, *Couronne* (Paris, 1857), p. 117; idem., *Histoire de Village* (Paris, 1860), p. 219; Daniel Stauben, *Scènes de la vie juive en Alsace* (Paris, 1860), pp. 41–53; Edouard Coypel, *Le Judaïsme: Esquisse des moeurs juives* (Mulhouse, 1876), pp. 109–10; Léon Cahun, *La Vie juive* (Paris, 1886), p. 33.

18. Moses Mahl, *Giddul Banim* (Lemberg, 1821), pp. 8–10.

19. David Biale, "Childhood, Marriage, and the Family in the Eastern European Jewish Enlightenment," in Steven M. Cohen and Paula E. Hyman, eds., *The Jewish Family*, pp. 45–61.

20. My calculations from marriage records. Archives départementales du Bas-

Rhin (hereafter A.D.B.R.) 4E 330, 4E 226, and Bischheim (1813–32)(1833–42)(1843–52)(1853–62); 5MI 1663 Strasbourg: Archives départementales du Haut-Rhin, 5E 105 and 5M 1 66R.50, colmar.

21. Lowenstein, "Voluntary and Involuntary Limitation," pp. 98–99.

22. Alice Goldstein, "Some Demographic Characteristics of Village Jews in Germany: Nonnenweier, 1800–1931," in Ritterband, ed., *Modern Jewish Fertility*, p. 123.

23. See, e.g., William Toll, *The Making of an Ethnic Middle Class: Portland Jewry over Four Generations* (Albany, N.Y., 1982), p. 46.

24. See, e.g., the memoir of Isidor Hirschfeld in *Juedisches Leben in Deutschland: Selbstzeugnisse zur Sozialgeschichte im Kaiserreich*, ed. Monika Richarz (Stuttgart, 1979), pp. 246–50; see also Toll, *The Making of an Ethnic Middle Class*, pp. 10–16.

25. See, e.g., Edmund Uhry. "Gallery of Memories," unpublished memoir, Archives of the Leo Baeck Institute; see also the memoir of Samuel Spiro, in Richarz, ed., *Juedisches Leben in Deutschland*, p. 146.

26. Marian Kaplan, "Priestess and Hausfrau: Women and Tradition in the German-Jewish Family," in Steven M. Cohen and Paula E. Hyman, eds., *The Jewish Family*, pp. 62–81.

27. My calculations from manuscript census data, A.D.B.R. VII M 719, 726, 733, 740 (Strasbourg, 1846).

28. My calculations from manuscript census data from the three towns and villages of Bischheim, Niederroedern, and Itterswiller, A.D.B.R. VII M 266 (Bischheim, 1836–46); VII M 562 (Niederroedern, 1836–66); and VII M 459 (Itterswiller, 1836–66).

29. Peter Gay, *The Bourgeois Experience* (New York and Oxford, 1984), 2 vols. I: *Education of the Senses*, p. 423.

30. *Archives israélites* 7 (1846), 110–11.

31. *Jewish Chronicle*, September 5, 1851, p. 377, and March 1852, p. 206.

32. *Jewish Chronicle*, September 17, 1875, p. 396. The *Archives israélites* (51 [1890], 59) also noted in response to anti-Semitic envy of Jewish success that that success can be laid at the feet of Jewish parents, all of whom encourage their children to attend school and to excel there and also provide them with living examples of self-discipline.

33. See, e.g., *Jewish Chronicle* 1 (1844–45), 239; September 5, 1851, p. 381; April 9, 1875, pp. 866–67; January 19, 1883, pp. 9–10. See also *Archives israélites* 9 (1848), 231–41; 13 (1852), 559–69, 608–17; 27 (1866), 490–91, 888–91; 30 (1869), 270–1; 35 (1874), 55–56; 46 (1885), 373–75; 56 (1895), 26; 61 (1900), 386–87. See, further, *The American Hebrew*, March 23, 1894, pp. 619–21; February 5, 1895, pp. 435–36; Feb. 12, 1895, p. 461; March 8, 1895, pp. 515–18.

34. These works were extremely popular and were published and republished from the late 1830s into the beginning of the twentieth century. Kompert and Auerbach were also translated into French and English. It should be pointed

out that Cahun's *La Vie juive* was illustrated with lithographs by Alphonse Lévy depicting scenes of Jewish life in Alsace.

35. Ismar Schorsch, "Art as Social History: Oppenheim and the German Jewish Vision of Emancipation," in *Moritz Oppenheim: The First Jewish Painter* [in English], ed. Barbara Gingold and Judy Levy (Jerusalem, 1983), pp. 39–51.

36. Léon Cahun, *La Vie juive* (Paris, 1886), pp. 97–98.

37. *Archives israélites* 20 (1859), 124.

38. See, e.g., *Archives israélites* 14 (1853), 306–17; 43 (1882), 177–78; 44 (1883), 98; 51 (1890), 258; 63 (1902), 25–26; 65 (1904), 65–67.

39. *Jewish Chronicle* 1 (1844–45), 55.

40. *Archives israélites* 13 (1852), 612.

41. *Archives israélites* 13 (1852), 612.

42. As cited in Kaplan, "Priestess and Hausfrau," in Steven M. Cohen and Paula E. Hyman, eds., *The Jewish Family*, p. 62.

43. *The American Hebrew*, March 8, 1895, p. 516.

44. *The American Hebrew*, March 23, 1894, p. 621.

45. *Archives israélites*, 65 (1904), 305–6.

46. As cited by Beth Wenger, "The Southern Lady and the Jewish Woman: The Early Organizational Life of Atlanta's Jewish Women," senior thesis, Wesleyan University, 1985.

47. *Jewish Chronicle*, March 12, 1875, p. 801.

48. *Archives israélites* 50 (1889), 399–400.

49. *Jewish Chronicle*, Dec. 3, 1875, p. 577.

50. *Archives israélites*, 56 (1895), 26.

PART IV

FAMILY RELATIONS AS METAPHOR

11

Sexual Metaphors and Praxis in the Kabbalah

MOSHE IDEL

Two major usages of sexual imagery, metaphors and praxis, occur in the kabbalistic literature. For describing these usages, it is reasonable to divide various types of sexual discussions into two main parts, according to their referents on the theological or theosophical plan. (1) When the relationship symbolized by the sexual imagery or praxis is between humans and God, I shall refer to it as "vertical symbolism." (2) When the relation the sexual imagery or praxis is pointing to is a process taking place between entities found on the same level, it will be referred to as "horizontal symbolism." "Vertical symbolism" can be found in the two main kabbalistic schools: the theosophical kabbalah, whose main chef d'oeuvre is the thirteenth-century *Zohar*, and in the ecstatic kabbalah, represented by the thirteenth-century writings of R. Abraham Abulafia and his followers; the "horizontal symbolism" recurs almost exclusively in the theosophical kabbalah.

Roughly speaking, the two main types of symbols occur already in the classical rabbinic texts, the Talmud and the midrash. However, the medieval kabbalists, who adopted the already existing sexual motifs, elaborated on details of rabbinic thoughts concerning sexual issues and sometimes integrated philosophical ideas, which contributed mainly to the formulations occurring in the ecstatic kabbalah.

Let us begin with the vertical symbolism. This type of symbolism includes two differing kinds of symbols.[1] The theosophical kabbalah refers to the divine manifestations as female partner whereas the kabbalists or the ideal figures of the remote antiquity (biblical or rabbinic heroes) are conceived of as playing the role of the male in their relation to the Divine. The ecstatic kabbalah, on the other hand, presents the mystic or his spiritual faculties as the female whereas the supernal powers (viz. the active intellect or God Himself) are viewed as the male partner. I would refer to the theosophical usage of vertical as well as horizontal symbolism as "descending symbolism."

This term, which was proposed and defined by Erich Kahler,[2] indicates a case when "symbolic representation detaches itself, descends to us, from a prior and higher reality, a reality determining, and therefore superior to, its symbolic meaning. That is to say, genuinely mythical and cultic works are not intended as symbolic representation, they are meant to describe real happenings."

In our case, the "higher reality" is the processes taking place in the infradivine world, namely, the domain of the *sephirot* ("the potencies and modes of action of the living God,")[3] which serve as archetypes for both the vertical and horizontal processes.

On the other hand, the vertical symbolism of the ecstatic kabbalah will be referred to as "ascending symbolism,"[4] this phrase expressing the elevation of a corporeal, human sexual act to the status of a metaphor for the relationship between the human soul and supernal entities.

I shall start with an analysis of the history of the vertical ascending symbolism.

Vertical Ascending Symbolism

It is a commonplace that mystical literatures incline to express the relationship between the mystic's soul and the divine by means of erotic imagery.[5] All the classical bodies of mystical writings can easily provide numerous examples, sometimes striking ones, wherein sexual images are openly and often employed. Kabbalah has nothing unique on this issue; it also extensively uses sexual images and metaphors. However, there is something novel in this body of literature that transcends the more common usage of erotic and sexual motifs. The difference lies not so much in the texts, but in their sociological contexts.

Unlike their Christian correspondents, the Jewish mystics who adopted sexual imagery in order to describe their experience of the divine shared with other Jews the conviction that actual marriage and fulfillment of the commandment of multiplying are a religious imperative. The kabbalists, therefore, can hardly be regarded as persons who employed sexual metaphors as a compensation for the frustration of the "real" erotic experiences.[6] Abraham Abulafia, Isaac of Acre, or any other kabbalists who will be mentioned later were seemingly married or, at least, persons who viewed sexual relations as religiously licit. Therefore, the very recurrence of this type of imagery in Jewish sources is evidence that the relatively common explanation offered by some scholars to the genesis of sexual imagery in the repressed libido can be no more than a partial solution.

A short survey of the vertical ascending symbolism evinces that it occurs in two major types of texts: the ancient classical Jewish literature and medieval kabbalistic literature. In the Bible and the talmudic-midrashic texts the relation between God and the Jewish people, sometimes designated as *Knesset Israel*, is described as the relation between husband and wife. This was also the main avenue adopted in the exegetical literature of the *Song of Songs* in medieval texts, which regarded the plain meaning of the biblical text to be concerned with the people of Israel and God. This is obviously a part of the national myth, which changes the entire nation into one entity standing in sexual relation to the other entity—the Divinity. This mythical relationship has little to do with mysticism; it is interested primarily in the whole nation as a unit whereas the particular Jew is rather neglected as a meaningful factor. The individual, according to classical Jewish texts, can take part in this bond with God by his participation in the significant great unity, *Knesset Israel* (the community of Israel). His activity, therefore, must be focused on becoming a part of this larger body. The erotic and sexual imagery occurs, in my opinion, solely on this plane: the relation of the mythical *Knesset Israel* with God. This bond mediates between the individual Jew and the divinity whenever this relation is expressed in sexual terms. It is only later, in the medieval period, that beside this mythical bond, expressed in marital terminology, a mystical relation between the individual and God made its appearance. The human soul or, sometimes, the human intellect was conceived of as female in its relation to a supernal "male" entity, be it the active intellect—viewed as a cosmic force—or God Himself.[7] This is the pattern adopted since the late twelfth-century by Jewish philosophers, and from them it infiltrated into the ecstatic kabbalah.

To illustrate this, I have chosen examples that permit us to perceive the neutralization of the mythical aspect of *Knesset Israel* as it appears in classical rabbinic texts or in the theosophical kabbalah,[8] and its transformation into an allegory of a human spiritual capacity.

In his *Gan Naul*, Abraham Abulafia writes: "The Song of Songs is only an allegory to *Knesset Israel* and God, the latter being a perfect bridegroom to her, and she is for Him a perfect bride, He—on the divine plane—she—on the human plane . . . and the human love does not unite with the divine one except after long studies and after comprehension of wisdom and reception of prophecy."[9]

Therefore, the attainment of "prophecy"—namely, of ecstatic experience—is tantamount to the union of a bride and her bridegroom. The nature of the bridegroom is obvious: God; the bride, however, named *Knesset Israel*, is human. On the basis of this passage alone it seems evident that *Knesset Israel* is conceived as an individual entity; after all, the reception of prophecy is, commonly, an individual experience. Furthermore, Abulafia let us know, in another work, that "the secret of *Knesset Israel* is . . . *Knesset I-Sar-El* (that which is gathered by the Prince removed ten [sephirotic] stages from God), since the perfect man brings everything together, he is called the community of Jacob."[10]

The transition from the perfect nation as the partner of God to the individual soul is evident in this comment. The wise man stands for the whole "community of Jacob," for he includes *Knesset* in his mind, the Active Intellect, which is represented by the word *Israel*. This ecstatic experience is described by Abulafia, again using strong erotic themes, as *unio mystica*: "This is the power of man: he can link the lower part with the higher one and the lower (part) will ascend to and unite with the supernal (part) and the higher (part) will descend and will kiss the entity ascending toward it, like a bridegroom actually kisses his bride, out of his great and real desire, characteristic of the delight of both, coming from the power of God (or His Name)."[11]

According to Abulafia, the final aim of ecstasy is the "pleasure of the bridegroom and bride," an expression recurring several times in his writings.[12] This union of the human and Divine represents a clear shift not only from the mythical to mystical, from national to individual, but also from the traditional terminology to the philosophical one. According to an anonymous treatise from the Abulafian school, "the rational faculty, named the rational soul, which received the divine influx, is called *Knesset Israel*, whose secret is the Active Intellect."[13]

Therefore "Israel," or "Knesset Israel," represents the human intellect, which is related, in a secret way, to the supernal Intellect. The nature of the secret seems to be the gematria,[14] *Israel* being tantamount to *Sekhel ha-Po'el* (the active intellect)[15].

Let us summarize the shift from the classical to the speculative view of *Knesset Israel* as the spouse of God: only when it was interpreted as referring to the individual was this term related to the mystical union between two monads. Only then could the kabbalist see himself as the "female" into whom the divine spark is sown and the spiritual son born. That is, a transmutation of the human spirit takes place as a result of contact with the divine.[16] It is important also to remark that the epithalamic symbolism[17] used by Abulafia is sometimes transcended by the occurrence of unitive symbolism.[18] For example, the passage previously quoted from *Or ha-Sekhel* appears immediately after the following passage: "The Name [of God] is composed from two parts[19] since there are two parts of love [divided between] two lovers, and the [parts of] love turn one (entity) when love became actuated. The divine intellectual love and the human intellectual love are conjuncted, being one."[20]

Before leaving this type of metaphors, it must be emphasized that an actual experience of a sexual contact is not essential for the ecstatic kabbalist. He may have experienced it or not in the past or still enjoy it (or not) in the present; the very act of sexual union plays no ritualistic role in the mystical experience.[21] By its nature, ecstatic kabbalah is mostly interested in spiritual processes, for which the corporeal actions would be only a hindrance.

Vertical Descending Symbolism

"If a man and woman are worthwhile, the divine presence dwells between them, if not—they shall be consumed by fire."[22] What is the significance of this talmudic dictum? Is it merely a warning intended to strengthen the laws of purity? Perhaps. This possibility notwithstanding, I should like to propose a more elaborate interpretation, which regards the act of union between husband and wife, when performed according to the Jewish ritual, as fraught with theurgical [23] meaning. Or, to put it otherwise, the perfect sexual union[24] actually influences the Divine Pres-

ence, causing it to dwell with the worthy pair. When the union is performed by impure persons, on the other hand, the result is fatal: fire
will devour them.

The pair of opposites, the favorable presence of divinity versus the
devouring fire, reminds us of the possibility inherent in another situation:
the entrance into the innermost Jewish sanctuary. Moses was able to
hear the divine voice from among the cherubim in the Tabernacle
whereas Nadav and Abihu were consumed by fire as they entered the
sanctuary.[25] Is this parallelism a sheer coincidence? Is there any significant affinity between the pure sexual union and the sanctuary? It seems
to me that the answer is yes. The divine presence was conceived as
dwelling between the two cherubim.[26] This biblical view was elaborated
in the Talmud; The cherubim turn toward each other when Israel performs the commandments, but when they sin the cherubim turn their
faces away from each other.[27] Therefore, by the fulfillment of the divine
will the cherubim change their position, as apparently described in another talmudic passage: "When Israel used to make the pilgrimage, they
(i.e., the priests) would roll up for them the *Parokhet* (curtain) and
show them the Cherubim which were intertwined with one another, and
say to them: 'Behold! Your love before God is like the love of male
and female.' "[28]

It seems, therefore, that the fulfillment of the divine will and the love
of God for Israel find their expression in the sexually oriented position
of the cherubim. But God's love for Israel is not tantamount to the love
of one cherub for another; the cherubim do not stand for God and
Israel. Only the nature of the love of male and female is a metaphor of
the divine love.

The dwelling of the divine presence between the cherubim and between the pure husband and wife are but particular cases of a more
general intention, expressed by the midrashic statement: "The natural
place of the Shekhinah was below."[29] The building of the Temple or
the performance of the commandments—and in our case those connected to the sexual act—are intended to restore the pristine state of
the divine presence.

Interestingly enough, a most important talmudic discussion on the
imperative to prepare a residence for the Shekhinah is again explicitly
connected to procreation.[30] There Ben Azai's refusal to marry in order
to devote himself to the study of Torah is sharply condemned by some
early sages; R. Eliezer even proclaims that whoever abstains from procreation will be punished by death, on the basis of the example of Nadav

and Avihu, who died, according to this interpretation, because "they had no children" (Num. 3:4).[31] An alternative explanation for the transgression of abstention is the fact that such an abstention causes the retraction of the Shekhinah from Israel, this view being sustained by the verse "to be a God unto thee and to thy seed after thee (Gen. 17:7). The anonymous sage continues: "[w]henever thy seed is after thee, the Shekhinah dwells [below], [whenever] there is no seed after thee, upon whom will the Shekhinah dwell? Upon trees and upon stones." Therefore, procreation is indispensable for attainment of the ideal state of the Shekhinah. Not only is She present during the very act of union between husband and wife,[32] but owing to the productive nature of this act She continues to dwell below.

The affinity between the presence of the Shekhinah on the cherubim in the Temple and Her dwellings on the pure human pair is, in my opinion, highly significant. It seems as if the religious role of the cherubim was transferred to human pairs; when the Temple was destroyed, its function was partially preserved by the human activity. This transfer was seemingly facilitated by the existence of a very ancient conception of the Holy of Holies as a bedroom. According to a Gnostic treatise preserved in Nag Hammadi: "The mysteries of truth are revealed, though in type and image; the bridal chamber however, remains hidden. It is the holy in the holy. The veil at first concealed how God controlled the creation, but when the veil is rent and the things inside are revealed, this house will be left desolate."[33] Or "There were three buildings specially for sacrifice in Jerusalem. The one facing west was called the 'Holy.' Another facing the south was called the 'Holy of the Holy.' The third facing east was called the 'Holy of the Holiest' . . . the Holy of the Holies is the bridal chamber."[34]

It seems that these Gnostic texts reflect an already existing Jewish perception of the Temple. According to *Midrash Tanhuma*, commenting on the reference to the royal bed in *Song of Songs* 3:7, the anonymous commentator asserts that " 'his [Solomon's] bed'— this is the Temple. And why is the Temple compared to the bed? Just as this bed serves fruitfulness and multiplication, so too the Temple, everything that was in it was fruitful and multiplied."[35]

Let us focus on the assertion that the veil "concealed how God controlled the creation." It seems plausible to assume that the Gnostic author intended to hint at a sexual act taking place in the holy of the holiest, for the latter is viewed as "a bridal chamber." At the same time, in this "bridal chamber" the way the world is governed can be visualized. The entities that were seen in the holy of holiest were related on the one hand to the cherubim—because of the sexual overtones—and on the other hand to the two attributes of God, *Middat ha-Raḥamim* (mercy) and *Middat ha-Din* (stern judgment), which represent the manner in which God "controls the creation." This thesis is based on the fact that Philo of Alexandria already identified the cherubim with the divine attributes.[36] In addition, identifications of the cherubim with masculine and feminine powers were known in ancient times even beyond the boundaries of Judaism.[37] Though the influence of Philo on the *Gospel of Philip* is possible, this thesis is by no means the only probable solution for the explanation as to how Jewish views of the holy of holies reached the Gnostic author. It is equally possible that Jewish traditions, contemporary to Philo but possibly independent of his writings, were known by the anonymous author.[38] We may conclude that a sexual perception of the holy of holies was in existence in ancient Judaism.

Shortly after the destruction of the Temple, we learn about a substitute for the Temple as the place where the Shekhinah may dwell. According to a view found in the talmudic context discussed earlier,[39] the presence of the Shekhinah requires the existence of at least twenty-two thousand children of Israel,[40] and each and every one has to contribute to the maintenance of this figure. The people of Israel are viewed, either as individuals or as a nation, as *Imago Templi*, a theme that extended its influence into both Christianity and Islam.

According to this conception, the pure union of male and female functions as a restorative act, enabling the Shekhinah to keep Her natural place amid the Jewish nation. At least partially, procreation is done for the sake of the divinity, it being an effort to reestablish the harmony that existed during the period the Temple was functioning. It seems, therefore, reasonable to suppose that the medieval kabbalistic dictum, "The dwelling of the Shekhinah below (or among Israel) is for Her (own) sake"[41] faithfully reflects a more ancient perception, which was only more clearly articulated by the kabbalists.

Let us elaborate upon another kabbalistic view of this theme. According to the classical rabbinic sources discussed earlier, the presence of the Shekhinah during the sexual act is conditioned by the ritual purity of the participants. No requisite of kavvanah (proper intention) is mentioned in these contexts. But the requirement of pure intention, described by the kabbalists as aiming to raise human thought to its supernal source while causing the descent of the Shekhinah afterward, was added in one of the early and most influential kabbalistic texts, *Iggeret ha-Kodesh*:

> It is well known to the masters of Kabbalah that human thought stems from the intellectual soul, which has descended from above. And human thought has the ability to strip itself [from alien issues] and to ascend to and arrive at the place of its source.[42] Then, it will unite with the supernal entity,[43] whence it comes, and it [i.e., the thought] and it [i.e., its source] become one entity.[44] And when the thought returns downward from above, something similar to a line appears, and with it the supernal light descends, under the influence of the thought that draws it downward, and consequently it draws the Shekhinah downward. Then the brilliant [45] light comes and increases upon the place where the owner of the thought stands . . . and since this is the case, our ancient sages had to state that when the husband copulates with his wife, and his thought unites with the supernal entities, that very thought draws the supernal light downward, and it (the light) dwells upon the drop [of semen] upon which he directs his intention and thought . . . that very drop is permanently linked with the brilliant light . . . since the thought on it [the drop] is linked to the supernal entities it draws the brilliant light downward."[46]

Therefore, the human mystical intention that has to accompany the sexual union can cause the supernal light—and the Shekhinah as well[47]—to descend on man during sexual intercourse. The husband has to elevate his thought to its source, to achieve an *unio mystica*, which will be followed by the descent of supernal spiritual forces on the *semen virile*.[48] Here *ascensio mentis*, *unio mystica*, and *reversio* are prerequisite stages of the ideal conception.[49]

It is worthwhile to compare this mystical conception of the sexual act to the tantric view. In both cases, the sexual act must be performed in a very mindful manner; a certain mystical consciousness is attained alongside the corporeal act. However, the usage of intercourse as a vehicle for spiritual experiences is evidently different. The mystical union of thought with its source is, in kabbalah, instrumental to the main goal— conception; the spiritual attainment is solely a preparatory phase in the process of procreation, which has to be performed with the cooperation of the Shekhinah. In the tantric systems, the mystical consciousness, the *bodhicitta*, is an aim in itself whereas the perfect state is obtained by the immobilization of the flow of *semen virile*.[50] The sexual act is regarded by the kabbalists as a life-giving act; with the tantric masters, the ejaculation is viewed as "death."[51] The kabbalists put mystical union in the service of procreation; tantra put fruitless intercourse into the service of mystical consciousness.

For the theosophical kabbalists, intercourse is not an aim in itself. The final goal or goals are procreation and preparation of appropriate *substrata*—human beings—to serve as residences for the Shekhinah. Either the human couple or its descendants come into direct contact with the Shekhinah, which descends on the man who performs the sexual act in purity. Therefore, a contact is evidently established between the human and the divine, during which the former retains his masculine nature.

In the texts analyzed earlier, the Shekhinah descends during proper intercourse. However, She does not play the role of the female and no mention of sexual relations between the male and the Shekhinah can be discerned in these discussions. It seems that the *Zohar* contributed an important concept in the domain of sexual motifs;[52] for the first time in a Jewish source[53] the righteous person is portrayed as standing between two females:[54] the human one—that is, his spouse—and the supernal one—the Shekhinah. The man is able to attain this status only when marrying a human woman, but afterward he is compensated by the presence of the Shekhinah whenever he separates from his earthly wife. This sexual description of human contact with the Shekhinah is primarily attributed to Moses, "Ish ha-Elohim" (lit. the man of God), a phrase interpreted by the kabbalists as "the husband of the Shekhinah."[55] However, even other righteous men are sometimes described in similar terms. According to the *Zohar*, marriage bestows the righteous not only with the opportunity to fulfill the requirement of procreation, but it also enables him to attain the mythical status of the human husband of "the world of the Womanhood" (*Alma de-nukba*). It is worthwhile to focus on this view—the ritualistic marriage is a prerequisite for the acquirement of the role of the mythical husband. The actual consummation of marriage is a sine qua non for it. However, afterward it may sometimes become an obstacle for the attainment of the spiritual experience. Note, for example, the opinion of R. Isaac of Acre: "Jacob, our ancestor, as long as he was [living] with the corporeal Rachel, outside the land of Israel, his soul could not unite with the supernal Rachel, the latter's residence being in the Holy Land; but as soon as he has reached the Holy Land, the lower Rachel died, and his soul united with the higher Rachel's."[56]

This combination of corporeal marriage as a first step, with the spiritual one as the second step, seemingly points to a synthesis of the theosophical importance of the marriage with the emphasis that the ecstatic kabbalah puts on the spiritual nature of the relation between man and God.[57]

Horizontal Descending Symbolism

The sexual symbolism that describes the relationship between the righteous and the Shekhinah assumes the female nature of the Shekhinah. The evolution of this concept is a complex issue, which cannot be discussed in this essay.[58] However, it is important to stress that, for the kabbalists, the feminine characteristic of the divine manifestation is only secondarily associated with her relation with righteous humans. Primarily, she is viewed as the feminine partner of the system of nine sephirot, which are regarded as the "world of the male" or of their representatives, the sephirot *Tiferet* or *Yesod*. Righteous humans, therefore, are imitating the parallel relationship between the supernal righteous entities, *Yesod* and Shekhinah. The real, archetypical processes take place in the divine world; here below we only reflect the mysterious dynamics of the infradivine world. Like righteous humans, who stand between two females—the human and the divine, so too the divine female stands between two males—the human and the divine.[59]

Because the relationship between righteous humans and the Shekhinah is, with the kabbalists, basically a mimesis of a supernal process, we may conceive it as being expressed by a "descending symbolism": The most important process takes place above,[60] and we use this symbolism in order to reflect a parallel phenomenon below. Thus, the vertical descending symbolism is rooted, according to the kabbalists, in the horizontal descending symbolism. The harmonious relation between *Tifereth* and *Malkhut*, or, as this relation was more commonly called, *Yiḥud Kudsha Berikh Hu u-Shekhintei"* (the unification of the Holy One, blessed be He, and His Divine Presence), is crucial for the welfare of the world. Only when the union between the two divine powers is achieved can the influx stemming from the *Eyn Sof* (the infinite one) be transmitted to the lower world. This harmony, which was disturbed by the primordial sin, as well as by sins in general, can be restored by the kabbalistic performance of the commandments, one of the most important of these being pure sexual relations. The human pair performing the sexual union is able to induce a state of harmony above. The sexual act is conceived as fraught with theurgical powers. With most of the kabbalists, this human act both reflects the higher structure and influences it. Therefore, marriage and sexual union have a tremendous impact on the upper worlds. This perception is one of the most important contributions kabbalah has made to the Jewish modus vivendi: Marriage and sex were transformed into a mystery that reflects a mysterious marriage above, whose success is crucial for both the divine cosmos and the lower universe. Reproduction, as the ultimate goal of the marital relations, became, in the kabbalistic weltanschauung, a secondary goal; although still most important for the human pair—mostly for the husband—the theurgical significance became more and more central as kabbalistic thought developed.

One of the earliest kabbalists, R. Jehudah ben Yakar (late twelfth to early thirteenth centuries), expressed the "descending" perception of the sexual union in a very concise manner: "and the commandment of union which concerns us is connected also to what G–d said to Shabbat:[61] Knesset Israel will be your spouse and it [Shabbat] is the Righteous, the foundation of the world,[62] and therefrom all the spirits and souls come . . .[63] this is the reason people are accustomed to celebrate the marriage on Shabbat."[64]

Here, *Knesset Israel* is conceived of as the bride of the Shabbat, which seemingly symbolized the ninth sefirah, *Yesod* (= bridegroom). Therefore, the human union, which generates the body, reflects the higher union, in the realm of the sephirot, wherefrom the souls emerge. We witness here, then, an interesting example of the transformation of an early midrash dealing with two mythic entities—*Knesset Israel* and Shabbat—into a full-fledged theosophical myth. One important factor in this shift is the overemphasis of the sexual polarity, which is apparently secondary in the midrash. Interestingly enough, one hundred years ago M. Joël pointed out the possibility that this midrash might have been composed based on the background of the Gnostic theory of syzygies (couples or pairs of entities, hierarchically arranged);[65] the medieval kabbalists exploited the mythical potentialities of this midrashic passage in order to elaborate their own mythical theosophy. The commandment of union is, according to R. Jehudah, an imitation of the supernal union, not only on the sexual level, but also as a custom that views Shabbat as propitious for such a union.

I would like to dwell on the way such a sexual reshaping took place. According to the wording of the midrash, Shabbat is implicitly viewed as a feminine entity whereas *Knesset Israel* is explicitly referred to as masculine: *Ben Zug* ("the [male] partner"). However, the roles change in the kabbalistic casting of this issue. Is this an arbitrary departure from the midrash, motivated by theosophic speculations? Indeed, as we have noted, Shabbat is viewed as masculine even in another early kabbalistic text, the *Book of Bahir*. However, it seems that we must also look for a more ancient conception, found, again, in the midrash. According to another passage in *Genesis Rabba*,[66] Adam could not find an appropriate mate among animals, and he exclaimed (like Shabbat) "each being has its partner, while I have no one." Here, the male is described as searching for a female mate. Therefore, I assume that this paradigm molded the kabbalistic apperception of the relationship between Shabbat and *Knesset Israel*.

The description of the union of the sephirot *Tiferet* or *Yesod* and *Malkhut* were labeled earlier as sexual horizontal descending symbolism. According to the definition offered by Kahler of "descending symbolism," which was adduced at the beginning of this essay, this term denotes a process that is symbolized by a system that is rooted in a higher level. As far as the lower sephirot are concerned, their relationship, expressed in sexual imagery, reflects an even higher sexual dichotomy described in the earliest kabbalistic treatises, where the sephirot *Ḥesed* and *Gevurah* were conceived respectively as a pair of masculine and feminine powers. Such is the case in R. Abraham ben David of Posquieres, who regarded the two divine attributes, seemingly *Ḥesed* and *Gevurah*, as *du-parzufim* (possessing dual characteristics), apparently as masculine and feminine.[67] Therefore, the lower sephirot reflect a higher syzygy. Indeed, a close scrutiny of the evolution of early kabbalistic symbolism evinces that the probably earlier sexual relationship of the two divine attributes, *Ḥesed* and *Gevurah*, influenced the same type of perception of the lower sephirot.[68] Again, this sexual understanding of the relation between *Ḥesed* and *Gevurah* may reflect a still higher syzygy of sephirot: *Ḥokhmah* and *Binah*, which were regarded respectively, as "father" and "mother." As the lower sephirot have to be in the status of *Yeḥud* ("union"), so too do the higher two sephirot, in order to attain the condition of "higher union."[69] According to important kabbalist sources, the two higher sephirot are mediated by a peculiar sephirah, *Da'at*, whose sexual overtones are almost explicit (*da'at* [knowledge] being the biblical term for sexual familiarity), mostly in the Lurianic kabbalah.[70] Therefore, sexual imagery played a most important role in the description of the nature of most of the divine attributes and the relations between them. Furthermore, according to the kabbalists the existence of the sygyzies in the divine world is a sine qua non for the achievement of the balance that ensures the existence of the divine structure. Thus, the masculine-feminine relationship is presented by them as an all-comprehensive dynamic, which pervades the entire divine world. The human sexual relationship is, therefore, viewed as a "participation mystique" in the divine hierogamy, both by reflecting it and by influencing the divine processes.

Moreover, some of the emanational phases in the autogenesis of the divine system are described in striking sexual symbolism. The seven lower sephirot were generated out of the union between *Hokhmah* and *Binah*, the seven sephirot being commonly considered the "sons" of the higher sephirot. According to a sixteenth-century kabbalist, the whole process of emanation can be described as the successive impregnations and births of the sephirot from one another, beginning with *Causa Causarum* and ending with the last sephirah.[71] According to R. Moshe Cordovero, a leading kabbalist of Safed:

> The issue of sexual union between the divine attributes is truly symbolized by our sexual union, after the corporeal part of it has been completely deleted; the conjunction of two attributes and their desire of union can be compared to, and explained by, their comprehension of the [supernal] spiritual season which consists in the influx of the light of *Eyn Sof* onto the attributes, and they [i.e., the attributes] love each other and desire each other exactly like the desire of man for his bride, after the corporeal part of it is deleted.[72]

Here the relationship between the divine attributes is not only compared to the structure of human sexual act, but also described as depending on a higher process taking place between the *Eyn Sof* and the sephirot. The usage of the term *onah* (season) has overt, sexual overtones (see Ex. 21:10), and the "light" symbolizes the semen[73] which the sephirot qua feminine entity receive from above. I assume that the supernal season is the eve of Shabbat, which was considered by the kabbalists as particularly proper for sexual relations.[74]

The anonymous author of *Iggeret ha-Kodesh* summarized the kabbalistic descending symbolism when he wrote: "All the issues we discussed[75] are the secret of the system of the order of the world and its structure, and the prototype of male and female [which are] the secret of the donor [of the influx] and [its] receiver,[76] and behold, the worthy union of man and his wife, is in the likeness of heaven and earth."[77,78]

The mainstream of kabbalah, the theosophical kabbalah, articulated earlier Jewish perceptions of human and divine existence, employing a multiplicity of sexual factors. Elements associated with the creation of humans in the Bible and midrash, with the cherubim in midrashic texts and perhaps with the divine attributes in Philo and talmudic-midrashic texts, were all structured into a comprehensive system that was apparently already evident in the very first kabbalistic sources.[79] This correlation between the various levels of reality permitted the kabbalists to regard the sexual union as an *imitatio Dei* from one perspective and as a theurgical act intended to induce a harmonious state in the supernal entities from another.

Moreover, kabbalists used these principles, as well as already existing motifs, in order to construct a bisexual system of the powers of evil. So, Sammael and Lilith are the "apes of God," who try to imitate the divine union in the demonic counterpart structure.[80]

A comparison between the various Jewish views on the sexual relationship and some ancient Christian and Gnostic views is pertinent at this final stage of our discussion.[81] The Philonic, the talmudic-midrashic, and the kabbalistic perceptions of sexuality are all unambiguously positive. The existence of two sexes is accepted as a fact that enables humankind to perpetuate itself without any pejorative insinuation of the nature of the sexual act. The return to the primal androgyne state of humans, which was commonly described by Gnostics,[82] or the endeavor to transcend the feminine plight by mystic transformations of the female into a "male," recurring in ancient Christian thought[83] and Gnosticism,[84] is alien to talmudic and theosophical kabbalistic weltanschauung.[85]

The cherubim can be viewed when intertwined, but they can also separate from each other. Human beings can unite in the sexual act without losing their specific sexual nature. The supernal divine manifestations are supposed to attain their ideal state when the opposite divine powers are united, a union that is explicitly described in sexual imagery. Nevertheless, nowhere is this union regarded as an annihilation of two sephirot, and the emergence of one, androgynous, alternative divine power. What is characteristic of the kabbalistic view is the emphasis on the attainment of a harmonious relationship between opposing principles, whose separate existence is indispensable for the welfare of the entire cosmos. Or, to put it in other words, theosophical kabbalah was not interested in a drastic restructuring of existence by either the transformation of the feminine into masculine or by their final fusion into a bisexual or asexual entity. Rather, the kabbalists were striving for an improvement of the processes going on between polar elements composing the terrestrial and the divine universes.

The kabbalists transported the human sexual relationship—not only the sexual polarity—into the supernal world; the processes there had to conform to the human sexual behavior. The Gnostic view attempted to copy the higher rule of androgyneity or asexuality in the lower world.[86] Gnostic—and to a certain extent also the Christian—attitudes toward sexuality represent an important aspect of their more comprehensive rejection of this world.[87] The Gnostic and Christian eschatologies present a spiritual escapism that aims at the restoring of the paradisiac androgyny or asexual status of the believer. At least in the Gnostic case, the uneasiness extends beyond this world to its evil creator, sexuality being regarded as an instrument implanted by him into humans in order to perpetuate his evil world. Christian asceticism is but a milder attitude toward the temporary plight of the world until the second arrival of the Savior. The sexual instinct was either suppressed or partially sublimated in the form of love of Christ.

Under the impact of the halakhic views, kabbalah dealt with the regulation of the libido rather than with its suppression or sublimation. This attitude toward sex and sexuality is generally this-world-oriented; the main effort was invested in the attempt to find the golden mean between the sexual asceticism cultivated by the Christian mystics and an uncommon emphasis on the centrality of the sexual processes, which could explode the regular texture of the family life.[88] The danger that haunted Jewish medieval kabbalah was not an exaggerated spirituality that disregarded the "carnal" love, but an outburst of positively perceived sexual relationships beyond the boundaries of halakhah.

The balance between a positive and natural attitude toward sexuality and its perception as a reflection of the supernal hierogamy also had its problems. When the halakhic regulations weakened, one of the main and immediate results was a removal of the sexual inhibitions. Shabbateanism and Frankism, two sects connected with mystical Judaism, deviated from kabbalah mainly by their transgression of incest interdictions, transgressions that were interpreted as the imitation of unrestrained relations in the divine world.[89] Both extreme Shabbateans and Frankists based their licentious behavior on classical kabbalistic texts.[90] Like the Gnostics,[91] the Shabbateans viewed the perfect man—in their case Shabbatai Zevi—as being free from all moral restrictions and as belonging to Gan Eden, a paradisiac state, as opposed to the lower world, described as "the heart" of the demonic world.[92] Moreover, the very core of Shabbatai Zevi's activity was once described as the restoration of the glory of sexuality, seemingly of the unrestrained sort: "The patriarchs came into the world to restore the senses and this they did to four of them. Then came Shabbatai Zevi and restored the fifth, the sense of touch, which, according to Aristotle[93] and Maimonides,[94] is a source of shame for us, but which now has been raised by him to a place of honour and glory.[95]

We witness here a clear case where metaphysics—in this case, kabbalistic theosophy—turned into an independent factor that shaped the behavior of persons. When put into the service of the metaphysical "idea," with ordinary sexual modes obliterated, orgiastic practices turned into a *via mystica* of the new aeon. No wonder the next important development of Jewish mysticism—Hasidism—was much more reticent in using sexual symbolism.

Finally, a remark on the metamorphosis of the above-mentioned attitudes toward sexuality in our own period may be pertinent. The ancient Jewish attitude toward sexuality as a mystery, as represented by midrashim describing the holy of holies, had a profound impact on Judaism in general and on kabbalah in particular. The supernal hierogamy and its lower reflection in the marital relations became one of the basic tenets of kabbalistic lore; at least on this point, kabbalah elaborated on an already existing Jewish topic.[96] This unequivocal view of sexuality had an important repercussion in modern psychoanalysis through Freud's appreciation of the libido.[97]

On the other hand, the reticent and sometimes ambiguous attitude toward sexuality and marriage in Christianity and Gnosticism found its expression in the works of Carl Jung and Mircea Eliade.[98] These scholars were not only deeply interested in the Gnostic mythology, but they even seemingly adopted several Gnostic *mythologoumena*, as atemporal truths[99] or even as spiritual guidance for our age.[100] Individual perfection is the ultimate goal of their idealization of androgyneity, as opposed to the creative interest, be it procreation or restoration of divine harmony, in the theosophical kabbalah. Any further comment would be superfluous.

NOTES

Abbreviations

Baer, *Philo's Use* = Richard A. Baer, Jr., *Philo's Use of the Categories Male and Female* (Leiden, 1970).

Eliade, *Yoga* = Mircea Eliade, *Yoga, Immortality and Freedom*, (Princeton, N.J., 1971).

Goldberg, *Schekhinah* = Arnold M. Goldberg, *Untersuchungen über die Vorstellung von der Schekhinah* (Berlin, 1969).

Idel, *Abraham Abulafia* = M. Idel, *The Mystical Experience in Abraham Abulafia* (Albany, 1988).

Idel, "Unio Mystica" = M. Idel, *Studies in Ecstatic Kabbalah* (Albany, 1988), pp. 1–31.

Idel, "Hitbodedut" = M. Idel, "Hitbodedut qua Concentration in Ecstatic Kabbalah" [in Hebrew] *Da'at* 14 (1985), 35–82.

Meeks, "The Image of the Androgyne" = Wayne A. Meeks, "The Image of the Androgyne; Some Uses of a Symbol in Earliest Christianity," *History of Religions* 13 (1974), 165–208.

Patai, *The Hebrew Goddess* = Raphael Patai, *The Hebrew Godess* (New York, 1978).

Scholem, *Les Origines* = G. Scholem, *Les Origines de la Kabbale* (Paris, 1966).

Scholem, *Major Trends* = G. Scholem, *Major Trends in Jewish Mysticism* (New York, 1967).

Scholem, *The Messianic Idea* = G. Scholem, *The Messianic Idea in Judaism* (New York, 1972).

Tishby, *The Wisdom of the Zohar* = Isaiah Tishby, *The Wisdom of the Zohar* [Hebrew], I, (Jerusalem, 1957), II, (Jerusalem, 1961).

1. I shall limit myself to self-evident *sexual* discussions in kabbalah, leaving aside a whole series of *erotic* imagery. Some of them were studied in George Vajda's *L'Amour de Dieu dans la théologie juive du Moyen Age* (Paris, 1957) or Chaim Wirszubski, *Three Studies in Christian Kabbala* [Hebrew] (Jerusalem, 1975), pp. 13–23; M. D. G. Langer, *Die Erotik der Kabbala* (Prague, 1923); see also nn. 9 and 79.

2. See Erich Kahler, "The Nature of the Symbol" in Rollo May, ed., *Symbolism in Religion and Literature* (New York, 1960), p. 65.

3. See Gershom Scholem, *On the Kabbalah and Its Symbolism* (New York, 1965), p. 100.

4. This term occurs also in Kahler's essay, however, in speculative contexts other than those discussed here; and I prefer, therefore, to propose my own definition for this phase; compare Kahler, "Nature of the Symbol," pp. 67–68.

5. See, e.g., A. E. Waite, *The Way of Divine Union* (London, 1915), esp. pp. 126ff.

6. See James H. Leuba, *The Psychology of Religious Mysticism* (London, 1925), pp. 116ff.

7. I consciously delete any discussion of Philo's parallel views because his literary *corpus* did not apparently influence kabbalah. Phenomenologically, the structure of Philo's thought is close to that of Abulafia's, both employing vertical ascending symbolism together with Greek philosophical terminology; again, in their writings, a neutralization of mythical elements is obvious. On Greek sexual puritanism, see E. R. Dodds, *The Greeks and the Irrational* (Berkeley, Calif., 1951), pp. 154–55. See also on Plotinus's usage of erotic imagery and its influence on the Renaissance, Edgar Wind, *Pagan Mysteries in the Renaissance* (New York, 1967), pp. 61–68.

8. See, our treatment of R. Jehudah ben Yakar's passage later in this essay in our discussion of "Horizontal Descending Symbolism."

9. Ms. München (Heb) 58 fol. 323$_r$. Scholem's statement that "older Kabbalists never interpreted the 'Song of Songs' as a dialogue between God and the Soul, i.e., an allegorical description of the path to *unio mystica*" (*Major Trends*, p. 226) must therefore be corrected. Abulafia indeed proposed such an allegorical interpretation, the ultimate aim of which is the *unio mystica*; his perception is closer to the philosophical interpretations than to the early kabbalistic one. However, he differs also from the philosophers, for he strove for an actual realization of the *unio mystica*, and thus allegorical interpretation turns into what I propose to call a spiritual interpretation or hermeneutic. On the philosophical perceptions of the *Song of Songs*, see A. S. Halkin, "Ibn Aknin's Commentary on the Song of Songs," *Alexander Marx Jubilee Volume* [English Section] (New York, 1950) pp. 389–424 and in Vajda, *L'Amour de Dieu*.

10. *Imre Shefer*, Ms. Paris (BN) (Heb) 777 p. 57.

11. *Or ha-Sekhel*. Ms. Vatican, 233 fol. 115$_r$.

12. See, e.g., Abulafia's *Hayye ha Nefesh*, Ms. Munich 408 fol. 65$_v$.

13. *Or ha-Menorah*, Ms. Jerusalem, National Library 8° 1303 fol. 28$_b$; compare to the collectanea stemming from the Abulafia circle found in Ms. New York, JTS Mic. 1771 fol. 34$_r$, where, again, *Knesset Israel* is connected to the rational soul.

14. An equation of the numerical value of the Hebrew letters in each word or phrase.

15. Both having the value of 541. On other philosophical allegorizations of *Israel*, see Marc Saperstein, *Decoding the Rabbis* (Cambridge, Mass., 1980), pp. 100, 248.

16. See Idel, *Abraham Abulafia*, pp. 190–203 and compare to Baer, *Philo's Use*, pp. 55–64.

17. Compare Scholem's view of mystical "communion," which is characteristic of Jewish mysticism, *The Messianic Idea*, pp. 203–205.

18. On *unio mystica* in Abulafia's doctrine, see Idel, "Unio Mystica," pp. 5–12, where additional material is quoted to substantiate the thesis that Abulafia asserted that total fusion with a higher entity— sometimes being God—is possible.

19. The value of the letters of the Tetragrammaton is 26, which is formed from 13 + 13; now "13" is the value of *Ehad*, that is, "one," and *Ahavah*, that is, "love." By the way of gematria, Abulafia evinces that it is possible to attain mystical union (One, One) with God (Tetragrammaton) by means of love (*Ahavah*).

20. Ms. Vatican 233 fol. 115,.

21. Nevertheless, marriage or sexual relationship is never presented by Abulafia or his disciples as an obstacle for attaining a mystical experience. We know for sure that Abulafia himself was married, and in his list of requirements for an ideal student (see *Hayye ha-Olam ha-Ba*, Ms. Oxford, 1582, fol. 33v–35r) no reference to sexual impurity can be found. See also Idel, *Abraham Abulafia*, pp. 143–4 on the nonascetic characteristic of Abulafia's mysticism.

22. b. Sotah 17a; cf. Pirke de-R. Eliezer, ch. 12, and R. Tuviah ben Eliezer's *Lekah Tov* on Genesis, 2:23. M. Kasher, *Torah Shelemah*, XXII, Appendix, p. 18, has already pointed out the possible connection between this dictum and the cherubim. See also Louis Ginzberg's apologetical view that this dictum reflects "another pagan conception which, in refined form, passed into the Cabala through the Talmud" (*On Jewish Law and Lore* [New York, 1970], p. 190).

23. *Theurgy*, in this essay, stands for the conception that human actions, mostly the commandments, are intended to change processes taking place in the supernal divine system. For more on my view of this concept, see M. Idel, *Kabbalah: New Perspectives* (New Haven and London, 1988), chaps. 7–8.

24. The formulation of R. Akiva's dictum does not explicitly refer to sexual union; however, this is the way the dictum was understood by the classical commentators, like Rashi. See also the rabbinic view that God participates in the process of producing the infant together with his father and mother; b. Niddah 31a and parallels. The affinity between these two rabbinic views was perceived and exploited by the anonymous kabbalist who composed the famous *Epistle on the Sexual Conjunction* attributed to Nachmanides; see the edition of C. Chavel in *Kitve ha-Ramban* (Jerusalem, 1964), II, 324–25.

25. Lev. 10:1. Here, as in the Sotah quotation, the verb *'achal* is used in order to express the idea of consummation by fire.

26. Num. 7:89.

27. See b. Baba Batra 99a. Interestingly enough, the two positions of the cherubim—separate or united—stand, according to some medieval interpreters of the Talmud, respectively for the curse and blessing occurring in the talmudic discussion of the cherubim in b. Yoma 54b; see R. Shemuel Edeles, *Novellae* ad locum, where he quotes R. Yom Tov Ashvili's view. Has this presumably later conception something to do with the perception of the cherubim as the two divine attributes, as found already in Philo?

28. b. Yoma 54a. See the interesting proposal of Menahem Kasher that this text may be connected to the perception that regards the *Song of Songs* as the holy of holies, and the secrets of the forbidden sexual unions in Mishnah Hagigah 2:1, as an esoteric topic; see "Zohar", *Sinai-Jubilee Volume* [Hebrew], ed. I. L. Maimon (Jerusalem, 1958), pp. 55–56. This argument merits a more elaborate analysis.

29. Genesis Rabba 19, 7 (p. 176). Midrash Rabba on *Song of Songs*, 5, 1. See also Bereshit Rabba p. 177, where it is implied that the righteous are persons who can cause the descent of the *Shekhinah*, who has left our world because of the sins of the sinners. Compare also to *Hebrew Enoch*, Ch. 5.

30. Yevamot 63b–64a.

31. On this issue see Avigdor Shinan, "The Sins of Nadav and Avihu in the Aggadah of the Sages," in A. Shinan, ed., *The Aggadic Literature—A Reader* [in Hebrew] (Jerusalem, 1983), pp. 182–83.

32. Cf. Bereshit Rabba, 8, 9 (p. 63); 22, 2 (p. 206).

33. *The Gospel of Philip*, trans. Wesley W. Isenberg, in *The Nag Hammadi Library*, ed. James M. Robinson (Harper & Row, 1984), p. 150. Some affinities between this treatise and Jewish concepts were pointed out by Jehudah Liebes, "The Messiah of the Zohar," in *The Messianic Idea in Jewish Thought* [in Hebrew] (Jerusalem, 1982), pp. 230–32; M. Idel "Jerusalem in Medieval Jewish Thought" [in Hebrew] (forthcoming). It is important to stress the fact that the relatively positive attitude toward sexuality and marriage occurring in Gnostic texts, as in this Gospel and parts of *Corpus Hermeticum*, are seemingly the result of Jewish influence.

34. *Gospel of Philip*, p. 142. See also p. 150: "The holies of holies were revealed and the bridal chamber invited us in." See also Robert M. Grant, "The Mystery of Marriage in the Gospel of Philip," *Vigiliae Christianae* 15 (1961), 129–40; J-M. Sevrin, "Les Noces spirituelles dans l'Evangile selon Philippe," *Le Muséon* 87 (1974), 143–93. J-M Sevrin, "Les rites et la Gnose," in Julien Ries, ed., *Gnosticisme et Monde Hellénistique* (Louvain-La-Neuve, 1982), pp. 448–50.

35. Buber's version, Num. fol. 17$_a$. Compare to Patai, *Man and Temple* (London, 1947), pp. 89–92, and on the perception of the holy of holies as *cletoris* in the *Zohar*, see Liebes, "The Messiah of the Zohar," p. 194. It seems plausible that the midrashic connection between *Apirion* (litter for a wedding procession) mentioned in the *Song of Songs*, III and the Temple and Tabernacle may have

something to do also to with sexuality and fertility; see *Song of Songs Rabbah* III, 15–19, ed. S. Dunski, Jerusalem and Tel Aviv, 1980, pp. 93–96.

36. See Erwin Goodenough, *By Light, Light* (New Haven, 1935), pp. 25–26, 359–69; idem, *Jewish Symbols in Greco-Roman Period*, 3 vols. (Princeton, N.J., 1954), IV, 132.

37. See Gedaliahu Stroumsa, "Le Couple de l'ange et de l'esprit: traditions juives et chrétiennes," *Revue biblique* 88 (1981), 46–47.

38. Liebes, "The Messiah of the Zohar," p. 231, even asserts that the anonymous Gnostic author was of Jewish extraction.

39. b. Yevamot, 64a.

40. This figure recurs in midrashic texts: see Goldberg, *Schekhinah*, pp. 357–59, 508–9.

41. See Nachmanides, *Commentary on Exodus*, 29:46, and a long series of other kabbalists afterward; compare also to R. Joseph Gikatilla's expression "the need of Shekhinah" in *Sha're Orah*, ed. J. ben Shelomo (Jerusalem, 1970), I, 67.

42. This view was taken over by the anonymous author of the *Iggeret* from Geronese Kabbalah; see Scholem, *Les Origines*, pp. 320–21. Our author is, seemingly, original in applying the already existing view of *elevatio mentis* to the procreative sexual process.

43. Literally, "secret"—"sod."

44. On this expression, see Scholem, *Les Origines*, p. 322 n. 192.

45. The expression "the light of the Shekhinah" (*or ha-Shekhinah*), which might influence this text, was in existence several centuries before the author of the *Iggeret*; see Georges Vajda, "Or Ha-Shekhina," *REJ* 134 (1975), 133–35, to which we may add *Midrash Tadshe*, ch. 11 (Epstein, p. 156), and Goldberg, *Schekhinah*, pp. 318–19.

46. Chavel, *Kitve ha-Ramban*, II, 373.

47. The presence of the Shekhinah is induced by the pure thought of the husband according to some additional statements (Goldberg, *Schekhinah*, p. 332), one of them asserting that whoever thinks of the exterior beauty of his wife does not think according to the "supernal pure thought," and thereby causes the Shekhinah to leave the pair.

48. I assume that to the ancient rabbinic view, concerning the presence of the Shekhinah during intercourse, the kabbalists supplied a certain magical perception. According to several medieval sources, man is able to prepare below an appropriate substratum, upon which he can draw a supernal influx named *Ruhaniat* in Arabic or *Ruhaniut* in Hebrew. In our text the *semen virile* stands for the substratum that is prepared to collect the supernal influx, named here "brilliant light" or Shekhinah.

49. Compare this view, which considers *union mystica* as a means, to R. Isaac of Acre's view, discussed later, where only after the corporeal relations is severed, the "higher" spiritual status of union is achieved.

50. See Eliade, *Yoga*, pp. 248–49, 266–68; idem, *The Two and the One* (New York, 1969), pp. 118–19.

51. See Eliade, *Yoga*, p. 249.

52. On the importance of sexual symbolism in the *Zohar*, see Scholem, *Major Trends*, pp. 225–29; Tishby, *The Wisdom of the Zohar*, II, 607–626; A. E. Waite, *The Holy Kabbalah* (New York, n.d.), pp. 377–405.

53. A parallel concept occurs also in Sufic material; see Idel, "Hitbodedut," p. 56 n. 117.

54. See Tishby, *The Wisdom of the Zohar*, I, 149.

55. See Idel, "Hitbodedut," p. 56 notes 117, 119, and 120.

56. *Ozar Hayyim*, Ms. Moscow—Günzburg 775 fol. 73$_v$, printed in Idel, "Hitbodedut," p. 56. n. 117.

57. Compare to the explanations offered by R. Moshe de Leon and the *Zohar* on the death of Rachel before Jacob's entrance to the Land of Israel. According to these texts, the interdiction to marry two sisters who are alive is stressed. Therefore, the ritualistic conception is chosen rather than the spiritual one. See I. Tishby, *Studies in Kabbalah and Its Branches* [Hebrew] (Jerusalem, 1982), p. 45. The transition from a corporeal concept of relation to women to a spiritual one is also evident in an important parable adduced by R. Isaac, on the "daughter of the King"; see Idel, "Hitbodedut," pp. 53–54. See also n. 49 earlier.

58. The generally accepted view of the Shekhinah, in ancient sources, as identical with the divinity, and therefore without any feminine characteristic, was formulated by G. Scholem and E. E. Urbach and endorsed by Goldberg in his monograph. On the other hand, Patai, *The Hebrew Goddess*, proposed a radically different conception of the Shekhinah, as a separate feminine entity, without, however, providing solid evidence. It seems that though the first view represents the common view of classical rabbinical sources, the second view is not totally absent.

59. Cf. *Zohar* I, 153b, and Liebes, "The Messiah of the Zohar," pp. 122, 179 n. 314, and 205 n. 407.

60. Compare Bertil Gärtner, *The Theology of the Gospel According to Thomas* (New York, 1961), p. 253: "[I]n the Gnostic systems the man-woman relationship is motivated basically by the structure of the heavenly world, the male and female powers which are striving after unity." The kabbalists also accepted, at least de jure, this rationale for their sexual behaviour; de facto, they visualized the higher worlds as ruled by the human sexual relationship as it was molded by the halakic regulations. Or, to put it otherwise, kabbalists viewed symbolism as a "descending symbolism" whereas, at least from a modern perspective, this symbolism is an ascending one. See also n. 79.

61. See *Genesis Rabba* XI, 8, pp. 95–96, adduced by R. Jehudah immediately afterward.

62. Cf. Prov. 10:26.

63. Compare to a parallel view occurring in *Sefer ha-Bahir* (ed. R. Margaliot, par. 157): "The Righteous is alone is his world . . . and he is the foundation of all souls . . . and Scripture [supports this in saying (Ex. 31:17)]: On the seventh he rested and was refreshed [= *vayinafash*; the same Hebrew root forms the word *soul = nefesh*]."

64. *Commentary of Prayer*, Shemuel Jerushalmi (Jerusalem, 1979), pt. II, p. 42. On Shabbat as a propitious time for sexual relations, see already t. Ketubot 62b, the *Zohar* (several times) and the text of R. Moshe Cordovero, n. 72. It seems that the kabbalist has a quasi-astrological perception of Shabbat; because it was regarded as the divine potency, namely, the *sephirah* (*yesod*), which presides over the process of fertility, it was thought that Shabbat is particularly proper for sexual activity; and see Erich Fromm, *The Forgotten Language* (New York, 1957), pp. 241–49.

65. M. Joël, *Blicke in die Religionsgeschichte* (Breslau, 1880), I, 107, 160–61.

66. XVII, 4, p. 156. See I. Tishby, *R. Azriel's Commentary on the Talmudic Aggadot* (Jerusalem, 1945), p. 17 and n. 15. It is highly probable that the identification of the cheribum with the two divine attributes is a continuation of an ancient tradition, found already in Philo and in *Midrash Tadshe*; see n. 36, and Patai, *The Hebrew Goddess*, p. 82. This issue will be elaborated in a separate study.

67. See Scholem, *Les origines*, pp. 232–33.

68. See Idel, "Jerusalem in Jewish Medieval Thought" (n. 33).

69. On the two levels of *Yehud*, or unification, see Tishby, *The Wisdom of the Zohar* II, pp. 261 ff.

70. See already in *Iggeret ha-Kodesh*, *Kitve ha-Ramban*, II p. 324.

71. See Abraham ben Eliezer ha-Levi's *Masoret ha-Hokhmah*, printed by Gershom Scholem, *Kiriat Sefer* [in Hebrew], 2 (1925–1926), 129–30. On the conception of the sexual life in the work of a contemporary of Cordovero, see the important discussion of R. J. Zwi Werblowsky, *Joseph Karo, Lawyer and Mystic* (Philadelphia, 1977), pp. 133–39.

72. See *Shiur Komah* (Jerusalem, 1966), 26_d.

73. Compare the tantric view referred by Eliade, *The Two and the One* pp. 40–41.

74. See earlier our discussion of R. Jehudah ben Yakar's text, as well as my discussion of Cordovero's passage in "The Magical and Theurgic Interpretation of Music in Jewish Sources from the Renaissance to Hasidism" [Hebrew] *Yuval* 4 (1982), 54–55.

75. Seemingly the divine powers that form the supernal *Merkavah*, namely the sephirotic realm; see *Kitve ha-Ramban* II, p. 324.

76. *Mashpia u-mekabbel*; these terms for masculine and feminine functioning entities are widespread in R. Joseph Gikatilla's later works.

77. These words may symbolically refer to the sephirot *Tipheret*, and *Malkhut*. Compare to the Upanishadic parallel referred by Eliade, *Yoga*, p. 254. It is worth remarking that already in the midrash, *Numbers Rabbah* par. 2, the cherubim stand for heaven and earth.

78. *Kitve ha-Ramban* II, 325.

79. See, e.g., the conception expressed in the *Alphabet of R. Akiba* in S. A. Wertheimer, ed. *Bate Midrashot* (Jerusalem, 1955), II, 357: "All of the creatures that we will in the future create are [to be created] one male and one female," and see the sources adduced in idem, n. 38. This view was adopted by R. Eleazar of Worms and R. Jacob ben Sheshet; see Ben Sheshet's *Meshiv Devarim Nekhohim*, ed. Georges Vajda (Jerusalem, 1969), p. 114. The issue of sexual polarity in supernal worlds in the views of the Ashkenazi Hasidism of the twelfth and thirteenth centuries is an important topic that must be meticulously inspected because it may constitute one of the main bridges between ancient Jewish views of sexuality and early kabbalah; see also n. 80 and Monford Harris, "The Concept of Love in Sefer Hassidim" *JQR* 50 (1959), 13–44.

It seems indeed that kabbalistic material influenced Leone Ebreo's thought, which was described as "the radical polarization of the entire universe in terms of male and female symbols." See T. Anthony Perry, *Erotic Spirituality: The Integrative Tradition from Leone Ebreo to John Donne* (University of Alabama Press, 1980), p. 15. See also M. Idel, "Kabbalah and Ancient Philosophy in R. Isaac and Jehudah Abrabanel, in M. Durman and Z. Levy, eds., *The Philosophy of Leone Ebreo* [Hebrew] (Tel Aviv, 1985), pp. 89–93.

80. See R. J. Zwi Werblowsky, "Ape and Essence," *Ex Orbe Religionum* (Leiden, 1972), II, 318–25; J. Dan, "Sammael, Lilith, and the Concept of Evil in Early Kabbalah," *AJS Review* 5 (1980), 17–25. The story of the development of the demonic bisexual structure has to be reconsidered, in my opinion, in the direction of an earlier appearance of the sexual relations between the heads of demons.

81. I consciously ignore the possibly more interesting comparison between the kabbalistic approach to sexuality and Hindu views, for I am interested in comparing conceptions that flourished in the same geographical region and could influence each other. Moreover, Gnosticism and kabbalah share the vision of the pleroma as being composed from syzygies and having hierogamic relations between them. Against this background, the discrepancies between them are even more startling.

82. See, e.g., the *Gospel of Thomas* and the *Gospel of Philip*; the pertinent texts were adduced in Eliade, *The Two and the One*, pp. 105–7; Baer, *Philo's Use*, pp. 72–74; William C. Robinson, Jr., "The Exegesis of the Soul," *Novum Testamentum* 12 (1970), 111–17; Meeks, "The Image of the Androgyne," pp. 188–97.

83. See *Gal.* 3:28; Wayne A. Meeks, "The Image of the Androgyne"; and

Carl Jung, *Mysterium Coniuctionis* (Princeton, N.J., 1977), pp. 373–74. This motif is well known already in Philo, but in my opinion, is unknown in Hebrew texts; see Baer, *Philo's Use*, pp. 45–55. See, however, his standard Jewish attitude toward marriage, idem, pp. 75, 94–95. Philo's views on "masculinity" and "virginity" as a mystical ideal were highly influential on the patristic literature and thereby on Christian thought in general; See Maryanne Cline Horowitz, "The Image of God in Man—Is Woman Included," *HTR* 72 (1979), 190–204.

84. Baer, *Philo's Use*, pp. 69–71.

85. As Meeks ("The Image of the Androgyne" p. 186) properly remarks: "In Judaism the myth (of androgyne) serves only to solve an exegetical dilemma and to support monogamy." However, the ecstatic kabbalah sometimes employs androgynous imagery, under the influence of Greek philosophy, mediated by Maimonides' works. Nevertheless, no ascetic movement emerged from this trend of thought; see n. 7 above. Another crucial difference between the Jewish and Greek view of androgyny is the positive Jewish perception of the separation between the male and female whereas with Plato this separation is viewed as a punishment. Compare, however, Thorlief Boman, *Hebrew Thought Compared with the Greek* (London, 1960), pp. 96–97; "the form of the myth is quite different from that in Genesis 2, but the meaning is exactly the same"! [My emphasis.] See also the Gnostic *Apocalypse of Adam*, tr. G. Macrae, in James H. Charlesworth, ed., *The Old Testament Pseudepigrapha* (New York, 1983), I, 712: "God, the ruler of the aeons, and the powers, separated us wrathfully. Then we became two aeons, and the glory in our hearts deserted us, me and your mother Eve." Compare also the accusation of a *matrona* that God created woman "by thievery" (Gen., Rabba, XVII, 7 p. 158) versus the answer of R. Jose, who stresses God's benevolence. On the possible Gnostic background of this passage, see recently Rosalie Gershenzon-Eliezer Slomovic, "A Second Century Jewish-Gnostic Debate: Rabbi Jose ben Halafta and the Matrona," *Journal for the Study of Judaism* 16 (1985), 20–22.

86. Or, as Jung put it very adequately, "Gnosticism . . . endeavoured in all seriousness to subordinate the physiological to the metaphysical"; see his *The Archetypes and the Collective Unconscious* (Princeton, N.J., 1980), p. 177. Meeks "The Image of the Androgyne," p. 207, uses the phrase "metaphysical rebellion" in his description of androgynous tendencies in Christian and Gnostic circles. It seems that with kabbalah the situation was completely different.

87. See Meeks, "The Image of the Androgyne," p. 207.

88. See the various midrashic discussions of God's ongoing paring couples since the end of the creation of the world, collected, translated, and analyzed by Aharon Agus, "Some Early Rabbinic Thinking on Gnosticism," *JQR* 71 (1980), pp. 18–30. Though Agus may indeed be right in his emphasis of the anti-Gnostic character of the rabbinic perception of God as an *arche-Shadkhen*,

some anti-Christian tendencies may also have contributed to the emergence of this view. I hope to deal elsewhere with this problem. See also Gershenzon-Slomovic, "A Second Century Jewish-Gnostic Debate," pp. 28–29.

89. See Scholem, *The Messianic Idea*, pp. 136–37.

90. They were designated as *Zoharisten* because of their frequent leaning on this work.

91. On the phenomenological affinity between radical forms of Shabbatean-ism and Gnosticism, see, e.g., Scholem, *The Messianic Idea*, pp. 132–33.

92. See Natan ha-Azati's *Treatise on the Menorah*, printed in Gershom Scholem's *Be-Iqvot Mashiah* (Jerusalem, 1944), p. 102; see also Scholem, *Sabbatai Ṣevi, The Mystical Messiah 1626–1676* (Princeton, N.J., 1973), pp. 810 and also 311–12.

93. *Nicomachean Ethics*, III, 10, 1118$_b$.

94. See *Guide of the Perplexed* II, 36, 40; III, 8, 49.

95. Quoted in Jacob Emden, *Sefer hit'abekut* (Lvov, 1877) 6$_a$, *apud* Scholem, *The Messianic Idea* p. 117. The presentation of Sabbatai Sevi as the redeemer of the touch sense is rather curious. Almost all the kabbalists refuted Maimon-ides's view and agreed on a positive perception of the sexual act; see already the stand of *Iggeret ha-Kodesh*, ch. 2 (Chavel, pp. 323–24).

96. This most important insight, shared by several authors, was ignored by the founders of the scholarly study of kabbalah like Scholem and Tishby. Cf. Patai, *The Hebrew Goddess*, pp. 119 ff; M. Kasher (in n. 28); Isaac Baer, "The Service of Sacrifice in Second Temple Times," [Hebrew], *Zion* 40 (1975), 101–4.

97. David Bakan's assertion that Jewish mystical tradition had indeed influ-enced Freud's views seems to be a sound approach, notwithstanding the diffi-culties the author had when he attempted to prove it by using historical arguments. It is enough to recognize that, at least regarding sexuality, the Jewish "nonmystical" attitude was not so far from the kabbalistic one and that the general positive approach to this issue was a common denominator for most of the Jews.

98. I refer primarily to their acceptance of the hermaphrodite or androgynic idea as a symbol for human perfection; see their works referred in notes 50, 82, 83, and 86. See especially Eliade's discussion of androgynisation in his *The Two and the One*, pp. 111–14.

99. Jung's perception of the androgyne as archetype is a fine example; ac-cording to him, androgyny as a "primordial idea has become a symbol of the creative union of opposites, a 'uniting symbol' in the literal sense." See Jung, *The Archetypes*, p. 174.

100. See Eliade, *The Two and the One*, p. 100, where he refers to androgyny as a symbol for the "wholeness resulting from the fusion of the sexes," "a new type of humanity in which the fusion of the sexes produces a new unpolarized

consciousness"; and also p. 114. Cf. his sympathetic description of orgiastic rituals in his *Patterns in Comparative Religion* (New York, 1972), pp. 356 ff, especially p. 361. For Eliade as a creative hermeneut who attempted to further a spiritual discipline, see W. L. Branneman Jr., S. O. Yarian, and A. M. Olson *The Seeing Eye* (University Park, Pa., 1982), pp. 57–71.

12

Literary Refractions of the Jewish Family

ROBERT ALTER

Literature does not reflect but refracts the world that it purports to represent in its fictions. This metaphor of refraction, which I adopt with gratitude from Harry Levin, provides an especially needed reminder when we are dealing with the literary mimesis of social institutions. The historian, the sociologist, the anthropologist assumes, sometimes perhaps too confidently, that the texts he or she analyzes—legal documents, chronicles, communal records, transcripts of interviews, and so forth—reflect social realities. Now it is perfectly possible to address the same order of questions to literary texts, and I hardly need to say that this has been done again and again. There are, to take an obvious example, innumerable discussions of how the novels of Balzac reflect France of the 1830s and 1840s, or, in a more canny contemporary recension, there have been expositions of how the ideology of the French bourgeoisie is "inscribed" in the formal moves of Balzac's fiction, in its assumptions about language, character, and causation. Against such critical inferences from text to world, I do not want to claim that there is no determinable relation between imaginative literature and social institutions, but only that the relationship is quirky, is never quite predictable, and always involves elements of distortion.

Precisely in this regard, the metaphor of refraction is helpful. Refraction, if I may quote a key phrase from Webster's definition, is "the bending of a ray or wave of light, heat, or sound as it passes obliquely from one medium to another of different density." Two elements here are beautifully appropriate to what occurs in the literary representation of social realities: the inevitable obliquity of the passage from life to literature and the difference in density between the medium of social existence and the medium of literature. To complicate the picture, all literary representations of social institutions involve a double mediation, first through the individual writer's experience, which may be atypical, extreme, or neurotically distorted, and then through the complicated warp of literary norms and conventions.

Mimetic fiction is informed by an impulse to generalize, to symbolize, to make the particular somehow exemplary—and often, I would add, exemplary of aspects of existence by no means limited to social institutions and their consequences in individual lives. Thus, an instance of a social institution in a fictional text is neither a laboratory specimen of a general condition nor an individual case study, though it may often oscillate over some ambiguous middle ground between the two. Let us recall the famous first sentence of *Anna Karenina*: "Happy families are all alike; every unhappy family is unhappy in its own way." It is, of course, the second clause that is to be the subject of Tolstoy's novel, as it is, indeed, of every novel, for about happy families there is scarcely anything to be narrated. (Nothing could indicate more clearly the institutional bias of literature in representing social institutions!) But that second clause operates in an odd, unsettling state of tension with the first clause, as if somehow the novel could make sense of the peculiarity of the particular only by setting it against the background of what is universally shared. As we read on, we discover that the Karenins and the Oblonskys are wretchedly unhappy, each in their own way, but their unhappiness is, after all, also exemplary just as the eventual happiness of Levin and Kitty is in certain regards decidedly peculiar. The very assertions, then, about what is typical and what is unique may be reversible (Nabokov, in fact, would actually reverse Tolstoy's terms in the first sentence of *Ada*), and that instability of the seemingly typical characterizes most fictional expressions of social realities.

I offer these words of warning because in my view the question we must ask is what writers make of the family rather than what picture of the actual family we can build by scrutinizing their texts. It does not, for example, seem to me feasible to draw valid general inferences about what happened to the Jewish family in America by canvassing a sampling of American Jewish novels. An instructive failed project of this sort is an essay published some years ago on the Jewish mother in contemporary American fiction by the critic Harold Fisch. According to Fisch, in the traditional Jewish family, the father was endowed with an aura of authority by virtue of the domestic religious system over which he presided. Once belief was eroded and the bonds of observance went slack, the father became a displaced person, powerless, pathetic, figuratively or literally constipated, while the possessive, overbearing, guilt-inducing mother, in this lopsided family configuration, now reigned supreme. In this way, the notorious Jewish mother of American fiction of the sixties was the clear symptom of a social pathology of post-traditional Jewish life.

Like most sweeping sociological generalizations, there is a grain of truth in all this, but I am skeptical about whether it is the sort of truth that would stand the test of statistical analysis. If this is more or less the image we get of Jewish mothers and fathers in, say, the early novels of Philip Roth, we are surely entitled to ask how much of this is typical of second-generation families of the Jewish middle class in the urban centers of the Northeast, how much is attributable to the personal experience of Philip Roth (the first refracting medium), how much to the generic and formal necessities of the kind of fiction he is writing (the second refracting medium), that is, a variety of erotic bildungsroman in which the plot of attempted self-discovery through exogamous union needs the possessive, rasping, anaphrodisiac mother as an obstacle to overcome.

What I am proposing for consideration, then, is not an overview of the modern Jewish family through the evidence of literary texts but rather some instances of how certain elements of the sociology of the modern Jewish family have been transmuted in fiction. I will focus on three major figures working in three different languages: Franz Kafka, S. Y. Agnon, and Saul Bellow. The three can by no means suggest all that has been made by modern writers of the Jewish family, but they may indicate three cardinal points on the map of possibilities. I will proceed in chronological order though there is no implication of a necessary historical chronology in my critical argument. The familial sequence will be from fathers to mothers to cousins.

Among the writings of Kafka, the primary document of his relation to the family is the *Letter to His Father*, a text of some twenty thousand words that he wrote in November 1919, just five years before his death, and that was never delivered to its addressee. Precisely because the *Letter to His Father*[1] is not a work of fiction, it offers an illuminating instance of how the materials of life are transformed when they are turned into fiction.

The letter is based on a ghastly contradiction that seems quite out of control for the writer (unlike his fiction, where contradictions are held in fiercely artful control). Intended as a gesture of reconciliation and, in a peculiar way, as an expression of frustrated filial love, it is one of the most terrible indictments imaginable of a father by his son. The son repeatedly confesses his own weakness, his impotence, his abiding sense of guilt, but he makes painfully clear through anecdote and analysis how the father is responsible for the catastrophe of his son's character. This is a lifelong contest between hopeless unequals: "[W]e were so different and in our difference so dangerous to each other that if anyone had tried to calculate in advance how I, the slowly developing child, and you, the full-grown man, would stand to each other, he could have assumed that you would simply trample me underfoot so that nothing was left of me" (p. 13). The perception of the father is an infantile one that seems never to have been altered by the growth of little Franz to adult proportions: "Sometimes I imagine the map of the world spread out and you stretched diagonally across it. And I feel as if I could consider living in only those regions that either are not covered by you or are not within your reach" (p. 115).

To what extent does any of this reflect the general condition of the Jewish bourgeois family in the Austro-Hungarian Empire around the turn of the century? (These are the same time and place, by the way, as those of Agnon's formative years, the Galician Agnon being just seven years Kafka's junior, though his greatest achievements would occur in the quarter century after the death of his Czech counterpart). Hermann Kafka, at least on the evidence of his son's letter, was an overbearing bully, a vulgarian, a monster of egotism, and in his modest way something of a sadist. Fortunately, none of these attributes can be referred to the sociology of the Jewish family. Kafka himself, however, does touch on certain notes of social generalization in the letter, and these demonstrate how the fateful peculiarities of individual character may be significantly reinforced by certain elements of shared cultural experience. The senior Kafka, as part of the vast immigration from shtetl to city that took place in Central Europe at this time, was preeminently a self-made man, and the force of self-assertion of this successful new member of the urban mercantile class was of a piece with his penchant for domination within the family: "You had worked your way so far up by your own energies alone, and as a result you had unbounded confidence in your opinion" (p. 21). Hermann Kafka had jettisoned the pious practice of the world of his childhood, retaining only a kind of tenuous and intermittent nostalgia for it that was expressed in little more than perfunctory attendance at synagogue services four times a year. His son, of course, sensed the emptiness of this vestigial reflex of observance, and in the letter he imagines that, had the religious situation been different, "we might have found each other in Judaism" (p. 75).

Kafka himself stresses the typicality of the predicament: "The whole thing is, of course, no isolated phenomenon. It was much the same with a large section of this transitional generation of Jews, which had migrated from the still comparatively devout countryside to the cities" (pp. 81–3). In the absence of authoritative tradition, the assertive father becomes an absolute arbitrary authority with all the force of the most punitive aspects of the God of tradition. (One sees that Harold Fisch's argument about the erosion of faith and the obtrusion of Jewish mothers can easily be turned around to explain overbearing fathers.) Kafka summarizes this displacement in a single, brief statement about his upbringing: "But for me as a child everything you called out at me was positively a heavenly commandment [*Himmelsgebot*]" (p. 27). The child, and the man-child after him, is forever at the foot of a towering Sinai, hearing the words hurled down at him in thunder, but the words frequently change, attach themselves to absurd or trivial objects, and are flagrantly violated by the very person who pronounces them.

In the *Letter to His Father*, all this amounts to an anguished account of the genesis of a neurosis, though, as I have just indicated, there is a sociological as well as a characterological component in the family situation that contributes to the inner crippling of the son. In the fiction these materials have been transformed into haunting narrative explorations of the dynamics of living in families, under political and spiritual constraint, and under the pressure of eternally elusive moral imperatives. That is why we read *The Trial*, *The Castle*, and the major short stories as great fictions of our dark times, not merely as the record of a cluster of obsessions. What the stories and novels do is to effect a symbolic reconfiguration of the family, the author using his own experience of the posttraditional Jewish familial matrix as the means to represent existence under a strictly lawlike, perhaps lawless, authority. Let me try to illustrate this process by some brief comments on the three remarkable stories, all of them written between 1912 and 1914, that constitute a kind of unintended small trilogy on the fate of filiation: "The Judgment," "The Metamorphosis," and "In the Penal Colony."

"The Judgment" is the starkest and most claustral of these three grim tales. The power of the story derives precisely from the fact that all reality has been stripped down to nothing more than the relation between the father and his son, Georg Bendemann. The only scene for action outside the dark rooms where the two Bendemanns live is the bridge from which Georg will fling himself at the end. There are only two other human figures, both of whom exist at the periphery of this world. One is the friend from Russia, who is variously a figment of Georg Bendemann's imagination, an alter ego, a bone of contention between father and son, and an alternative image of a son for Bendemann senior. The other figure in the background is Georg's putative fiancée.

Now, one of the recurrent topics of the *Letter to His Father* is Franz Kafka's inability to marry, which he attributes to his sense of devastating weakness vis-à-vis the powerful paterfamilias whose role he cannot hope to emulate, whose place he does not dare usurp. In the letter this notion has the status of a symptom and the tonality of a tormented whine. Translated into the narrative invention of "The Judgment,"[2] the idea assumes archetypal force: The conflict between the two Bendemanns becomes the immemorial conflict between father and son in which every attempt of the son to take a sexual partner is construed as a betrayal, a thinly veiled project to displace the father and possess a surrogate of the mother. "Because . . . the nasty creature," thunders Bendemann père, referring to the fiancée, "lifted her skirts . . . you made up to her, and in order to make free with her undisturbed you have disgraced your mother's memory, betrayed your friend, and stuck your father in bed so he can't move" (p. 85). The intuitive rightness of invented detail in this symbolic reconfiguration of the family is uncanny: the thigh wound laid bare by the father, which suggests both threatened castration and past prowess in battle; the fact that the father, through the strength of his claimed insight into the son's motives, suddenly grows "radiant" and is able to rise powerfully from bed. The final stroke of the story, the paternal death sentence that the son finds irresistible, is at once the most fantastic and the most symbolically resonant moment of the tale: It carries us back far beyond the Jewish bourgeois familial setting of the

Kafkas of Prague into an archaic shadow world of absolute patriarchal authority where the self-assertive impulse of the young is crushed with savage force.

In "The Metamorphosis"[3] the stroke of fantasy occurs at the very beginning, in the famous first sentence that announces Gregor Samsa's transformation into a gigantic insect. Everything thereafter in the novella follows with a harshly realistic logic from that initial fantastic fact. The sense of unworthiness, of rejection, that Kafka articulates in the *Letter to His Father* is startlingly objectified by this conversion of man into dung beetle—a pariah within the family, an object of embarrassment and loathing, and an insuperable obstacle to normal family existence. The family as institution is more clearly the central focus of this story than of the other two we are considering. Although the trappings of contemporary urban life are in evidence—the cramped apartment, the economic endeavors of Gregor and his father—this does not, ultimately, seem a "representation" of the early twentieth-century bourgeois family but rather a narrative study of the delicate hydraulic system of the nuclear family as such. Here, too, we have the rivalry of power between father and son, in which, as the son becomes weaker (wounded by an apple embedded in his insect belly, he is like an "old invalid" [p. 122]), the father grows in strength; but that relationship is complicated by the crisscrossing connections among all four members of the family. The crippled son futilely seeks refuge from the hostility of the father in the possibility of maternal solicitude; for a while he imagines that his sister, who is the one given the task of nurturing him, is his secret ally, but this proves a delusion. In the end it dawns on him that the only way he can serve the family is through his death. This frightening tale, then, proves to have a kind of happy ending, whatever ironic inferences one might choose to draw about the conclusion. Gregor's death has a redemptive force: With the noisome giant bug at last out of the way, father, mother, and the suddenly blooming daughter can leave the foul atmosphere of their apartment/prison, walk out into the fresh air of spring, think again of action, renewal, and a clean, fresh place to live. To state in shorthand the distance that has been traversed from experience to art, the cramped psychic space of life in the family of Hermann Kafka has been transformed into a scapegoat story—and, alas, all too many families have their scapegoats—where the well-being of the whole is achieved at the cost of the unassimilable individual.

"In the Penal Colony"[4] presents more complications of narrative elaboration than our two other stories, and I can hardly pretend to offer a serious interpretation of it in this rapid overview. Like so many Kafka texts, it has been read in very divergent ways: as a theological tale about the transition from the Old Dispensation to the New; as a political fable, uncannily prescient of the concentration camp universe; as a psychological study of the insidious dialectic between sadism and masochism; and much more. The point I want to stress is that it is precisely through the symbolic reconfiguration of family experience that such a multiplicity of readings becomes possible—because the family, after all, is the matrix of our psychological lives; of our political, moral, and theological imaginings. In contrast to both "The Judgment" and "The Metamorphosis," no literal family is present here. The setting is a kind of Devil's Island somewhere in the tropics. The explorer who comes to witness the operation of the terrible torture machine explained in such loving detail by the officer provides a zone of mediation and distancing absent in the other two stories: When he pushes off from the shore in his boat at the end, whipping away the outstretched hands of the soldier and the prisoner with a heavy knotted rope, we get a sense that he—and all of us with him—is literally putting behind him the nightmare world of the Old Commandant.

And yet this distanced, fabulous world of perfectly programmed punishment is fraught with familial energies, energies one sees expressed on a much lower plane of significance in the *Letter to His Father*. The relationship between the Old Commandant and the officer is manifestly one of father and son, and the officer, in attempting, however futilely, to replicate the dead Commandant, is a kind of Hermann Kafka under the aspect of eternity, or at least under the aspect of political morality. "My guiding principle is this," he tells the explorer, "Guilt is never to be doubted" (p. 145). At the end of the story the failed authoritative father will try to become the submissive son, stripping himself and placing his own body under the teeth of the dreadful Harrow.

The notion of divine commandment (*Himmelsgebot*), which was the young Franz Kafka's sense of his father's words, here undergoes a grotesque transmogrification, for this is a story about supposedly revelatory, indecipherable inscriptions. When the explorer confesses that he can't make out the labyrinthine tracings on the paper the officer shows him, the officer comments, "It's no calligraphy for school children. It needs to be studied" (p. 149). In the end the machine that is to inscribe the injunction of justice in the body of the transgressor goes haywire, and the redemptive revelation of the language of the law turns into sheer mayhem.

The three stories, then, mark a course of growing elaboration and imaginative transformation of the familial materials: from the symbolic confessional mode of "The Judgment" to the fantasy and expiative ritual of "The Metamorphosis" to the invented exotic world of "In the Penal Colony," where the writer's personal awareness of an overpowering father and his perception of the displacement of tradition in his own home produce a fable that resonates in multiple registers, leading us to reflect on the failed project of perfect justice, the stubborn human need for punishment, the abuses of political authority, the historical transition from an era of harsh retribution, the breakdown of revelation, the threat of the indecipherable that subverts any confident use of language.

On the surface, it might seem that the case of Agnon is incommensurate with that of Kafka, for the Hebrew writer's fictional world is so much more varied in topic, genre, and tone. In over sixty years of literary activity, Agnon produced cunningly artful imitations of pious tales, nostalgic reminiscences of his childhood, subtle psychological studies of contemporary types, panoramically realistic novels (though the realism is always tinctured with something else), satires, a whole spectrum of symbolic fictions, and also some dreamlike expressionistic stories that in fact have been compared with Kafka's. But beneath this variety of literary kinds, one detects a family constellation only a little less obsessive than that encountered in Kafka. For Agnon, it is the looming figure of the mother rather than the father that constantly overshadows the existence of the son. In Agnon's case, we know lamentably little about the specific circumstances of the Czaczkes (his original family name) ménage in turn-of-the-century Buczacz; and considering the almost total neglect of serious literary biography by Hebrew scholarship, we are not likely to find out much before the last remaining witnesses will have vanished. The actual etiology, then, of Agnon's imagination of the family may be inaccessible, but the pattern articulated in his stories and novels is itself eloquent. In Agnon's world of origins, the mother reigns; the father is strangely recessive or actually absent. Occasionally, she is seen as a thinly veiled object of erotic yearning, like the mother of Yitzhak Kumer, the protagonist of *Just Yesterday* (1946, still untranslated)—he recalls her last lingering kiss and in that recollection recoils in guilt from attachment to another women—or, like the mother of Jacob Rechnitz in the symbolic novella "Betrothed," who is confused in her son's mind with the mother of his fiancée, whom in turn he eerily confounds with her own daughter.

A Simple Story (1935), the novel that is Agnon's masterpiece of psychological realism, offers the most clear-cut instance of domination by the mother as against attraction to the mother. Tzirel Hurvitz, the strong-willed self-assured, grasping shopkeeper—a kind of fictional soul sister to Hermann Kafka—possesses her son without ever having really nurtured him: she blocks his way to the poor cousin who is the woman he longs for, marries him off, out of social and economic calculation, to a woman he doesn't want, enlists him despite himself in the family business, and is ultimately responsible for his attempted escape into madness.

As the related fates of Hirschel Hurvitz in *A Simple Story* and Jacob Rechnitz in "Betrothed" will suggest, powerful or powerfully desired mothers in Agnon tend to make weak sons, and the passivity, the debility, the impotence of Agnon's male figures have long been observed by critics. This kind of protagonist is prominent as early as "The Hill of Sand" (1920, but based on a story written in 1911, when Agnon was only twenty- three), with its touch-me-touch-me-not central character wandering through a labyrinth of castration symbols, and as late as the posthumously published novel *Shira* (1971), the story of a hopelessly blocked scholar alternately mothered by his prematurely aging wife and obsessed by his domineering, elusive, weirdly androgynous mistress. (Both these works are untranslated).

The examples I have touched on illustrate how Agnon could spin out of his own obsessive concern with mothers and sons a long series of variations on a single psychological type or, if we stress relationship rather than character in these fictions, a series of studies of the psychopathology of erotic life. The psychopathology of the erotic, let me stress, is by no means limited to the overtly modernist phases of Agnon's writing as we may infer from the disquieting story of the unconsummated marriage in "The Scribe's Legend" (1919), an ostensibly pious tale where the values of piety are ironically subverted from beginning to end. If, as I argued at the outset, a fictional representation is never just a case study because of the exemplary, generalizing force of fictional mimesis, what is finally most arresting about Agnon's preoccupation with these family materials is his ability to address through them a range of large questions involving the cultural and spiritual predicaments of our century. This reach of implication is evident, among the works I have already mentioned, in *Just Yesterday*, "Betrothed," and *Shira*, but I would like to follow out a little more closely the move from family to culture and history in another text, the 1951 novella "Edo and Enam,"[5] which I think is one of Agnon's most original symbolic fictions.

"Edo and Enam," as a story about the mystique of archeology and the quest after lost civilizations, would not at first blush seem to have a great deal to do with families. The lonely scholar, Dr. Ginath, becomes famous by deciphering the hitherto unknown language of Edo and by publishing the beautiful Enamite hymns, said to stand as the missing link at the very dawn of human history. In the course of the story, it emerges that his source for both the language and the hymns is a somnambulistic woman named Gemulah, who has been brought to Jerusalem as a wife from her exotic mountain homeland by Gabriel Gamzu, an antiquarian discoverer of rare books and manuscripts. The symbolism of this strange and evocative tale has been expounded all too many times in Hebrew criticism (and often in all too allegorical a manner), and rather than add my own voice to that chorus, I should like to comment on how the familial concerns define the lines of the symbolic picture and give it coherence and dimension.

The contemporary world of "Edo and Enam," as most readers readily notice, is one of epidemic homelessness, where houses are simply unavailable or are broken into or are threatened with destruction. The theme of the destroyed house is pervasive in Agnon's fiction, but here it is correlated with the theme of disrupted conjugality. The paradigm is provided in an anecdotal inset about a certain Günther and his bride, who have been married for over a year but, unable to find an apartment, live in separate rented rooms, meet at bus stops and park benches, and, one concludes, have had no opportunity to consummate their union. Near the end of the story, we learn that the marriage between Gemulah and Gamzu is also unconsummated: "I am no married woman," Gemulah proclaims to Ginath when the two are discovered together by Gamzu. "Ask him if he has ever beheld my naked flesh." Not even adultery is fulfilled: Ginath's relation to Gemulah is the cool connection of self-interested amanuensis to informant, as much as she passionately longs for another order of intimacy with the scholar. As for the Greifenbachs, the couple in whose home Ginath lives, there are no indications in the story about their conjugal arrangements, but, after ten years of marriage, their union remains without offspring (and, in the ambiguous chronology of the story, they could be married nearly twice that long, for they are referred to as having already been a couple in 1929, and the principal action presumably takes place around 1946 or 1947).

Finally, the narrator himself, though a husband and father, is separated from his wife and children during the main time sequence of the story and so participates, albeit temporarily, in the general pattern of disrupted conjugality.

What has happened, in short, is that the psychological theme of the weak son, erotically impaired by Oedipal guilt or by maternal domination, has been projected here onto a global scale and translated into nonpsychological terms. It is a preeminent instance of what I referred to in the case of Kafka as a symbolic reconfiguration of family materials. The novella gives us a world of ineffectual males, either incapable of or unwilling to achieve conjugal consummation. In the thematic confrontation of modernity and the archaic, this universal slackening of the sexual bond serves us an apt image of a culture that has lost its élan, its sense of direction and purpose, its faith in its capacity for self-perpetuation.

Against this contemporary panorama of failed relations between the sexes, the story offers two ironically unattainable alternatives, one mythic and the other archaic. In the long dialogues between Gamzu and the narrator, mention is made a couple of times of the perfect conjunction between male and female in the heavenly constellations, or, according to the kabbalah, between the angels of the Shekhinah, the female aspect of the Godhead, and the angels of the *Kudsha Brikh Hu*, the male aspect of the Godhead. In a still more pointed antithesis to the flaccid males of the contemporary scene, Gemulah's archaic world is marked by a practice to which our attention is repeatedly drawn in which the suitor, emulating the biblical story of the seizure of young women by the men of the tribe of Benjamin, must forcibly "snatch" his bride from all rivals. The contrast between modern exhaustion or sterility and archaic vitality is emphatically clear.

"Edo and Enam," however, is more intriguingly ambiguous than my account of it so far would indicate. In her archaic realm, Gemulah is nurturing mother (she nurses the injured Gamzu back to health when, blinded, he stumbles into her land); in contemporary Jerusalem, she is, alternately, an invalid daughter, a dangerous she-demon, an elusive object of desire, to her husband. But the most devious ironic turn of the tale is that the whole vision of an archaic realm of vital origins proves to be illusory. The language of origins Gemulah speaks is revealed as a concoction, less language than idiolect, a project of secret intimacy shared solely by daughter and father, from which the exogamous suitor, the male outsider, Gamzu, is excluded.

At the heart of the archaic, then, we discover a kind of incestuous circularity that generates still another version of sexual exclusion. Language itself, instead of being anchored in history or, according to Gamzu's kabbalistic perspective, in the cosmos, is fictive; and the Oedipal aspiration of modern culture to return to the source can attain no more than the pseudoarchaic, the flirtation with an immemorial vitality proving to be a seduction by death. What happens in the family as Agnon perceives it turns out to be homologous with what happens in culture, but in the larger arena, the consequences seem more portentous. At the very end of the tale, the narrator tells us that, after a writer's death, his soul shines out in his work for anyone with eyes to "make use of its light," as presumably will be the case with Ginath's publications. But remembering the ultimately fictive basis of Ginath's discoveries, the deceptive lunar luminosities with which they are associated, we may also recall an earlier remark by the narrator about the alluring light of the moon: "Happy is he who makes use of its light and comes to no harm."[6]

The family in the fiction of Saul Bellow unsettles the nice symmetry of our instances from Kafka and Agnon and so provides a salutary reminder that there are very different possibilities for turning perceptions of the family to literary purposes. The crucial distinction between Bellow and the two earlier writers, a distinction deeply implicated in the different character of his fictional enterprise, is that he is chiefly interested in the extended family, not in the nuclear family. He began his career in the 1940s with *Dangling Man* in a stark Modernist mode (Dostoevski cum Kafka), but from the early fifties onward his novels and stories encompass not isolate individuals and overmastering parents but a welter of disparate, squabbling, ambivalently loving siblings, uncles and aunts, cousins near and distant. This attraction to familial sprawl is inseparable from the zest, the panoramic sweep, and the element of formal looseness in Bellow's fiction. Nothing he has written exhibits the tightness, the inexorability of "In the Penal Colony" or "Edo and Enam," but it may well be that such formal rigor in fiction is dependent on the imaginative concentration on the tight four-square zone of the nuclear family, and any reaching beyond those limits entails a certain untidiness. Bellow himself seems perfectly aware of the opposition in this regard between his work and that of the moderns. In his recent story "Cousins"[7] (from which I will draw all my examples), the narrator, Ijah Brodsky, reports his ex-wife as having explained his fascination with collateral relatives in the following terms: "Her opinion was that through the cousins . . . I indulged my taste for the easier effects. I lacked true modern severity. Maybe she believed that I satisfied an artist's needs by visits to old galleries, walking through museums of beauty, happy with the charms of kinship, quite contented with painted relics, not tough enough for rapture in its strongest forms, not purified by nihilistic fire" (p. 288). In modernists like Kafka and Agnon, one indeed sees true modern severity, the purging fires of nihilism. Bellow at his best offers a more human warmth and also a compound of wry amusement, curiosity, puzzlement, and compassion instead of the intensities of rapture.

As fiction moves from the nuclear family to the larger network of relatives, the whole enterprise of symbolic reconfiguration is set aside. There is nothing symbolic about Bellow's cousins and aunts and uncles, no implication of multiple registers of meaning. The Jewish immigrant extended family draws him because it offers such a splendid sampling of human variety, and it is the extravagant particularity of individual character that engages him. But the simile Ijah Brodsky tries on for size, of visiting old galleries, undersells his own, and his author's, activity as a cousin-watcher, for the impulse is anthropological, in the older, philosophical sense of the term, and therefore also ultimately metaphysical.

In the story "Cousins" the language of zoology and, in particular, of evolutionary theory abounds in the characterizations of the relatives: species, forms of life, extinct types, kinds of creature, and so forth. What range of possibilities for humanity are manifest in these individual figures, known more or less intimately as members of the same family, belonging, as the narrator notes, "to the same genetic pool, with a certain difference in scale" (p. 236)? At one point Brodsky is led to speculate—and it is a notion that underlies a good deal of Bellow's fiction—that each human being is born with something that deserves to be called an original self, not reducible to common denominators, not explicable through general patterns and external determinants. That would provide a metaphysical warrant for the cognitive seriousness of Bellow's scrutiny of disparate individuals in his fiction: "The seams open, the bonds dissolve, and the untenability of existence releases you back to the original self. Then you are free to look for real being under the debris of modern ideas, and in a magical trance, if you like, or with a lucidity altogether different from the lucidity of *approved* types of knowledge" (p. 268).

What does this enterprise of trying to fathom human variety through collateral relatives have to do with the Jewish family? It is a common-place that in Western urban societies the extended family has long been in a state of dissolution, and it is obvious that such vestigial forms of it as persist are by no means limited to Jews. Nevertheless, Bellow has his Ijah Brodsky propose that in Jews the corrosive effects of modern-ization, the devastation of genocide, have produced a certain instinct of reversion to the premodern familial system: "Jewish consanguinity— a special phenomenon, an archaism of which the Jews, until the present century stopped them, were in the course of divesting themselves. The world as it was dissolving apparently collapsed on top of them, and the divestiture could not continue" (p. 246). It is hard to say whether sta-tistical evidence could be mustered to support this assertion, but it does seem to have an intuitive rightness. The Jewish family, like other kinds of family, is inevitably flung out to all points of the compass in the centrifuge of contemporary life, yet one may detect surprising tugs back to the center, perhaps especially over the last decade, as we enter the second generation after that most terrible collapse of the modern world on the Jewish people.

In any case, the literary treatment of the family, as I have been arguing all along, has very little to do with statistics because the writer does not *report* social institutions but picks up hints from them that he imagi-natively elaborates into a certain vision of human possibilities or, we might add, of impossibilities, as the case may be. When the terms the writer works with are drawn from the tightly looped psychosexual circuits of the nuclear family, what he does amounts in one way or another to deriving from the family a defining model of relations between man and woman, strong and weak, old and young, man and God, individual and authority, nature and culture, present and past. I am not enough of a determinist to believe that everything the writer sees is distorted into the image of the family, but we do, after all, internalize our childhood families, and that predisposes us to see things in a certain way, to integrate them according to certain patterns, perhaps at times even to penetrate to underlying principles that might otherwise escape us.

The extended family, on the other hand, as the example of Bellow suggests, offers the most immediate access to the endless heterogeneity of human types. The bulging familial grab bag of Bellow's story—hood-lum, lawyer, businessman, cab-driving philosopher, vulgarian, aesthete, introvert, female powerhouse—is something most of us experience in our own extended families. The fact that Bellow chooses to begin his catalog with a criminal is instructive. Most extended-family closets have capacious enough corners to contain a skeleton or two—cousin Sam, the embezzler; Uncle Max, the crooked kosher caterer; Eddie, the brother-in-law from Jersey City who was an addicted gambler and ran into trouble with the mob. For the law-abiding citizen, the criminal may often seem alien, someone who has stepped to the other side of a fatal dividing line; but the criminal in the family confronts us with kinship, reminds us that this, too, is a permutation of the human stuff we are made of: After all, we remember Max fooling around at Hebrew school or Sam gulping down milk by the quart at the open icebox door in Aunt Gitta's kitchen, and we are faced with hints of ourselves in their physical lineaments.

If, as I have intimated, there is some complicated linkage between the nuclear family and symbolism, there would seem to be a connection between the extended family and what we call realism in fiction. This is not to suggest that the great realists deal only with the extended family (Zola often does; Dickens usually does not), but rather that they typically show the nuclear family to be implicated in larger familial and social contexts. By contrast, the creators of modern symbolic fiction conjure with an enclosed, imploded nuclear family.

The two modes of fiction, to be sure, rarely exist as pure entities and can combine in a variety of ways; but for our present purpose, I would define realism as the fictional invention, based on close observation, of verisimilar individual personages whose principal interest for us is the peculiar heft of their individuality, not their capacity to serve as conduits to some higher plane of signification. The generalizing impulse of fictional mimesis is in this case more implied, operating mainly in that pondering of divergent human possibility to which we are invited. "Human absorption in faces, deeds, bodies, drew me toward metaphysics," Bellow has his Ijah Brodsky say (p. 232). The Jewish family is not exactly "portrayed" in Bellow's fiction, but it provides him a special opening for contemplating through particulars humanity at large. The realist and the symbolist, then, arrive at the threshold of metaphysics by very different routes, but it is there that finally they both bring their familial concerns, for what the imaginative writer seeks to uncover in the recesses of family life is not a sociological schema, but the secret hints of meaning about what we are and where we are headed.

NOTES

1. Franz Kafka, *Letter to His Father*, trans. Ernst Kaiser and Eithne Wilkins (New York, 1953). Subsequent references to this and other works are acknowledged by page number, in parentheses, following each quotation.

2. "The Judgment," in *The Complete Stories*, ed. Nahum N. Glatzer (New York, 1946).

3. "The Metamorphosis," in *The Complete Stories*.

4. "In the Penal Colony," in *The Complete Stories*.

5. S. Y. Agnon, "Edo and Enam," in *Two Tales*, trans. Walter Lever (New York, 1966).

6. Ibid., pp. 225–26. I have modified the translation to make it conform more closely to the Hebrew.

7. Saul Bellow, "Cousins," in *Him with His Foot in His Mouth* (New York, 1984).

Index